Yeats, Shakespeare, and Irish Cultural Nationalism

Yeats, Shakespeare, and Irish Cultural Nationalism

Oliver Michael Hennessey

FAIRLEIGH DICKINSON UNIVERSITY PRESS

Madison • Teaneck

Published by Fairleigh Dickinson University Press
Copublished by The Rowman & Littlefield Publishing Group, Inc.
4501 Forbes Boulevard, Suite 200, Lanham, Maryland 20706
www.rowman.com

16 Carlisle Street, London W1D 3BT, United Kingdom

British Library Cataloguing in Publication Information Available

Library of Congress Cataloging-in-Publication Data

Hennessey, Oliver, author
Yeats, Shakespeare, and Irish Cultural Nationalism / Oliver Hennessey.
pages cm
Includes bibliographical references and index.
ISBN 978-1-61147-626-2 (cloth : alk. paper) — ISBN 978-1-61147-627-9 (electronic)
1. Yeats, W. B. (William Butler), 1865-1939—Knowledge—Literature. 2. Shakespeare, William,
1564-1616—Influence. 3. National characteristics, Irish, in literature. 4. Influence (Literary, artistic,
etc.) 5. Nationalism in literature. I. Title.
PR5908.L5H46 2014
821'.8—dc23
2014022020

∞™ The paper used in this publication meets the minimum requirements of American
National Standard for Information Sciences Permanence of Paper for Printed Library
Materials, ANSI/NISO Z39.48-1992.

Printed in the United States of America

Neath Ben Bulben's buttoks lies,
Bill Yeats, a poet twoice the size
Of William Shakespear, as they say,
Down Ballykillywuchlin way.

Let saxon roiders break their bones
Huntin' the fox
thru dese gravestones.

Ezra Pound, "Neath Ben Bulben's Buttoks Lies"

Contents

Acknowledgments

Although recently completed, this book began life as a 2006 Ph.D. dissertation at the University of Alabama, entitled "Yeats-speare in Shakespace." I owe a debt of gratitude to the members of my dissertation committee—especially Professors Gary Taylor, Brandie Siegfried, and Sharon O'Dair—for their guidance. After some years of neglect, I returned to the project as a junior faculty member at Xavier University of Louisiana in 2009. Now titled "Making Yeats-speare," the manuscript took on a new structure and focus. Chapter 3, on "Yeats's Late Shakespeare," was completed over the summer of 2010 with the help of a summer stipend from the National Endowment for the Humanities. Numerous passages were polished and tweaked by colleagues in my critical writing circle, a small group of Xavier and Tulane faculty: thanks to David, Kathleen, Nicole, Jeremy, Violet, and Robin. I must thank Professor Andrew Murphy for reading the draft manuscript; his generous and extensive remarks saved me from a number of factual errors and strengthened the book immeasurably. Finally, I offer much thanks to my editors at Fairleigh Dickinson University Press, and at Rowman & Littlefield—Harry Keyishian, Brooke Bures, and Amie Brown—for their wise guidance through production.

This book is lovingly dedicated to my wife, Kara Shaw Hennessey, and to our son, Jameson. Sláinte!

William Shakespeare in Yeats's Irish Revival

There is no great literature without nationality, no great nationality without
literature.
—W. B. Yeats, *Letters to the New Island*

To illustrate the confluence of culture and politics which had, over the course
of the nineteenth century, implicated Shakespeare's works within the framework of nationalist ideologies, two anecdotes should here suffice. Both concern 1916, a year of enormous significance in both Irish and English nationalism. On Easter Monday, 1916, Patrick Pearse and his followers led an
armed insurrection in Dublin against British rule, seizing key buildings in the
city center and proclaiming the existence of an independent Irish nation.
Three months later, across the English Channel on the battlefields of northern
France, July 1916 brought carnage on an industrial scale during the Somme
Offensive. Both the battles of the First World War and the military engagement (and subsequent executions) of the Easter Rising have, of course, received much historical attention, and both are often regarded as watersheds
in the political consciousness of England and Ireland, respectively. After
1916, no longer could British citizens disregard the human cost of modern
war. In Ireland, 1916 ushered in a version of Irish nationalism hitherto championed by a minority, so that, as Richard English writes, the "most emphatic
achievement of 1916 was to destroy a constitutional, parliamentary, conciliatory version of nationalism (a nationalism founded on the principles of compromise, trust, tolerance, and opposition to political violence or coercion)."[1]
As ever in the history of Irish nationalism, political violence proved divisive,
in this case further separating Ireland's "two political communities,"[2] nationalist and Unionist.

1

This, however, is a book about literary nationalism, and accordingly, the events with which I am concerned are not military, but cultural. That being said, they are decidedly political. The year 1916 was also the tercentenary of the death of William Shakespeare. On Wednesday of Easter week, the pro-Union *Irish Times* greeted Dublin's citizenry—at least those who read the *Times*—with the following headline: "How many citizens of Dublin have any real knowledge of the works of Shakespeare? Could any better occasion for reading them be afforded than the coincidence of enforced domesticity with the poet's tercentenary?"[3] Under military curfew, following the Rising, acquiescent *Times* readers might well have been asking themselves, which of Shakespeare's plays *does* fit these tumultuous times? *Julius Caesar*, perhaps, with its dramatization of conspiracy, coup, and murderous, fickle crowds of the angry and confused; or might it have been *Henry V*, a play whose ironic chorus can only comment upon, and not halt, the imperialist vigor of an English monarch rampant?

As a part of the tercentenary celebrations, the year 1916 also saw publication of *A Book of Homage to Shakespeare*, a tome dedicated to the veneration of "the greatest Englishman." "The very purpose of the book," Coppélia Kahn argues, was "to assert the continuity of a single national identity, 'England,' from the medieval past to the imperial present, by invoking Shakespeare."[4] Edited by Sir Israel Gollancz, professor of English literature at King's College, London, and honorary secretary of the Shakespeare Tercentenary Committee, *A Book of Homage* contains "166 tributes to Shakespeare by scholars, novelists, poets, literati and public figures from both sides of the Atlantic and around the globe."[5] The memorial aptly reveals the architecture of an imperialist discourse that had championed the Elizabethan playwright as the epitome of "Englishness"—a term connoting both racial purity and a certain celebrated cultural sensibility.[6] This Shakespeare stood for an English literary inheritance which validated, post hoc, the exporting of English culture to the nation's colonial territories.[7] A heady mixture of Shakespeare worship and imperial enthusiasm is manifest, for instance, in the work of one contributor, William Pember Reeves. Reeves's central metaphor functions by fastening the popular-critical commonplace of Shakespeare's far-ranging imagination onto a romantic vision of global exploration:

> The mind of Shakespeare voyaged forth with them.
> They bore his universe of tears and mirth
> In battered sea-chests to the ends of earth,
> So that in many a brown, mishandled tome,
> —Compacted spirit of the ancient home,—
> He for who man the human chart unfurled
> Explored eight oceans and possessed the world.[8]

Shakespeare's dramatic corpus here becomes a kind of secular scripture, while also signifying the "spirit" of a heroic, archaic England. Finally, the poem moves to conflate the voyagers with Shakespeare himself: Shakespeare is England; England is Shakespeare. The construction of this overtly English Shakespeare has of course been the subject of numerous critical studies in recent years. Richard Halpern, for instance, reminds his readers in *Shakespeare among the Moderns* about one of the more imperialistic appropriations of England's national poet by the British Empire Society, "whose 1907 report bore the ominous motto: 'Using no other weapon but his name.'"[9] "With branches throughout the United Kingdom," writes Halpern, "as well as in Demerera (British Guiana), Johannesberg, and later in India, the Society had as its principal object, 'To promote greater familiarity with Shakespeare's works among all classes throughout the British Empire.'"[10] That this was the case should come as no surprise to those who study Shakespeare reception, particularly in the nineteenth century. Institutionalized in the English Civil Service exam of 1853, this Victorian Shakespeare loomed large as the cultural centerpiece of English imperial discourse. In the specific case of the *Times*, the use to which the newspaper puts Shakespeare indicates a number of the signifying qualities of "Shakespeare" (the man, the works, the icon) that had coalesced in a process contiguous to the development of English cultural imperialism. For those with power, "Shakespeare" was a force for political conservatism and Anglicization. He respected order and scorned the mob. His plays were examples of individual artistic genius, and stood metonymically for the genius of the Anglo-Saxon character.[11] Disseminated through the multiple capillaries of public discourse—newspapers, school examinations, academic essays, performances, policy papers, and ephemera—this version of Shakespeare was a construct of numerous interpretations, solidified by critical consensus, popularized by its insertion into the discourse of nationalism, and deployed globally.

SHAKESPEARE AND NATIONAL CULTURAL CAPITAL

How had Shakespeare come to occupy such a position of cultural authority? How were his name, his plays, and his reputation mythologized by men and women promoting a diverse array of political agendas: adult literacy, women's rights, the moral development of children, nationalism, imperialism, and cultural and racial chauvinism? Literary historians have now covered much of this territory in studies of Shakespeare's reception and appropriation.[12] Larger critical monographs have charted the development of Shakespeare's literary reputation and attendant cultural capital from—borrowing the subtitle to Gary Taylor's book—the Restoration to the present. In addition, numerous scholarly articles have been published over the last few decades in academic journals of Shakespeare studies, postcolonial studies, and literary history, many attending to specific historical events, or to the role played by individual artists or cultural figures in championing, inflating, redirecting, or critiquing the notion of Shakespeare's particular genius and the special quality of Englishness it has come to embody. In one such study, Diana E. Henderson neatly summarizes the story of Shakespeare's preeminence thus: "William Shakespeare wrote poetic stories for the stage. Many of his plays were palpable hits; some were not. He died. Or rather, a man died and 'Shakespeare' lived on and kept growing, becoming, as centuries passed, the bearer of English history, an encyclopedia of phrases, a source of profound inspiration, and fodder for many professions."[13] Such books and articles—many of which are referenced in this book—comprise the critical context of my work here and have profoundly impacted my thinking. More rarely, however, have historians of Shakespeare's cultural legacy focused on a specific writer's relationship with Shakespeare in such a context in monograph length. So, before moving on to specifics, it might be worth justifying the necessity for such an endeavor. Why should we care what William Butler Yeats thought and wrote about Shakespeare? For those interested in such matters, Yeats's Shakespeare is worthy of study on the basis of Yeats's own value as a poet and dramatist, because of his work on behalf of Irish cultural nationalism, and because of Yeats's hybrid identity. Given the importance of the Irish Literary Revival within Irish nationalism in the late nineteenth century, Yeats's Shakespeare is also a part of the history of an independent Irish state, as well as the undisputed twentieth-century elevation of Irish literature into the realm of the greatest imaginative works written in the English language.

The aim of this book is, therefore, to assess the role played by Shakespeare in Yeats's cultural politics, and in his work on behalf of the Irish Literary Revival. In doing so, we will necessarily query Edward Said's labeling of Yeats as a "poet of decolonization."[14] Historians of English and Irish nationalisms demonstrate that the relationship between the two countries was never simply one of aggressive, asymmetric colonialism. Epitomizing this nuanced approach is Richard English, who reminds us that the "geographical proximity between Britain and Ireland had produced a cultural and physical intermingling which set these islands' relationship apart from any other British colonial experience," and so "Irish people experienced the British empire as colonized and also as colonist."[15] For Richard English, then, the term "quasi-colonial" is more suitable in capturing "the ambiguity of the experience."[16] Similarly, Andrew Murphy, whose work I have drawn on significantly here, sees an "imperfect otherness" characterizing English assessments of their Irish neighbors from the early modern period onward.[17]

Because of his hybrid identity, part English, part Irish Protestant, and his upbringing in Sligo and London, Yeats's relationship with Shakespeare was inevitably complex and evolving. This is not a point of conjecture, but one readily articulated in his writing:

There are moments when hatred poisons my life and I accuse myself of effeminacy because I have not given it adequate expression. . . . Then I remind myself that though mine is the first English marriage I know of in the direct line, all my family names are English, and that I owe my soul to Shakespeare . . . and to the English language in which I think, speak, and write, that everything I love has come to me through English; my hatred tortures me with love, my love with hate.[18]

In this way, Yeats was part of a literary tradition to which he belonged as an Anglophone writer with solid ties to England. However, Irish revivalist writing meant reforging another, indigenous literary tradition that had become largely extinct outside the oral culture of communities in rural, predominantly western Ireland. What remains for critical appraisal are the ways in which Yeats's cultural-nationalist project responded to the presence of Shakespeare in a literary canon feeding claims of English cultural superiority. Thus a central concern here is one of intertextual politics. Was the centrality of Shakespeare to Yeats's aesthetic and political projects characterized by collusion or iconoclasm? In order to explore this question, I am necessarily drawing upon well-theorized concepts of appropriation, collaboration, and cultural capital.[19] The key concept here is that of "appropriation," and in her introduction to *Shakespeare and Appropriation*, Christy Desmet explains how contemporary studies of Shakespeare's influence have built upon Harold Bloom's famous "quasi-Freudian"[20] "anxiety of influence"[21] to consider the sociopolitical forces that shape the interaction between writers and the Shakespearean texts they take up. Appropriation, explains Desmet, "implies an exchange, either the theft of something valuable . . . or a gift, the allocation of resources for a worthy cause,"[22] and the metaphor works particularly well when we understand Shakespeare's reputation as a kind of commodity possessing cultural capital, which confers "symbolic value and legendary status on cultural projects from both highbrow and lowbrow culture."[23] Since Yeats's writing on Shakespeare emerges from his essays and articles promoting the ideals of his literary nationalism, it is useful to think in these terms: writing about, or even referencing, Shakespeare in newspaper articles or revivalist periodicals constituted a "theft," or perhaps more generously, a reallocation of Shakespearean "resources." In terms of Yeats's more creative, literary uses of Shakespeare—in poetic allusions and historical verse drama—we might employ Diana E. Henderson's concept of diachronic "collaboration,"[24] whereby artists at a historical remove from Shakespeare regard themselves as cooperating with, and therefore "recovering," Shakespeare for modernity. Both "appropriation" and "collaboration," in this sense, describe Yeats's use of Shakespeare, so that just as we can see Yeats drawing upon Shakespearean capital on behalf of the Revival, and to shore up his own artistic prestige, he also becomes one of many writers of the modern age who have "wrestled with the relationships between Shakespeare's modernity and historicity."[25]

Shakespeare signifies in Yeats's thought in a number of ways, reflecting the various contours of his aesthetics, his mysticism, and his nationalism. What we can say for certain is that Yeats's Shakespeare was never a purely literary figure. Rather, thinking about Shakespeare's art and his milieu allowed Yeats to develop ideas for a new national culture and to theorize the place of a Protestant, Anglophone poet within it. Yeats read and wrote about Shakespeare. As a child he idolized and imitated Henry Irving's Hamlet. In 1901 he visited Stratford-upon-Avon to see the Benson Cycle of history plays. He modeled his nationalist theatrical movement in part on what he regarded as the symbolist theatre of "merry England." Later in life, he firmly implicated Shakespeare and the Renaissance in his idealist vision of cyclical history. As a poet, a dramatist, and an Irish cultural nationalist, Yeats returned frequently to Shakespeare's art and engaged throughout his career with the critical and popular discourses concerning Shakespeare's plays, his putative racial characteristics, and above all, his cultural authority.

YEATS'S REVIVAL AND INTERNATIONAL LITERARY SPACE

Yeats's brand of cultural nationalism, like much of his thought, was simultaneously idiosyncratic and of its time, and the Irish Literary Revival as a whole emerged from a variety of sources, both international and indigenous to Ireland. In his sweeping study of nationalism in Ireland, Richard English refers to "the magnificent Yeatsian variation, with its emphasis on a Protestant-inclusive understanding of national dignity."[26] So, it is first important to understand that Yeats's nationalism was directed primarily toward the integration of the Protestant minority into a unified nation and to the ennobling of Ireland at home and overseas via the resuscitation of its ancient culture. Indeed, the Literary Revival was primarily a Protestant endeavor, and its historians have interpreted it as an anxious response to the vulnerability of the Anglo-Irish, Protestant community within Ireland.[27] Reviving Irish culture meant reestablishing the link between contemporary Irish arts—poetry, painting, drama, dance, and song—and a body of folklore, myths, and legends. But what characterizes Yeats's approach specifically was his interest in ritual magic as a revivalist technology, and his conviction that Ireland's authentic self was essentially feudal and heroic. Given to thinking in antitheses, Yeats constructed his ideal nation in opposition to the industrial modernity of contemporary England, and as we shall see, the issue of epistemic change in England proved central to his assessment of the English canon, and to his thinking about the cultural and spiritual life of the two neighboring islands.[28] Following Terence Brown, we might also view the Revival as "an expression of Irish Victorianism,"[29] and as we shall see, Yeats's Shakespeare was initially a Victorian one. In his assessment of the Revival, Brown has pointed out how, "until very recent times," literary historians have tended to understand the work of Hyde, Gregory, Yeats, and Synge in terms of their individual talents and the "compelling . . . inheritance"[30] of Irish mythology, rather than as a product of their cultural milieu. A case of not seeing the forest for the trees, Brown argues that a critical refocusing is necessary to reframe our understanding of Irish Protestantism so that it is seen "not only as one more lamentable attribute of a colonial class which largely sets its face against the emergent nation but as a much more interesting element in a complex of ideas and modes of feeling and action which compromise the Irish Victorian world in which that Revival came to life."[31]

So, the Revival can be understood as a cultural program with indigenous roots in the activities of an anxious Victorian, Protestant literati. It is also important to consider the role of Irish literary societies in the development of revivalist coterie culture, another significant domestic element.[32] However, the Revival's elevation of folk materials also connects it to an older, broader current of European cultural activity associated with the symbiotic evolution of romanticism and literary nationalism in Europe during the late eighteenth and nineteenth centuries. My guide here is Pascale Casanova, whose important monograph, *The World Republic of Letters*, theorizes the competition among nation-states for literary-capital acquisition within the context of nationalist struggles for cultural authority and autonomy. I want to spend a little time on Casanova here, not only to narrate the origins of the literary nationalism practiced by the Irish Revival, but also because her theory of an international, autonomous literary space—the "world republic of letters"—helps us to understand the direction of Yeats's cultural nationalism away from an initial provincialism and toward a more cosmopolitan outlook. Moreover, I will return periodically to Casanova in order to demonstrate how Yeats's Shakespeare contributes to the process by which Shakespeare has been globalized and stripped of a straightforward English affiliation over the course of the twentieth century.

In her account of the "Herder effect," Casanova describes the profound impact of Johann Gottfried Von Herder—German philosopher, theologian, and literary critic—on the cultural politics of literary nationalism. Countering the ubiquity of French belles lettres in Europe at the end of the eighteenth century, Herder shattered literary-historical paradigms by asserting the rights of all epochs and cultures to be judged on their own terms. French claims of cultural superiority could therefore be circumvented by changing the location of a nation's artistic fertility from its relationship with Greco-Roman antiquity to its indigenous folk materials. No longer the preserve of literary elites, literature was reconfigured as a product of a nation's people, whose linguistic vitality gave it a power and status requiring no history of classical aesthetic elaboration. In doing so, Herder "changed the rules of the international literary game."[33] As a response to French literary and linguistic hegemony in Europe, therefore, Herder posited a new model for accruing national literary capital, one which altered the structural relations between nation-states competing for cultural cachet and linguistic prestige. Widely disseminated, Herder's theories were mined for a few key ideas, which "provided the theoretical basis for the attempt made in politically dominated territories, both in Europe and elsewhere, to invent their own solutions to the problem of cultural dependence."[34] "Henceforth," claims Casanova, "all the 'little' nations in Europe and elsewhere were able, on account of their ennoblement by the people, to claim an independent existence that was inseparably political and literary."[35]

One of a number of such movements among the politically disenfranchised nations of Europe, the Irish Revival posited the rediscovery (translation, publication, and dissemination) of national legendary material as a literary renaissance that promised to unify the people of Ireland under the aegis of a shared cultural heritage and collective historical memory. Indeed, the intellectual debt owed to Herder by the Irish revivalists, and Yeats in particular, is carefully examined in Casanova's chapter on "The Irish Paradigm."[36] As a function of the broader claims of romantic thought, the Herderian revolution refigured Shakespeare as perhaps the most powerful literary resource for Anglophone writers on the periphery of European literary space, and this was particularly the case for Irish Protestant revivalists like Yeats. As social and literary historians have demonstrated, England and Ireland had shared a history of assimilation, not merely one of conquest and colonialism: Elizabethan literature, for instance, frequently registers English concerns about the "degeneration" of the Old English in Ireland, and Shakespeare famously embodied fantasies of Irish assimilation in *Henry V* via the proto-British nationalist Macmorris: "What ish my nation? Ish a villain and a basterd and a knave and a rascal?"[37] Yeats himself was a hybrid, an Anglo-Irishman with literary ties to London as well as Dublin. Empowered by Herder's idealization of popular folk culture, then, the Irish Literary Revival looked to build cultural capital by excavating, transcribing, and translating Irish materials. But for the inheritors of Anglo-Protestant Irishness, this strategy proved tricky, since it constructed an Irish literary tradition within which they could not claim an entirely authentic position. The twin revivalist strategies of de-Anglicization and constructing an indigenous literary tradition, and the attendant difficulties of doing so in English, within the parlors of the Protestant literati, and via literary works largely devoid of overt references to the history of Irish political struggles, meant that Yeats's work on behalf of the Revival was always open to charges of a potentially counterproductive validation of English letters. As we shall see, domestic opposition to the work of the Revival came both from figures such as the Trinity College don, Edward Dowden, who considered the focus on Irish writers too provincial, and conversely, from Catholic nationalists such as David Patrick Moran—described by Richard English as "a very talented if myopic zealot"[38] —who beat the drum for explicitly nationalist Irish drama.

Again, Casanova is useful here. She theorizes that the function of the literary figure in the politics of nations seeking independence, or recognition as nations capable of competing internationally, is to increase literary capital, hence the Irish Revival's translation and reworking of indigenous folk material.[39] But capital can also be borrowed, as, I argue, is the case with Yeats's use of Shakespeare. Shakespeare could be appropriated by Irish writers, for instance, but the cost of doing so was potentially validating claims of English cultural superiority. Yeats's Shakespeare was thus necessarily a fraught, hybrid entity, and he frequently situated Shakespeare in an idealized, nonnational literary space with recourse to his esoteric religious philosophy, simultaneously, however, Yeats's thought went beyond de-Anglicizing the "Bard," locating in both Elizabethan language and sensibility an affinity with the inhabitants of Ireland's West. That this was a delicate balancing act is registered in Yeats's incessant claims that his art belonged to a disinterested realm that should not be mired in transient national concerns.

Examining the connection between nationalism and its literatures, literary space, and literary capital, Casanova establishes that national literature is never in fact solely "national," in spite of its appropriation by national authorities as a "symbol of identity."[40] Building on the work of Benedict Anderson, she theorizes national literature as a phenomenon arising alongside print capitalism and the formation of the European nation-states in the late fifteenth and early sixteenth centuries, and so following the elevation of the vernacular as an administrative, and then a literary language. Because of this, she claims, the "accumulation of literary resources is necessarily rooted in the political history of states."[41] However, as national literature became officially interpreted as the repository and representative of national character, the same forces that worked to construct distinct national identities by asserting recognizably different national characteristics made literature similarly relational and competitive. According to this account of literary history, then, vernacular literature developed from, and contributed to, national competition and self-identification. But, having achieved legitimacy, and having accumulated "specifically literary resources," literary space gradually "achieve[d] independence and determine[d] its own laws of operation."[42] By this logic, the end result of official literary competitiveness and self-definition among nations was the creation of a nonterritorial literary space, the "world republic of letters." This is a process we can see enacted in miniature in Yeats's work. His initial, intensely topographical work broadens out over the early decades of the twentieth century. Early in his thought, Shakespeare appears as a rustic folklorist, a man of the people, imbuing his work with characters and symbols culled from rural England and its thinly veiled pagan structures of thought and feeling. For Yeats, the significance of Shakespeare's drama was both its engagement with the magical thinking of its early modern audience and the organic nature of its situation within the socioeconomic structures of a highly idealized, stratified, and feudal England on the cusp of what Yeats regarded as an epistemic rupture, characterized by the ascendency of capitalism, Puritanism, and empirical philosophy.

YEATS'S SHAKESPEARE: SYMBOLIST, ARTIST, AND MAGICIAN

What did Yeats's Shakespeare look like? It should first be acknowledged that nowhere did Yeats claim that Shakespeare was an occultist or practitioner of magic; however, we can find in Yeats's writings many suggestions that Shakespeare might have been a mystic, and that he inherited the sensibility of a premodern folk accustomed to mystical thinking. Yeats's own esoteric activities encompassed many forms of ritual magic and philosophical speculation, and I borrow here from Kathryn Ludwigson to distinguish between the two: "In his trust in the ability of human faculties to penetrate into the hidden recesses of the supersensory realms of Nature and in his confidence that by magic the human spirit could exercise lordship over Nature, the mystic and the mage, though unlike, became one in Yeats."[43] An ability to access the "supersensory realm," as we shall see, characterizes much of Yeats's evaluation of Shakespeare as an artist, and this belief accounts in large part for the manner in which he appropriated Shakespeare's drama into his own occultist cultural nationalism. We can determine in Yeats's early essays a number of claims about the man from Stratford, his work, and his milieu, which, taken together, demonstrate the Irishman's construction of Shakespeare as a producer of a symbolist dramatic verse capable of inducing visionary meditations via its deployment of images drawn from an otherworldly repository known as the *anima mundi*. Further, as I examine here in some detail, Shakespeare's historical position at the cusp of modernity marks him, per Yeats, as premodern, and thus the inheritor of a Neoplatonic, idealist weltanschauung.

Yeats's view of the Renaissance shifted throughout his career.[44] Initially, Yeats followed William Morris in idealizing the Anglo-French Middle Ages, but by the late 1890s the Renaissance figured as the last flowering of an ideal, organic society of aristocratic values and adventurers with an accompanying literary culture that drew from the simple songs and ancient tales of the rural folk and permeated high culture in the form of lyrics of outstanding aesthetic beauty and vast metaphysical scope. Classical Athens at the time of Pericles constituted such a prized cultural apotheosis, as did Byzantium around one thousand years later. Given this idealized view of the European Renaissance, it is not difficult to see the contours of Yeats's thinking about the Irish Literary Revival and the role of his own coterie within it. The context of Yeats's statements about the Renaissance is typically a culturally nationalist one, such that, as Andrew Murphy handily surmises, "In writing about the Renaissance Yeats is always also writing about Ireland."[45] Yeats occasionally viewed the Elizabethan age through a more pejorative lens, as when he writes about Edmund Spenser, a poet who, in Yeats's view, subsumed his poetic talents to political allegory and thus presaged an epistemic turn to positive materialism, the soul-deadening empirical philosophy of the modern age, and, crucially, an epistemology alien to rural Ireland. By this thinking, then, Shakespeare was a relic, a throwback, and his work registered the impact of an imminent cultural catastrophe. Indeed, Yeats's famous tussle with Trinity College's Shakespearean, Edward Dowden (discussed in chapter 1), can be understood as an attempt to enlarge the visibility of indigenous Irish writers, and, further, to boost Irish cultural capital by asserting the premodern, and thus "Irish," status of England's culture hero. Within the rhetorical scheme of Yeats's cultural nationalism, Shakespeare was both English and "ancient," a term, as we shall see, employed to describe an international and atemporal affiliation among premodern cultures, whether in Elizabethan England or the rural margins of twentieth-century Ireland.[46]

The trope cluster I have just outlined is visible, for instance, in "The Symbolism of Poetry," an essay published in *The Dome* in April 1900, which responds to Arthur Symons's influential book, *The Symbolist Movement in Literature*. In his opening preamble, Yeats situates Shakespeare as a poet "on the edge of modern times,"[47] attacks journalists for their misguided assumptions that great art does not require a profound philosophical framework from which inspiration must arise, and then indicts England as a country where "journalists are far more powerful and ideas less plentiful than elsewhere" and where "great art . . . is perhaps dead."[48] Revolting against a literature brought forth from the "scientific movement,"[49] Yeats lauds a new breed of writer that has "begun to dwell upon the element of evocation, of suggestion, upon what we call the symbolism in great writers."[50] Although in this essay Yeats generally avoids explicit statements of the use of symbols in occultist rituals, he employs a series of terms—"evocation," "the divine life," and "the buried reality"[51] —which employ the rhetoric of esoteric organizations like the Hermetic Order of the Golden Dawn, to which Yeats belonged. In fact, Yeats does reference the "secret history" of occultism when he suggests that the source of creative inspiration is "the lowest of the Nine Hierarchies."[52] However, Yeats does not hesitate in attributing mystical qualities to symbols, which "call down among us certain disembodied powers whose footsteps over our hearts we call emotions"[53] and are capable of luring us "to the threshold of sleep, and it may be far beyond it."[54] Distinguishing between "emotional" and "intellectual" symbols (the best symbols combine both qualities), Yeats goes on to explain how "the purpose of rhythm . . . is to prolong the moment of contemplation, the moment when we are both asleep and awake . . . to keep us in that state of perhaps real trance, in which the mind liberated from the pressure of the will is unfolded in symbols."[55] Great art, whether consciously or not, employs complex patterns and symbols whose effect is to move the reader or listener into a higher plane of reality. Symbolical art is therefore a mystical art, and to illustrate this, Yeats quotes from Burns, from Nash, and from Shakespeare:

> Timon hath made his everlasting mansion
> Upon the beached verge of the salt flood;
> Who once a day with his embossed froth
> The turbulent surge shall cover[.][56]

The implication is clear: Shakespeare is a symbolist.

"I believe in the practice of what we have agreed to call magic, in the evocation of spirits, though I do not know what they are, in the power of creating magical illusions, in the visions of truth in the depths of the mind when the eyes are closed,"[57] writes Yeats in another essay from 1900, entitled "Magic." Well known to Yeatsians as an early statement of the poet's mystical religious philosophy, and precursor to his longer expositions of mystical doctrine, *Per Amica Silentia Lunae* (1918) and *A Vision* (1925 and 1937), "Magic" sets out three doctrines "which have, as I think, been handed down from early times":[58]

> 1. That the borders of our minds are ever shifting, and that many minds can flow into one another, as it were, and create or reveal a single mind, a single energy.
> 2. That the borders of our memories are as shifting, and that our memories are a part of one great memory, the memory of Nature herself.
> 3. That this great mind and great memory can be evoked by symbols.[59]

Following this tripartite credo, the essay recounts a series of anecdotes concerning the poet's own visionary experiences, including two prolonged accounts of collective visions.[60] Again, while this essay is familiar to Yeats scholars, I want to outline its implications for my object of scrutiny here: Yeats's Shakespeare. About halfway through, Yeats reflects on the nature of these collective visions:

> At the time these two visions meant little more to me . . . than a proof of the supremacy of imagination, of the power of many minds to become one, overpowering another by spoken words and by unspoken thought till they have become a single, intense, unhesitating energy. One mind was doubtless the master; I thought, but all the minds gave a little, creating or revealing for a moment what I must call a supernatural artist.[61]

This essay was written only a few months before Yeats's trip to Stratford to see the Benson History Cycle, at the same time that he was developing rituals for a new, Irish occult society—the Celtic Mysteries—and at the beginning of his work as a dramatist for the Irish Literary Theatre. What we see, then, in the publications that followed his Stratford visit and accompanied his work for the Irish dramatic movement is a reiteration of this key concept of the supernatural artist, whose symbolic, rhythmical art possesses the capability for inducing collective visionary experiences. Returning to the above passage, Yeats depicts the supernatural artist as a collective. Led by a powerful magician or evoker of symbols—"One mind was the master"—the "supernatural artist" is created from all of the participants: "all the minds gave a little." As I discuss in more detail in the second chapter, the poet or director as supernatural artist underpins Yeats's aspirations for a "Shakespearean" Irish verse drama that would unify Ireland's Protestants and Catholics, de-Anglicize Ireland's urban bourgeoisie, and usher in an organic Irish nation. In this new Ireland, disparate social classes would unite under the aegis of a shared religious philosophy, which in turn would be manifested in the revived mystical aesthetics. However, for drama like Shakespeare's to produce collective meditative experiences of the kind recounted in "Magic," a sympathetic audience was required: the artist must fit the times. As we shall see, this theory accounts, in part, for Yeats's increasing frustration with the tastes and mores of Dublin playgoers, who tended to find his strange, ritualistic plays unappealing.

In completing this overview of Yeats's Shakespeare as a supernatural artist, we must turn finally to his essay on Edmund Spenser. Written as an introduction to *Poems of Spenser: Selected and with an Introduction by W. B. Yeats* (1906), the essay was composed in 1902, and thus shortly after "The Symbolism of Poetry" and "Magic." "Allegory and, to a much greater degree, symbolism," writes Yeats in a familiar vein, "are a natural language by which the soul when entranced . . . communes with God and with angels."[62] However, he continues a little later, "I find that though I love symbolism, which is often the only fitting speech for some mystery of disembodied life, I am for the most part bored by allegory, which is made, as Blake says, 'by the daughters of memory,' and coldly, with no wizard frenzy."[63] This is the gist of Yeats's analysis: Spenser, a talented poet, subsumed his art to the pragmatism of self-advancement "to justify himself to his new masters."[64] In a well-known phrase, Yeats notes that while Spenser "wrote of knights and ladies . . . he fastened them with allegorical nails to a big barn-door of common sense."[65] In stark contrast, "The dramatists [of the Elizabethan age] lived in a disorderly world . . . following their imagination wherever it led them. Their imagination, driven hither and thither by beauty and sympathy, put on something of the nature of eternity."[66] While Yeats doesn't go as far as Marx, who famously labeled Spenser "Elizabeth's arse-kissing poet," he identifies

Spenser's primary flaw as a harnessing of poetry to politics, this a frequent trope in his critique of current Irish popular nationalism. As for his status as an Elizabethan agent of colonization in Ireland, Yeats expresses regret: "When Spenser wrote of Ireland he wrote as an official, and out of thoughts and emotions that had been organized by the State. . . . Could he have gone there as a poet merely, he might have found among its poets more wonderful imaginations than even those islands of Phaedria and Acrasia."[67] The significance of the essay for my argument here is its articulation of an artistic shift in the late sixteenth and early seventeenth centuries away from an art whose symbolism was unfettered, toward one whose allegorical nature greatly lessened its emotive affect by making its referents concrete, worldly, and political rather than abstract, universal, and religious. As Yeats makes clear in this essay, and elsewhere, the reason for this shift lay with what he would later call the turning of the gyres. Here, it is pinned on the advent of "that new Anglo-Saxon nation that was arising amid Puritan sermons and Marprelate pamphlets."[68] "This nation," he continues, "had driven out the language of its conquerors, and now it was to overthrow their beautiful haughty imagination and their manners . . . and to set in their stead earnestness and logic and the timidity and reserve of a counting-house."[69] The implications of this historical change in terms of Yeats's Shakespeare and his position within Yeats's cultural nationalism are profound. Based upon this interpretation of historical change, Yeats de-Anglicized Shakespeare, claiming that the Elizabethan's sensibility—his "delight in great persons . . . his indifference to the State . . . his scorn of the crowd [and] his feudal passion"[70] —effectively cut him off from a pernicious "English" modernity. This, then, is the central claim of this book: in the context his occultist cultural nationalism, Yeats claimed Shakespeare for Ireland.[71]

APPROPRIATING SHAKESPEARE: YEATS'S NATIONALIST RECEPTION

No simple case of "bardolatry" or "bardicide," Yeats's Shakespeare is a complex and evolving figure, but one always central to Yeatsian aesthetics and to his nationalist cultural agenda. By piecing together a diverse array of references, allusions, and lengthier ruminations, I have endeavored to provide a detailed analysis of the manner in which Yeats interpreted and appropriated Shakespeare's works, characters, and cultural authority to advance publicly the Irish Revival, and as part of a broader move to write himself into the history of Irish nationalism. Certainly, Yeats deployed Shakespeare differently in the 1920s and 1930s than he did in the 1890s and 1900s. However, throughout we can identify three points of continuity: Yeats's Shakespeare follows the contours of his cultural nationalism; Yeats's Shakespeare maps onto the dominant and emergent paradigms in Shakespeare reception, but is always distinctly Yeatsian, thus defying too simple a categorization; and finally, Yeats's Shakespeare adds to a now weighty body of evidence concerning the fundamental importance of Yeats's occult beliefs, especially as they pertain to questions of Irish ethnicity and nationhood. In each chapter, then, I adduce a series of prose fragments to narrate the development of Yeats's thinking about Shakespeare, and to demonstrate how it adheres to these three key precepts. As Philip L. Marcus points out, "Yeats was not content with merely letting his creative productions serve as *exempla* of the literary ideals he held in the 1880's and 1890's: he worked actively to transmit the ideals to others."[72] Much of Yeats's prose can therefore be considered propaganda for his cultural nationalism, and so it is these writings that I have primarily examined In order to form a comprehensive assessment of his Shakespeare.

Chapter 1 thus situates Yeats and Shakespeare within the context of claims being made by two prominent nineteenth-century academics. Oriented around racial philology, character critique, and biography, the work of Matthew Arnold and, later, Edward Dowden broadly outlines what we can identify, with some reservation, as a "Victorian" Shakespeare, imbued above all with moral and cultural authority. Yeats's early Shakespeare emerges toward the end of the century first in response to Arnold's dissection of the "Celtic" sensibility and then as a rejoinder to Dowden's influential study of Shakespeare's "Mind and Art." In both cases, Yeats intervenes in essentially academic discourses, appropriating and reorienting their terms. So, this first stage in the development of Yeats's Shakespeare constitutes a series of essays that de-Anglicize Shakespeare and position him as the representative of a loose confederation of ancient peoples, whose proclivity for magical thinking and visionary spiritualism figures them as both the precursors to, and natural enemies of, a modern, English, industrial, and utilitarian culture. In both cases, what is really at stake is cultural authority, and while Yeats's disagreement with Arnold can be read as a straightforwardly nationalist maneuver, his rejection of Dowden's exegesis of the history plays should be understood as an intranational matter of cultural politics, part of an effort to elevate the status of the Literary Revival and ultimately to relocate the center of Ireland's literary world from the academy to the stage.

Eventually, Shakespeare comes to occupy a predominantly literary space in Yeats's discourse, but only after the failure of Yeats's attempts in the opening decade of the twentieth century to popularize a highly symbolic, "Shakespearean" Irish drama with an avant garde, occultist stagecraft capable of unifying Ireland's social strata via shared visionary experience. I read this nation-building stage of Yeats's Shakespeare as emerging from his visit to Stratford in 1901, his involvement with the Hermetic Order of the Golden Dawn, and his concomitant efforts to construct a set of occult rituals for a new Irish religious society: the Celtic Mysteries. The new Irish drama was intended to rapidly renew Irish literary capital; more than this, however, Yeats's writings for the movement's periodicals reveal the poet-playwright exploring the possibility of a drama capable of awakening a premodern sensibility in its urban audience. The story of this phase in the life of Yeats's Shakespeare comprises the second chapter of this book, and an occult Shakespeare is surely one of the more bizarre products of twentieth-century reception. However, while the increase of Irish literary capital during the initial revivalist period had suggested to Yeats the return of a nation and the revival of a pan-European, ancient race, the third stage of Yeats's Shakespeare registers disappointment with the provincialism and official, Jansenist culture of the new nation. As I detail in chapter 3, Yeats's later Shakespeare reflects a change in the dominant nationalist discourse in Ireland during the fifteen or so years leading up to Irish sovereignty. Put another way, after 1916, the competing nationalisms of the earlier years—including Yeats's revivalism— lost out to a political nationalism that posited the formation of a sovereign, Catholic, Irish-speaking state as its primary goal, and called for the policing of indigenous literary output to ensure the adequate representation of this official identity without competition. Ironically, in spite of Yeats's initial focus on indigenous Irish literature, the most serious challenge to Yeats's cultural agenda was internally generated provincialism, and at the end of his life we witness Yeats browbeating his domestic cultural foes with recourse to a reconfigured, scornful, high-culture Shakespeare.

While the body of this book therefore follows this three-stage chronology, chapter 4 steps back to consider the impact of literary modernism on Shakespeare reception and evaluates the extent to which Yeats's Shakespeare resembles the new anthropological approach advanced by writers like T. S. Eliot and Wyndham Lewis, as well as the influential hermeneutic developed by G. Wilson Knight, who essentially read the plays as long symbolist poems. Influenced by the work of anthropologists such as Sir James Frazer, Eliot in the 1920s championed a new critical approach to Elizabethan drama that emphasized its basis in primitive rituals and its supposedly universal mythic dimensions. Throughout Yeats's writings on Shakespeare, we find similar tropes and motifs, particularly the attention to a mythic and ritualistic power in Shakespeare's plays. As I argue in chapter 4, however, Yeats's Shakespeare differs from Eliot's since he locates the origins of this archetypal power in the realm of the spirit, rather than in the historical transmission of ancient religious rites. Again, we see here the manner in which Yeats's Shakespeare appears to reflect emergent paradigms, while simultaneously conforming to the idiosyncrasies of an eclectic religious philosophy. Considering the similarities between Yeats's approach to Shakespeare's drama and those of modernist writers, G. Wilson Knight—himself a spiritualist— emerges as a Shakespearean whose thinking more clearly aligns with that of

Yeats. Yeats's Shakespeare—as with his later poetry—is thus "modernish," rather than "modernist." Finally, applying Pascale Casanova's model of an autonomous literary space wrought from international literary-capital competition to Shakespeare's works, I argue that Yeats's Shakespeare has not received adequate scrutiny in terms of its contribution to the twentieth century's development of a transnational Shakespeare, divorced from a straightforwardly English national affiliation.

In writing this book I am heavily indebted to a number of previous studies, which have focused on Yeats's Shakespearean influences from either purely aesthetic positions, or as part of much larger postcolonial works like Declan Kiberd's accomplished *Inventing Ireland: The Literature of the Modern Nation*. However, while some studies marginalize Yeats's interest in Shakespeare as it pertains to Irish drama, others finesse his occultism, thus contributing to a long tradition of critical squeamishness in the treatment of Yeats's religious pursuits. But as Kiberd makes clear, Yeats required unofficial literary space and institutions to pursue his revivalist brand of cultural nationalism.[73] Instead of dismissing Yeats's occult interests, we need to understand them as fundamental to this requirement: esoteric principles and occult societies were never far from his mind, and they allowed him to experiment with alternate strategies of literary visibility, revivalist aesthetics, and, moreover, self-construction. Recent critics have therefore begun to take seriously his assertion that "the mystical life is the centre of all that I do and all that I think and all that I write."[74]

Since Yeats's views on Shakespeare and his milieu fluctuated throughout his career, this study takes something of a diachronic approach. Many of these shifts, signifying eddies in a larger current, rather than drastic changes of direction, have been examined in Rupin Desai's *Yeats's Shakespeare*,[75] and I need to acknowledge the debt this project owes to Desai. Yet Desai's analysis—now over forty years old—bears the hallmark of an earlier period of criticism less inclined to theorize Shakespeare reception and make assessments concerning the role played by literature in ratifying, promoting, or indeed opposing socially oppressive modes of thought and representation, as well as the material practices and institutions in which they are housed. Not so here. Yeats's thinking about Shakespeare needs to be adequately contextualized in terms of the material circumstances that produced it. It is therefore within the sociocultural context of Yeats's work that this relationship with Shakespeare is best understood, and Diana E. Henderson reminds us that "an analysis of artists' sociopolitical location is neither distant from nor anathema to a literary or formal understanding of art itself."[76] Given the signifying power of Shakespeare at this time, in this specific political situation, how indeed can we come to a critical understanding of Yeats's Shakespeare if we maintain the (political) position of the autonomy of art, or if we leave the phenomenon with Desai as an outcome of a relatively innocent literary intertextuality? To be fair, there are a few instances in *Yeats's Shakespeare* where the question of national allegiance is raised:

> It may seem astonishing that Yeats nowhere resents Shakespeare's obvious pride in England's conquests abroad; he completely overlooks the pulsating fervor for England's supremacy in the history plays. . . . Yeats must have felt that, in the ultimate analysis, Shakespeare's sympathy and understanding for the oppressed was a truer index of his feelings that the turgid homage to England for her victories over her weaker neighbors, a homage which was undoubtedly intended to cater to the appetite of a popular audience. [77]

But such moments where Desai's analysis seems to want to break through into postcolonial critique are short-lived. These are points of departure from which this study takes its direction. The stated aim of Desai's book is to explore fully "Yeats's regard for Shakespeare,"[78] and his work falls into three sections: first, he identifies references to Shakespeare's craft in Yeats's prose, explicates them, and indicates how they might have impacted the Irishman's appreciation of Shakespeare as an artist; second, he examines Shakespeare's position within the esoteric religious beliefs reflected in his poetry, and articulated in *A Vision*; and third, he examines Shakespearean "echoes" in Yeats's plays. Yeats's cultural nationalism is therefore rarely considered, while his occultism is treated as a purely intellectual and textual phenomenon, eliding the importance of his involvement with ritual magic and communities of like-minded adepts. [79]

Rather than situating Yeats's Shakespeare in a predominantly literary milieu, with the politics of the Irish literary revival forming a "background" in line with older forms of historicist criticism, I prefer to think in terms of Bryan Reynold's "Shakespace" to position Yeats's Shakespearean work within a wider, interactive network of cultural significations: "the articulatory space through which discourses, adaptations, and uses of Shakespeare have suffused the cosmopolitan landscape transhistorically."[80] I therefore adopt a different approach to Desai, foregrounding the material conditions of production: the rituals of the Golden Dawn and squabbles among its leadership; the experience of Yeats's visit to Stratford; his attempts to ritualize a "Shakespearean" Irish verse drama; and post-Treaty Jansenist restrictions on Irish cultural production. Fundamentally, then, this study is concerned with the role of Shakespeare within the discourse of Irish cultural nationalism. By following the construction and dissemination of Yeats's Shakespeare, I am not merely outlining another chapter in the ideological history of Shakespeare reception, though this is certainly a significant aspect of this study. Instead, I hope this book will contribute to a fuller understanding of Yeats's nationalist thought, his identity politics, his aesthetic philosophies, and the role played by England's national culture hero within these multiple contexts. As such, the story of Yeats's Shakespeare deserves critical attention as the convergence of fascinating chapters in the history of Shakespeare reception and Irish cultural nationalism.

NOTES

1. Richard English, *Irish Freedom: The History of Nationalism in Ireland* (London: Macmillan, 2006), 227.
2. Ibid., 228.
3. Cited in Declan Kiberd, *Inventing Ireland: The Literature of the Modern Nation* (London: Vintage, 1995), 268.
4. Coppélia Kahn, "Remembering Shakespeare Imperially: The 1916 Tercentenary," *Shakespeare Quarterly* 52, no. 4 (2001): 458.
5. Ibid., 457.
6. Kahn argues that the *Book of Homage* constitutes a "cultural performance" in which "English society 'performs' a certain past with Shakespeare in the lead role." However, as she sees it, the 166 multicultural tributes to Shakespeare work ironically, but "always respectfully," to "stage the contradictions of empire." Kahn, "Remembering Shakespeare," 457.
7. Curiously, Douglas Hyde, head of the Gaelic League, also submitted a poem in Gaelic of twenty-seven stanzas, along with a translation which Israel Gollancz edited to remove lines that might seem offensive to English ears. As Werner Habicht notes, the poem included "a refrain promising that everyone, even Irish mythical heroes and England's foes could be pacified if sent to 'Stratford on the Avon.'" See Werner Habicht, "Shakespeare Celebrations in Times of War," *Shakespeare Quarterly* 52, no. 4 (2001): 450.
8. William Pember Reeves, "Dream Imperial," in *A Book of Homage to Shakespeare*, ed. Israel Gollancz (Oxford: Oxford University Press, 1916), 312. Cited in Kahn, "Remembering Shakespeare," 461.
9. Richard Halpern, *Shakespeare among the Moderns* (Ithaca, NY: Cornell University Press, 1997), 21.
10. Ibid.
11. Perhaps the best-known iteration of this Shakespeare comes from Thomas Carlyle, who, in his lectures "On Heroes and Hero-Worship," championed Shakespeare as a "Saxon" culture hero, and envisaged a "Saxondom covering great spaces of the globe." See Thomas Carlyle, *On Heroes, Hero-Worship and the Heroic in History* (1841), notes and intro. Michael K. Goldberg (Berkeley: University of California Press, 1993), 96.
12. See, for instance, Gary Taylor, *Reinventing Shakespeare: A Cultural History from the Restoration to the Present* (Oxford: Oxford University Press, 1991); Jonathan Bate, *The Genius of Shakespeare* (Basingstoke and Oxford: Picador, 1997); and Samuel Schoenbaum, *Shakespeare's Lives* (Oxford: Oxford University Press, 1993). On the appropriation of Shakespeare in texts and performance, see Diana E. Henderson, *Collaborations with the Past: Reshaping Shakespeare across Time and Media* (Ithaca, NY, and London: Cornell University Press, 2006); Thomas Cartelli, *Repositioning Shakespeare: National Formations, Postcolonial Appropriations* (London and New York: Routledge, 1999); Christy Desmet and Robert Sawyer, eds., *Shakespeare and Appropriation* (London and New York: Routledge, 1999); and Richard Halpern, *Shakespeare among the Moderns* (Ithaca, NY: Cornell University Press, 1997). On the "Victorian" Shakespeare, see in particular Adrian Poole, *Shakespeare and the Victorians* (London: Arden, 2004), and Gail Marshall and Adrian Poole, eds., *Victorian Shakespeare*, 2 vols. (Basingstoke and New York: Palgrave Macmillan, 2003).
13. Henderson, *Collaborations*, 2.
14. Edward Said distinguishes him with this label. See "Yeats and Decolonization," in *Celtic Revivals: Essays in Modern Irish Literature*, ed. Seamus Deane (Minneapolis, MN, 1990), 80. Said situates Yeats's early work of the 1890s, in particular, in a phase of anti-imperialist resistance preceding the liberationist movements of the mid-twentieth century, thus placing him in ranks of revolutionary nationalist writers like Tagore, Senghor, Neruda, Vallejo, Césaire, Faiz, and Darwish. However, this label has proved somewhat controversial. In "Yeats,

Nationalism and Post-Colonial Theory," for instance, Stephen Regan asks whether "to call Yeats a *revolutionary* nationalist . . . is to overstate and exaggerate his political commitment." See Stephan Regan, "W. B. Yeats: Irish Nationalism and Post-Colonial Theory," *Nordic Irish Studies*, 5 (2006): 89. Given the multifarious nature of Irish nationalism at the end of the nineteenth century, Regan argues further, we must be careful in parsing Yeats's overtly nationalist statements and rhetorical maneuvers: "What Yeats was seeking in the 1890s was a way of re-establishing his own cultural identity—and that of his class—in a country that was witnessing a strongly emerging Catholic nationalism. There was, to put it bluntly, more than one kind of nationalism at work in late nineteenth century Ireland." Regan, "W. B. Yeats," 95. Indeed, it is one argument of this book that Yeats's Shakespeare is fundamentally an expression of this complex of identities and allegiances.

15. English, *Irish Freedom*, 124. English's analysis of Irish cultural nationalism is astute, and of particular significance for my work is the attribution of a quasi-religious function to the tenor of its cultural goals: "Cultural nationalists in Ireland thought in terms of the contemporary awakening of an historically embedded culture, and saw the struggle for such cultural revival as necessary to the nation's survival. The flaws of such an Anglicized present could be judged, arraigned and condemned against the standard of an imagined Gaelic past—a past supposedly pristine, harmonious, distinctive and dignified. It was a politics of decline. . . . The present was unsatisfying and the villain—in this case England—was repeatedly identified; the people had lapsed from the true faith but could be reconverted by cultural-nationalist preachers." English, *Irish Freedom*, 238–39.

16. Ibid., 125.

17. Murphy writes that "the standard tropes of colonial stereotyping are always likely to unravel in the encounter with the imperfect Otherness of the Irish." Andrew Murphy, *But the Irish Sea betwixt Us* (Lexington: University Press of Kentucky, 1999), 7.

18. See "A General Introduction for My Work," in W. B. Yeats, *Essays and Introductions* (New York: Macmillan, 1961), 519.

19. On the concept of cultural capital, see Pierre Bourdieu, *Distinction: A Social Critique of the Judgment of Taste*, trans. Richard Nice (Cambridge, MA: Harvard University Press, 1984).

20. Desmet and Sawyer, *Shakespeare and Appropriation*, 7.

21. Harold Bloom, *The Anxiety of Influence: A Theory of Poetry* (New York: Oxford University Press, 1973).

22. Desmet and Sawyer, *Shakespeare and Appropriation*, 4.

23. Ibid., 5.

24. Henderson, *Collaborations*, 12–13. Henderson sees the "modern" Shakespeare emerging after the French Revolution and during the Industrial Revolution, when "a sense of radical Change generated the energies and systems conventionally deemed to constitute the modern era." Henderson, *Collaborations*, 18. Because of the social, economic, and political changes, writes Henderson, "'modern' now signified not merely 'of the present' but also a particular historical configuration of institutions and attitudes. These changes likewise affected the conceptualization and representation of Shakespeare, most notable in his overt political deployment in the service of the imperial nation-state . . . and in a more thoroughgoing acknowledgment of historical distance from his world (as in the gradual shift from contemporary to period costuming)." Ibid., 18–19.

25. Ibid., 18.

26. English, *Irish Freedom*, 237.

27. See, for instance, Terence Brown, *Ireland's Literature: Selected Essays* (Mullingar: Lilliput, 1988); R. F. Foster, *W. B. Yeats: A Life*, vol. 1, *The Apprentice Mage: 1865–1914* (New York and Oxford: Oxford University Press, 1998); and Kiberd, *Inventing Ireland*. Also see especially R. F. Foster, "Protestant Magic: W. B. Yeats and the Spell of Irish History," *Proceedings of the British Academy* 75 (1989): 243–66.

28. Ludwigson usefully summarizes Yeats's cultural agenda as follows:

> Yeats reacted to the rationalism bequeathed by the eighteenth century and to the scientific movement of the nineteenth. He hated science and industrialism, longed for a return of Ireland to the heroic values of the past, and hence fostered the Celtic

revival. He envisioned the creation of a heroic, passionate concept of life based on the folklore of the uneducated in Ireland, which through poetry and art might be made a subject worthy of study among the educated in all countries and which might also become a political passion unifying the Irish people. The catalyst he used in hope of bringing about such a change was the irrational: magic, Theosophy, Cabala, Spiritualism, folklore, and evoked moods.

Kathryn Ludwigson, *Edward Dowden* (New York: Twayne, 1973), 130.

29. Brown, *Ireland's Literature*, 58.

30. Ibid.

31. Ibid.

32. For a brief but useful assessment of the role of such societies, see Philip L. Marcus, *Yeats and the Beginning of the Irish Renaissance* (Ithaca, NY, and London: Cornell University Press, 1970), 65–70. A much more thorough account can be found in R. F. Foster's biography, *W. B. Yeats: A Life*, vol. 1, *The Apprentice Mage: 1865–1914*, particularly chapter 2, "Explorations: Dublin, 1881–1887."

33. Pascale Casanova, *The World Republic of Letters*, trans. M. B. DeBevoise (Cambridge, MA: Harvard University Press, 2007), 77.

34. Ibid., 75.

35. Ibid., 77.

36. Ibid., 303–23.

37. William Shakespeare, *Henry V* (3.3.61–62). William Shakespeare, *The Norton Shakespeare (Based on the Oxford Edition)*, ed. Stephen Greenblatt, Walter Cohen, Jean E. Howard, and Katherine Eisaman Maus (New York: Norton, 1997).

38. Richard English, *Irish Freedom*, 237.

39. Defining "capital" in this noneconomic sense, Casanova writes that it is first "constituted by things, material objects [such as] texts—collected, catalogued, and declared national history and property." Casanova, *World Republic*, 14. Furthermore, the age of a nation's literary texts contribute to its capital, since "the older the literature, the more substantial a country's patrimony, the more numerous canonical texts that constitute its literary pantheon in the form of 'national classics.'" Ibid. Casanova divides such canonical texts into "classics," "works that stand above temporal rivalry," and "universal" works, which "transcend all particular attachments or qualities." Ibid. Shakespeare, Dante, and Cervantes are examples of works which "summarize at once the greatness of a national literary past, its historical and literary legitimacy, and the universal (and therefore ennobling) recognition of its greatest authors." Ibid., 15.

40. Ibid., 34.

41. Ibid., 35.

42. Ibid., 37.

43. Ludwigson, *Edward Dowden*, 135.

44. For a thorough account of Yeats's thinking about the English Renaissance and its writers (Spenser and Jonson in particular), the interested reader should turn to Wayne Chapman, *Yeats and English Renaissance Literature* (London: Palgrave Macmillan, 1991). A useful summary can also be found in T. McAlindon's essay, "Yeats and the English Renaissance," *PMLA* 82, no. 2 (1967): 157–69.

45. Murphy, "An Irish Catalysis," 216.

46. Much recent work has focused on the implications of Yeats's studies of English Renaissance writers for his cultural nationalism. Declan Kiberd, for instance, suggests that "hidden in the classic writings of England . . . lay many subversive potentials, awaiting their moments like unexploded bombs." He continues: "The young Irish man and woman could use Shakespeare to explore, and explain, and even perhaps to justify, themselves." Kiberd, *Inventing Ireland*, 268. Typically, however, critical studies tend to foreground Spenser, rather than Shakespeare. In one such essay, for instance, David Gardiner examines Yeats's work on *The Selected Poems of Edmund Spenser with an Introduction by W. B. Yeats* and argues that Yeats constructed Spenser as an Anglo-French court poet as a means of reconciling the disparate demands of an Irish cultural nationalism and an English literary tradition with which he identified: "Claiming his own Norman descent from the Butler Earls of Ormond, Yeats asserted that the nation to which

Spenser had 'true' allegiance was the 'Anglo-French.'" David Gardiner, "'To Go There as a Poet Merely': Spenser, Dowden, and Yeats," *New Hibernia Review* 1, no. 2 (1997): 131. The manner in which Yeats supplements Edward Dowden's Spenser book to promote an Irish literary tradition mirrors his critique of Dowden's Shakespeare and, as I argue in chapter 1, his de-Anglicizing of England's national poet.

47. W. B. Yeats, *The Collected Works of W. B. Yeats*, vol. 4, *Early Essays*, ed. Richard J. Finneran (New York: Scribner, 2007), 113.

48. Ibid., 114.

49. Ibid.

50. Ibid.

51. Ibid.

52. Ibid., 112. George Bornstein and Richard J. Finneran attribute this allusion to Dionysius the Areopagite, who "sought to combine Neoplatonic mystical elements with Christianity." W. B. Yeats, *Early Essays*, 393–94.

53. Ibid., 116.

54. Ibid., 118.

55. Ibid., 116.

56. Ibid., 115.

57. Ibid., 25.

58. Ibid.

59. Ibid.

60. Yeats writes that one such vision was inspired by his request "to have some past life of mine revealed." It proceeds as follows:

> A man in chain armour passed through a castle door, and the seeress noticed with surprise the bareness and rudeness of the castle rooms. There was nothing of the magnificence or the pageantry she had expected. The man came to a large hall and to a little chapel opening out of it, where a ceremony was taking place. There were six girls dressed in white, who took from the altar some yellow object—I thought it was gold, for though, like my acquaintance, I was told not to see, I could not help seeing. Somebody else thought that it was yellow flowers, and I think the girls, though I cannot remember clearly, laid it between the man's hands. He went out for a time, and as he passed through the great hall one of us, I forget whom, noticed that he passed over two gravestones. Then the vision became broken, but presently he stood in a monk's habit among men-at-arms in the middle of a village reading from a parchment. He was calling villagers about him, and presently he and they and the men-at-arms took ship for some long voyage. The vision became broken again, and when we could see clearly they had come to what seemed the Holy Land. They had begun some kind of sacred labour among palm-trees. The common men among them stood idle, but the gentlemen carried large stones, bringing them from certain directions, from the cardinal points I think, with a ceremonious for-mality. The evoker of spirits said they must be making some masonic house. His mind, like the minds of so many students of these hidden things, was always running on masonry and discovering it in strange places.

W. B. Yeats, *Early Essays*, 28–29.

61. Ibid., 31.

62. Ibid., 265.

63. Ibid., 275.

64. Ibid., 265.

65. Ibid.

66. Ibid., 267.

67. Ibid., 268.

68. Ibid., 263.

69. Ibid.

70. Ibid.

71. Yeats does not dismiss all of Spenser's poetry in this manner. "I have put into this book only those passages from Spenser that I want to remember and carry about with me," he writes. W. B. Yeats, *Early Essays*, 274. In his final section of the essay, in fact, Yeats explains that he has chosen passages which "have enough ancient mythology, always an implicit symbolism," and then proceeds with a fascinating anecdote: "Once I saw what is called, I think, a Board School continuation class play *Hamlet*. There was no stage, but they walked in procession into the midst of a large room full of visitors and of their friends. While they were walking in, that thought came to me again from I know not where. I was alone in a great church watching ghostly kings and queens setting out upon their unearthly business." Ibid., 275. Again, then, the visionary potential of Shakespeare's drama is emphasized. In this case, however, "that thought" refers to a boyhood experience of being alone in "some old building" and imagining that a "procession of strange people doing mysterious things" was about to emerge from a doorway. Ibid. Both cases—the *Hamlet* production and the boyhood imaginings—result from a passage from the *Faerie Queene* that Yeats claims he must have read as a child, and then later forgotten: "It was only last summer, when I read the Fourth Book of the *Faerie Queene*, that I found I had been imagining over and over the enchanted persecution of Amoret." Ibid.

72. Marcus, *Irish Renaissance*, 61.

73. See in particular the chapter, "The Last *Aisling*—A Vision," in *Inventing Ireland*, 316–26.

74. This is taken from Yeats's famous letter to John O'Leary, July 1892. See *The Collected Works of W. B. Yeats*, vol. 3, *Autobiographies*, ed. Douglas Archibald and William O'Donnell (New York: Scribner, 1999), 210–11.

75. Rupin Desai, *Yeats's Shakespeare* (Evanston, IL: Northwestern University Press, 1971).

76. Henderson, *Collaborations*, 13.

77. Desai, *Yeats's Shakespeare*, 6.

78. Ibid., xiii.

79. I should also mention two recent examinations of Yeats's Shakespeare. In 2013, a special issue of *Yeats Annual*, entitled "The Living Stream: Essays in Memory of A. Norman Jeffares," appeared with an essay by Denis Donoghue on this topic. See "Yeats's Shakespeare: 'There Is a Good Deal of My Father in It,'" *Yeats Annual* 18 (2013): 69–95. In addition, Adam Putz covers much of the same ground as myself in his book, *The Celtic Revival in Shakespeare's Wake: Appropriation and Cultural Politics in Ireland, 1867–1922* (New York: Palgrave Macmillan, 2013). Unfortunately, due to the very recent publication of Putz's book, I have been unable to respond to his work substantively.

80. Bryan Reynolds, *Performing Transversally: Reimagining Shakespeare and the Critical Future* (New York and Basingstoke: Palgrave Macmillan, 2003), 9.

Chapter One

De-Anglicization

Yeats, Victorian Shakespeare, and Cultural Authority

> Matthew Arnold asks how much of the Celt must one imagine in the ideal man
> of genius. I prefer to say, how much of the ancient hunters and fishers and of
> the ecstatic dancers among hills and woods must one imagine in the ideal man
> of genius?
> —W. B. Yeats, "The Celtic Element in Literature"

In his "Reveries over Childhood," Yeats recalls a time when, aged "ten or twelve,"[1] his father took him to see Henry Irving play Hamlet. He writes of his father's preference for Ellen Terry in the role, remarking how he "did not understand why I preferred Irving to Ellen Terry, who was, I can see now, the idol of himself and his friends."[2] He continues as follows: "I could not think of her, as I could think of Irving's Hamlet, as but myself, and I was not old enough to care for feminine charm and beauty. For many years Hamlet was an image of heroic self-possession for the poses of youth and childhood to copy, a combatant of the battle within myself."[3] As was the case for many children in Victorian Britain, Shakespeare loomed large in Yeats's early imagination, both as a treasury of fantastic stories and as a mammoth figure of cultural authority. Earlier in the pages of his autobiography, Yeats compares his stentorian grandfather, William Pollexfen, to King Lear: patriarchal, terrifying, prone to irruptions from some profound subterranean passion. Here, Yeats remembers the impact of Irving's Hamlet on his young imagination, a palimpsest of male figures—Shakespeare, Hamlet, Irving—impressing upon him the weight of Shakespearean masculinity, embodied in the most admired Shakespearean actor of the day. Irving's Hamlet, so the adult Yeats says, offered him "an image of heroic self-possession," a mask with which to project strength, authority, and power, qualities that the shy

25

young Anglo-Irish boy did not yet possess. Many years later, in his essay "At Stratford-on-Avon," Yeats would pick a fight with the most famous Shakespearean academic of the day, Edward Dowden, demolishing an entire school of criticism with the kind of ad hominem appeal his younger self would surely have appreciated: "These books took the same delight in abasing Richard II. that school-boys do in persecuting some boy of fine temperament, who has weak muscles and a distaste for school games."[4] Hamlet and, later, Richard were close to Yeats's heart: persecuted, misunderstood noblemen with a poet's sensibility and minds always on the verge of a self-induced madness.

Growing up in the latter half of the nineteenth century, Yeats could hardly have avoided Shakespeare. As Adrian Poole puts it, "If not a god, Shakespeare was the most powerful of ghosts, and ghosts tend to inhabit at least as much as they inspire and liberate."[5] Yeats would surely have approved of Poole's metaphor; as much a spiritualist as a poet and playwright, he encountered numerous ghosts in his career, and the spirit of Shakespeare occupied his mind at key points in his life, guiding him in his poetry and his drama, and lending weight to his cultural agenda on behalf of Irish nationalism.[6] Literary historians have given a great deal of attention to the Victorian Shakespeare, although Victorian *Shakespeares* might be a better term, since "the Bard" and his works had so thoroughly suffused the cultural landscape of the period. Shakespeare on the stage; Shakespeare for children; Shakespeare for women and for the working classes; Shakespeare for the empire; Shakespeare for moral edification; Shakespeare bowdlerized; Shakespeare mythologized; and above all, Shakespeare nationalized: such was the diversity of sites and discourses in which the Victorian Shakespeare operated. Referenced, alluded to, and imitated in literary works, the Victorian Shakespeare was also a mass of textual fragments, and we might again borrow from Poole to indicate the sheer quantity and variety of such literary appropriations in nineteenth-century texts:

> If we think of what a particular writer such as Dickens owes to Shakespeare, no single metaphor will be adequate to its range and complexity, whether derived from economics, law, physiology, psychology, theology, or even literary theory. Think for example . . . of borrowing, stealing, appropriating, inheriting, assimilating; of being influenced, inspired, dependent, indebted, haunted, possessed; of homage, mimicry, travesty, echo, allusion and intertextuality.[7]

Moreover, if the two "key sites" of Shakespeare dissemination at the time were the schoolroom and the theatre, Katheryn Prince reminds us that he also "circulated within a diverse array of less formal engagements, for instance as a popular topic for women's reading groups."[8] Indeed, the Shakespeare of this book—Yeats's Shakespeare—emerges from the pages of Yeats's essays and articles, many published in the newspapers and in the various periodicals associated with the Irish Literary Revival. Perhaps the most significant Shakespeare of the Victorian period (if taken as a whole) was the academic Shakespeare, and Michael Taylor sums up this period as "the age of Grammar and Lexicography, the golden age of the philologist and the academic editor, described by M. C. Bradbrook as 'the Industrial Revolution of Shakespeare studies.'"[9] Yeats's Shakespeare was decidedly nonacademic, as was Yeats, in the sense of the institutionalized, professionalized study of English literature established at the end of the nineteenth century, and epitomized in Ireland by Edward Dowden, Trinity don and friend of Yeats's father. That being said, Yeats's Shakespeare emerges initially from two interventions within the realm of academic Shakespeare, engagements with two academic giants of the period: Matthew Arnold and Edward Dowden.[10]

Of course, we should be wary of construing the nineteenth century as a singular "period," tempting as it can be to align history with the reigns of individual monarchs. In terms of Shakespeare reception, Adrian Poole sees "half-truths"[11] in "contemplating three main phases"[12] in the nineteenth century. The first, consisting of the romantic poets; the novels of Sir Walter Scott; the performances of Kean, Kemble, and Siddons; and the criticism of Hazlitt and Coleridge, comes to an end in the 1830s, giving way to a forty-year "period of consolidation"[13] during which "Shakespeare infiltrates the imagination of all the major creative writers."[14] It is during this phase that Shakespearean biography takes off, and his works reach a broader audience through a proliferation of new editions of his texts. Finally, and most importantly for this study, Poole sees 1875 ushering in a "new epoch" in the theatre, marked by Henry Irving's Lyceum Theatre and his "brooding Shakespeare."[15] Subsequently, this epoch triggered a reaction against the dominant modes of Shakespearean staging from the spectacular to a fashion for "more authentic staging."[16] Finally, writes Poole, Shakespeare came to be seen as an obstacle to the development of a new theatrical aesthetic. On the stage, then, the story of nineteenth-century Shakespeare is one of increasing cultural authority and ubiquity—both "lowbrow" and "high"—followed by a filial revolt. In his "Dublin Epilogue," Poole reminds the reader that Irish writers played a significant role in these later developments, such that even though their "dealings with Shakespeare are of very different kinds . . . they help to draw a line that separates a Victorian from a post-Victorian Shakespeare."[17] "Dowden, Stoker and Wilde fall on one side of this line," he writes, "Shaw, Yeats and Joyce on the other."[18] Poole's historical scheme is of course open to debate,[19] as is the clarity of the demarcation he offers in regard to his Dubliners. There can be little doubt that Yeats's drama does position him among those who sought to break from nineteenth-century dramatic traditions of illusion and stage realism (a topic I explore in the second chapter); however, as mentioned above, Yeats's Shakespeare develops initially from his interventions in two distinctly Victorian academic fields: philology, with its racial subtext, and a biographically oriented character critique. As such, Yeats's Shakespeare in his first flush is largely a Victorian Shakespeare.[20] This assertion constitutes the primary thrust of this chapter. Moreover, I want to demonstrate here how this early version of Yeats's Shakespeare adheres to the three precepts I set out in the introduction: that he follows the contours of Yeats's evolving cultural nationalism, that he maps onto—but imperfectly so—the dominant paradigms in Shakespeare reception of the times, and that he demonstrates the primacy of Yeats's esoteric metaphysics in his work, especially as they pertain to questions of Irish ethnicity and nationality. What is really at stake in Yeats's writing about Shakespeare, in his disputes with Arnold and Dowden, is Yeats's own authority as a nationalist writer and ultimately the foremost figure in the Irish Revival. His argument in the case of Arnold's work is an explicitly nationalist one: the "Celt" is not subordinate to the "Saxon," whether in language, literature, or life. With Dowden, Yeats's Shakespeare responds to a specifically intranational struggle concerning the professor's political Unionism and disdain for the seemingly nativist cultural agenda of the Revival. Indeed, any assessment of Yeats's Shakespeare must attempt to parse the young poet's relationship with Dowden. As an Anglo-Irishman of Methodist stock, an affirmed political Unionist, a public opponent of the Irish Literary Revival, and a professional literary critic, Dowden's background and cultural politics simultaneously aligned him with, and separated him from, the younger Yeats's trajectory. Although literary historians have long situated the origins of the public dispute between the two men in the 1895 "Dowden Controversy" (as Yeats called it), the exact nature of Yeats's revolt against the Trinity academic proves harder to unravel. Dowden had encouraged the young poet, helping him to publish his early poetry. Later, in failing health, Dowden was to suggest Yeats as a replacement chair of English.[21] In the 1890s, however, Yeats excoriated Dowden, and in 1901, in the pages of his essay "At Stratford-on-Avon," Yeats extrapolated from Dowden's Shakespeare criticism a philosophical materialism and utilitarian mode of thought he considered inimically English. In both cases—Arnold and Dowden—we see Yeats working via a process of engagement and appropriation: he enters a preexisting discourse, adopts its terms, and then supplements them (Arnold) or inverts them (Dowden). Despite his own avowed opposition to all matters "Victorian," a descriptor he associates with a pernicious English modernity, Yeats's Shakespeare began life among the nineteenth-century academic colossi, and on their terms.

Most of all, the Victorian Shakespeare was a figure of moral and social authority, and it is this characteristic that enabled his deployment ideologically in both progressive and conservative cultural politics. Poole calls him the "Great Image of Authority" and demonstrates how, for the Victorians,

"Shakespeare was . . . a way of expressing all sorts of beliefs, ideals, desires, and fears about authority."[22] In an age of increasing religious skepticism, Shakespeare might even be considered the ultimate authority, and Gary Taylor notes how "the scientific assault on received religion perhaps made literature the more secure idol for a modern civilization."[23] "In this cultural environment," he writes, "Shakespeare's artistic supremacy had ceased to be debated; it was simply assumed."[24] In the field of Shakespeare reception and appropriation, ideological critique has concentrated primarily on the ways in which Shakespeare's authority has been exploited to oppress the marginalized and consolidate the power of the ruling classes. However, as Prince reminds us in her work on Victorian periodicals, "Shakespeare [in periodicals] signified meanings ranging from archetypal authority figure to friend and ally of the disenfranchised,"[25] and such publications reveal that "he was also used to resist hegemony and to claim alternative kinds of political and cultural power."[26] Prince's assessment is equally germane to the analysis of Yeats's Shakespeare, who responds to the paradox of Yeats's cultural politics—nationalist, folk oriented, but elitist—and indeed to the complexities of his social identity. As a cultural program with political interests, the Irish Revival grappled with foes both domestic and international. Engaging with these opponents, Yeats drew rather conventionally upon the authority of Shakespeare, and indeed upon the authority of Shakespeareans. But Yeats also had recourse to alternative authorities: the esoteric societies to which he belonged as an adept and practitioner of magic. As such, I agree with Denis Donoghue, who, in a recent essay on Yeats's Shakespeare, moves to qualify the position maintained by Yeats scholars, "that Yeats received his first sense of Shakespeare from his father, presumably in early conversations with him in London and Dublin."[27] "Our main authority for this conclusion," he continues "is William M. Murphy, who maintains that the ideas expressed in Yeats's essay on Shakespeare, 'At Stratford-on-Avon,' are 'completely his father's, though not specifically acknowledged.'"[28] Donoghue rightly "demur[s] at Murphy's word, 'completely'";[29] Yeats's Shakespeare, as with a great deal of his aesthetic philosophy, owes much to his father's influence, but more to his own evolving thought. If, as a youth, Yeats wrapped himself in the cloak of Irving's Hamlet, as an adult he donned the black cape of the magus. This fusion of the orthodox and the esoteric defines much of Yeats's work and accounts for the manner in which his Shakespeare defies a facile categorization even as it reflects the dominant and emergent paradigms of the nineteenth and early twentieth centuries. Whether deliberate or not, his early foray into "Shakespace" should be understood broadly as a move whose effects were to de-Anglicize Shakespeare, appropriate Shakespearean cultural capital for the Revival, and undermine the cultural authority of the Irish academy.

AN OCCULT HERMENEUTIC

As we will see, Yeats's primary technique for supplementing and so de-Anglicizing the dominant academic Shakespearean paradigms—biography, character critique, philology—relied fundamentally upon an epistemological reorientation, and his Shakespeare can be seen as an appropriation of trends in Shakespeare criticism into the framework of a highly idiosyncratic occult nationalism. Before delving into the specifics of Yeats's response to Arnold and to Dowden, I want to define the tenets of his esoteric religious philosophy around the turn of the century, and to isolate those specific principles deployed in the construction of Shakespeare: visionary spiritualism; an idealist, esoteric account of historical change; and the pursuit of gnosis (secret wisdom) through ritual magic. As is well known, Yeats's distaste for scientific positivism and his proclivity for Neoplatonic thought underpin his revivalist aesthetics and account for his initial allegiance to Blavatsky's Theosophists and his subsequent membership of the Hermetic Order of the Golden Dawn, which he joined in 1890. Eclecticism and open-mindedness perhaps best describe the evolution of Yeats's spiritual beliefs, and certainly the occult organizations with which he associated drew upon a wide range of arcane lore and esoteric scholarship for their rites and philosophical principles: Far Eastern philosophy, Cabbala, Rosicrucianism, and spiritualist practices such as séances and divination, for instance. Denis Saurat's definition of "the occult" as "a strange and monstrous alliance" of "all the conquered religions: Gnostic beliefs, Neo-platonism, Hermeticism, Manicheanism, Mithraism, Zoroastrianism"[30] captures perfectly the mishmash of traditions plundered by MacGregor Mathers in his construction of the Golden Dawn's rituals and belief system. Of course, the topic of Yeats's attraction to and participation in occult societies has now been examined in some detail, and I would direct the interested reader to the collection of essays edited by George Mills Harper, *Yeats and the Occult*, for a thorough investigation of the topic.[31] Here, however, it is sufficient to differentiate between two important terms that I will be using in my analysis of Shakespeare's construction and deployment: "mysticism" and "occultism."[32]

In his accomplished monograph, *The Birth of Modernism: Ezra Pound, T. S. Eliot, W. B. Yeats, and the Occult*, Leon Surette argues for the centrality of the late nineteenth and early twentieth-century Occult Revival in the aesthetic philosophies of avant-garde European artists and writers. French symbolism and Poundian imagism, he argues, share a concern with the transformative power of visual symbols that is not purely aesthetic, but instead bears witness to occultist techniques for inducing visions. In the 1890s, under MacGregor Mathers's tutelage, Yeats learned such techniques, which required the adept to focus on specific symbolic shapes and colors. Having fixed these symbols in the mind's eye, the visionary might then travel "through" the symbol, as if through an open door, into the transcendent realm of higher reality. Significantly, in his 1901 essay "Magic," Yeats wonders if artists are in fact the "successors" of "the masters of magic,"[33] capable not only of access to this realm, but also of "casting forth enchantments, glamours, illusions" over their audiences, and "especially tranquil men."[34] As we shall see, this is a concept central to Yeatsian dramaturgy, and one which he inevitably applied to Shakespeare's dramatic effect. In *The Birth of Modernism*, Surette also draws a straight line from the so-called modernist treatment of myth and history to the "secret histories" of occultists, which posit supernatural or transcendental forces as the primum mobile of human history and identify a tradition of secret knowledge, or "gnosis," passed down from antiquity and encoded in hermetic texts. Yeats's own *A Vision* (1922) might be seen as his contribution to this tradition. In his introduction, moreover, Surette supplies the following working definition of occultism, and distinguishes it from mysticism pure and simple:

> Occultism, then, can reasonably be regarded as metaphysical speculation—speculation about the nature of ultimate reality and of our relation to it. Typically nontheistic and monistic, it is also typically mystical. All varieties of occultism . . . assume the possibility of direct contact between living human beings and ultimate reality, the noumenal, the transcendent, or the divine. Contact with ultimate reality can be achieved either through a spontaneous mystical revelation or through some ritual initiation such as those of the mysteries of Eleusis. The possibility of illumination through initiation distinguishes the occult from mysticism and connects it to secret societies such as Masonry.[35]

This is a useful way of thinking; what makes occultism different from mysticism is the concept of self-transformation through initiation rites, an emphasis on the study of occult lore, and the conviction that progressing through the various levels or orders of an occult organization could lead ultimately to the development of powerful visionary—even magical—abilities. One might be born a seer, but one needed to study to become a magus. In *Yeats and the Occult*, for instance, William H. O'Donnell explains how "this principle that mortals could be turned into magi was the central organizing principle for the Golden Dawn's ritual initiations, which chart the progression from Neophyte, through four ranks of the Outer Order, to the Inner Order with its three 'Adeptus' grades."[36] Yeats was undoubtedly a mystic from childhood on, but as a member of the Inner Order of the Golden Dawn, he was also an accomplished occultist who participated in—and in some cases helped to craft—secret rituals, and who studied texts in the hermetic tradition. The last decade of the nineteenth century, in particular, was a period in which Yeats's occult activities became increasingly important to him on both a personal and intellectual level. Many of Yeats's influential patrons and admirers, not to mention his muse, Maud Gonne, were members of the Golden Dawn, and the draft of his unpublished semiautobiographical novel, *A Speckled Bird*, bears witness both to the significance of the society in Yeats's thought, and to the series of acrimonious squabbles that led to a split in the membership of the London branch, and to the eventual expulsion of Mathers himself. Yeats's Shakespeare was therefore constructed primarily during the 1890s during a period when Yeats was working hard to craft a public literary reputation, to negotiate the politics and personalities of the Golden Dawn, and to define his role more clearly as an Irish cultural nationalist.

What we see, then, in Yeats's earlier writing on Shakespeare is first and foremost the attribution of mystical affect to his drama via its lyricism and symbolism. In doing so, Yeats adopts what Leon Surette terms an "occult allegoresis,"[37] a hermeneutic derived from "the symbolic theory of Friedrich Creuzer [which] reads myths as accounts of transcendental experiences that have been esoterically concealed beneath an exoteric surface."[38] Yeats also points to the inclusion of supernatural beings from English folklore—the fairies in *A Midsummer Night's Dream*, for example—as a sign of the play-wright's own mysticism and participation in the folk beliefs of the rural, early modern English. Valorizing magical thinking within the English and Irish folk traditions allows Yeats to connect them, and to then draw a contrast between the contemporary English and their early modern culture hero.[39] A proclivity for mysticism thus replaces the pragmatic, business-minded bard constructed by many Victorian biographers and imperial apologists. Having established Shakespeare's mystical credentials, Yeats then takes on the Trinity College Shakespearean, Edward Dowden, engaging with the professor's exegesis of Shakespeare's English kings, but reversing the signification of their character attributes such that Richard II—an effete and incompetent figure in Dowden's reckoning—is elevated through what Yeats identifies as the experience of spontaneous mystical revelation. England's greatest king, it turns out, was an impractical seer, precisely the charge laid by Matthew Arnold at the feet of "the Celt."

"Because of occultism's focus on a mystery or incommunicable wisdom," writes Surette, "occult writing has two principle themes: contact with the noumenal, or 'reality'; and the secret tradition, namely, the lives and teachings of enlightened individuals and of the communities of 'seekers' after illumination."[40] If contact with the "noumenal" makes King Richard a seer, and Shakespeare a symbolist working within a Neoplatonic, folkloric imaginary, the emphasis of the secret tradition on communities of enlightened truth seekers underpins the critical reorientation Yeats undertakes following his disagreements with Arnold and Dowden. As a producer and legitimizer of a positivist epistemology, academe constituted a natural opponent for Yeats, the occult nationalist, and in Yeats's writing, professor Dowden in particular stands for the academy's complicity in what Yeats saw as a debasing modernity which had spread from England across the sea to Dublin, and which threatened to colonize Irish minds utterly. As such, occult organizations offered an alternative institutional model and—in combination with an avant-garde theatre—suggested a means by which writers of the Irish Literary Revival might lead a cultural transformation and a rejection of bourgeois, "English" modes of self-representation. Indeed, it was precisely the symbolic, ritualistic nature of Elizabethan drama; contemporary, avant-garde stagecraft; *and* occultist rites that led Yeats to devote a majority of his energies at the start of the twentieth century to constructing rituals for a new, nationalist secret society—the Celtic Mysteries—and writing verse drama for the Irish National Theatre. While Yeats's use of Shakespeare in the new Irish drama comprises the topic of the second chapter of this book, his initial foray into academic criticism merits consideration here as a part of what I am arguing is an important intervention by Yeats in a literary-critical discourse with significant implications for Irish cultural nationalism.

YEATS'S "ANCIENT FISHERS": DE-ANGLICIZING THE BARD

Yeats's Shakespeare is, therefore, first visible in the fascinating dialectic between Matthew Arnold's essay "On the Study of Celtic Literature" (1866) and Yeats's response, "The Celtic Element in Literature" (1897). What emerges from Yeats's early foray into "Shakespace" is a neoromantic bard whose drama channels the symbols and sensibilities of a vibrant Elizabethan folk culture; his drama is replete with lyrical passages of natural imagery and, occasionally, representations of folkloric characters whose roots can be traced to a pre-Christian era. This construction of Shakespeare as a people's poet finds a philological basis in Arnold's writing; the Englishman's central thesis is that a "Celtic" substratum exists in English letters, visible in some of the more lyrical and folkloric passages in Shakespeare's plays. The Shakespeare that develops from Yeats's treatment of this subject is not radically different from Arnold's. As we shall see, Yeats does not disagree entirely with Arnold; rather, he adopts Arnold's terms and supplements their signifieds. Specifically, he reorients the signification of the word "Celt." Furthermore, he situates his Shakespeare within the structures of two of his most important, and critically dismissed, ideas: the existence of magic, and the cyclicality of historical epochs. These two strains of thought were to later find their textual apotheosis in *A Vision*, but they appear early in Yeats's thought, here making possible a careful de-Anglicization of "the Bard" by offering alternatives to Arnold's ethnography. Yeats's belief in magic, and his theories about what would later be called "gyres," are both central to his thinking about Shakespeare, both on the page and in the Irish National Theatre.

So, Yeats's nationalist Shakespeare emerges at the end of the nineteenth century, before his seminal visit to Stratford in 1901, and does so as an intervention in a philological discourse similar to those uncovered by Edward Said in his influential study of Orientalism. It should be noted that Arnold's essay on the "Celtic Element" in English literature was conceived as a lecture, given at Oxford University as a part of Arnold's call for establishing a chair of "Celtic." Ostensibly a philological recuperation of the "Celtic" sensibility in English letters, Arnold clearly intends a discursive assimilation of the Irish, thus naturalizing the position of Ireland as a colonized territory. Politically, Arnold was no Irish nationalist; as Declan Kiberd points out, "in 1886, during the Home Rule crisis he proclaimed himself a staunch critic of Gladstone's proposal, arguing that the 'idle and impudent Irish could never properly govern themselves.'"[41] The study of Celtic literature proposed by Arnold was really an exploitation of Herder's liberating theses to deflect Irish claims to an autonomous literary space: a fascinating case of subversion and containment. However, this discursive maneuver was not without its own fissures. Pointing to Shakespeare for evidence of a "Celtic" lyrical influence offered Irish writers a claim to the Shakespearean inheritance and its attendant cultural capital. In many ways, then, Yeats's response to Arnold's "defense" marks the public debut of Yeats's Shakespeare, whose form and function was to shift over the next several decades to follow the contours of Yeats's nationalist projects.

Arnold's foray into racial hermeneutics represents an interesting juncture in Victorian thinking about national literature, and about Shakespeare in particular. Establishing a racial pedigree for the man from Stratford was a pseudoscientific game with national and imperial implications, and the tussle between German and English philologists, physiognomists, and amateur scholars of various stripes has been well documented.[42] As Richard Halpern neatly surmises in *Shakespeare among the Moderns*, "While these competing racial theories were equally chimerical, all harnessed Shakespeare's literary reputation to the politics of imperialism."[43] Following the demise of French literary hegemony in Europe, the nineteenth century witnessed a structural change in literary space that saw England's chief rivalry shift to the east. An Anglo-Saxon racial categorization fed into both English and German cultural triumphalism—each side claiming Shakespeare as their own—and in *On Heroes, Hero-Worship, and the Heroic in History*, Thomas Carlyle famously elevated Shakespeare to the status of a Saxon culture hero, a metonym for the British imperium, and the "ideological glue of Empire."[44] Hence, both Shakespeare and the Elizabethan era were enshrined as British cultural capital. In this context of competing claims to Shakespeare and to Saxon racial superiority, Arnold's essay actually constitutes a departure from the exclusive discourse of Anglo-German competition. "Arnold's insistence on the Celtic strain in Shakespeare's genius was an attempt to formulate a more liberal racial politics than Carlyle's," writes Halpern, "which might soften the antipathy the English felt towards their Irish subjects by positing a great Indo-European unity in which both races shared."[45] As previously mentioned, Arnold stopped short of endorsing a separate state for the Irish, reading in "Celtic" poetry the signs of a racial predisposition toward subservience: too dreamy and "ineffectual," the "Celts" were not capable of self-governance. Although Arnold's essay did not advocate political emancipation, it did have an interesting, unintentional effect. By rhetorically assimilating the "Celt" into a racial discourse privileging the Anglo-Teutonic qualities of English letters, Arnold opened up fissures which made possible further critical interventions by subaltern voices.[46] Declan Kiberd, for instance, notes how, "as early as 1897," Yeats was "expanding the meanings of 'Celtic' to global dimensions, sensing that the ancient was due for a return."[47] Most fascinating in W. B. Yeats's response, "The Celtic Element in Literature," is therefore the Irishman's strategy of rhetorical appropriation and subversion, and what emerges from Yeats's critical intervention is an "ancient" Shakespeare aligned with the tenets of an esoteric cultural nationalism, and divorced from an Anglo-Saxon racial signification.[48] Indeed, Kiberd sees this discursive reorientation as a central strategy of Irish revivalists: "The modern English, seeing themselves as secular, progressive and rational, had deemed the neighbouring islanders to be superstitious, backward and irrational. The strategy for revivalists thus became clear: for bad words substitute good, for *superstitious* use *religious*, for *backward* say *traditional*, for *irrational* suggest *emotional*."[49] In Yeats's romantic idealization of the rural Irish, the signifiers of Irish barbarity are connected to ideas or images that are given a positive valence by the precepts of Yeats's aesthetic philosophy, and much of the Irish Literary Revival was concerned in this way with rendering a discourse polysemous. This is one of the functions of Yeats's early Shakespeare: to confuse and reorient the Arnoldian account of English racial and cultural evolution, a master narrative of Celtic assimilation and Anglo triumphalism.

Of course, before examining this nascent Shakespeare, we need to look carefully at Arnold's essay, its teleological assumptions, and the spaces it creates for discursive resistance. Arnold's broader project took the form of a fight against an encroaching philistinism, and "On the Study of Celtic Literature" takes up arms against a bourgeoisie ignorant of "the Celt," or the "Celtic genius." "[E]ven as a matter of science," writes Arnold, "the Celt has a claim to be known, and we have an interest in knowing him, yet this interest is wonderfully enhanced if we find him to have actually a part in us."[50] Arnold's grounds for knowing "him" are thus twofold: first, the objective interests of "science," and second, the prospect of a greater understanding of "us." Literature here is rendered a body of empirical data through which to sift for signs of the "Celtic genius," just as cranial measurements might supply physiognomical clues: "the language and physical type of our race afford certain data for trying it, and other data are afforded by our literature, genius, and spiritual production generally."[51] Interestingly, Arnold's thesis seems to be calling for an awareness of hybridity, a collapsing of absolute difference. Citing the latest "discoveries" of philology, he points out how the Celtic languages—Gaelic and Cymric—belong to the same family as the Aryan ones. At root, then, the Saxon "us" and Celtic "them" are related. When "we" ask "what are we? what is England?"[52] the answer tentatively proposed by Arnold is: "[a] vast obscure Cymric basis with a vast visible Teutonic superstructure."[53] The Celt is buried beneath the Teuton, but "he" supports the entire structure: out of sight, buried, but nevertheless a subterranean presence of some significance. Arnold's archeological language is really political metaphor masquerading as Victorian empiricism: he is digging down to uncover the signs of a shared past. Yet while Arnold claims that "philology carries us towards ideas of affinity of race which are new to us,"[54] his history of ethnic interaction is underwritten by Anglocentric scientific and industrial discourses of modern "progress." The ability to see this march of progress, indeed to partake in it, depends upon a certain national disposition: "The excellence of a national spirit thus composed is freedom from whim, flightiness, perverseness; patient fidelity to Nature,—in a word, *science*,—leading it at last, though slowly, and not by the most brilliant road, out of the bondage of the humdrum and common, into the better life."[55] This, for Arnold, is the English genius: "energy with honesty."[56] Despite shared Indo-European roots, it is the English who manifest progress; they perfect a synthesis of flawed Germanic and Celtic elements. Anglo-Celtic ethnic history is thus the story of "a subject race['s] . . . blood entering into the composition of a new people, in which the stock of the conquerors counts for the most, but the stock of the conquered, too, counts for something."[57] Arnold's exposition is hardly conciliatory. The Celts are to be respected insofar as their ancestors have contributed "something" to the creation of the English master race; by extension, those Celts who remain separate from the English are flawed, outdated, unlikely to thrive in modernity, or perhaps even survive: "[s]entimental,—*always ready to react against the despotism of fact . . .* so eager for emotion that he has not patience for science [my italics]."[58] While the Germans are lacking in emotion, the Celts' "rebellion against fact" has doomed them not just to mediocre literature, but also to political oblivion, since "[t]he skillful and resolute application of means to ends which is needed both to make progress in material civilization, and also to form powerful states, is just what the Celt has the least turn for."[59] Arnold's recuperation of the Celt, then, is in truth a recuperation of those qualities he sees as Celtic inasmuch as they are not Germanic and insofar as they have helped construct the modern English: superior to the Celts in material, scientific propensity, and superior to the Germans in the affective qualities of their art.

Lest his audience should read Celtic emotionality as attractive in of itself, Arnold qualifies it by drawing a comparison with the descendants of ancient Greeks and Romans:

> He is sensual, as I have said, or at least sensuous; he loves bright colours, company, and pleasure; and here he is like the Greek and Latin races; but compare him with the talent the Greek and Latin (or Latinised) races have shown for gratifying their senses, for procuring an outward life, rich, luxurious, splendid, with the Celt's failure to reach any material civilisation sound and satisfying, and not out at elbows, poor, slovenly, and half barbarous.[60]

Here Arnold rewrites a history of conquest and exploitation as one of innate failure. In doing so he repeats many of the ethnic slurs articulated in four hundred years' worth of English accounts of Irish barbarity: they are primitive, unsuited for modern life, and dirty. They are in fact "half barbarous." Unlike earlier accounts, such as those we find in the early modern period, these qualities are innate, not performed. The Celts are detached from their land: they are "colossal, impetuous, adventurous wanderer[s]."[61] "They" are potentially unstable in terms of gender, "hav[ing] something feminine in them . . . peculiarly disposed to feel the spell of feminine idiosyncrasy."[62] "He" possesses a mystical and superstitious relation to the natural world, "attracted [to] the secret of natural beauty and natural magic,"[63] and last, but by no means least, "he" is "undisciplinable, anarchical, and turbulent by nature."[64] In making a case for the Celt, Arnold reiterates accusations of barbarity that had circulated since the twelfth-century Gerald of Wales composed the seminal treatise on Irish ethnicity: *Topographia Hibernia*. But here these familiar tropes are hardened into explicitly racial dogma. Transhumance, superstition, belligerence, material inferiority, proximity to nature—these things no longer signify barbaric behavior; they signify "the Celt."

I want to see Arnold's lectures as important in the history of imperialist discourse on Ireland, not just because they demonstrate the ways in which earlier, fluid accounts of difference harden into scientific classifications and collapse both subjects and objects into ontologically simpler groups, but also because they open up cracks, areas for intervention and resistance. According to Arnold, the qualities of English poetry derived from the Celts are "its turn for style, its turn for melancholy, and its turn for natural magic."[65] But his highly impressionistic exposition of these "Celtic" elements in English literature relies primarily on Arnold's mandarin intellectual cachet for its hermeneutic; the audience is to believe the speaker not necessarily because of the weight of evidence, but because of the status of the speaker as professor of poetry at Oxford University, the situation of his epideictic rhetoric (a lecture series given to undergraduates), and the respective authority of the writers from which he culls his examples, the most important of which is Shakespeare. Arnold's call at the end of the series for the establishment of a chair of "Celtic" at Oxford is a move designed to make Ireland an object of institutional academic knowledge/power in much the same way as "the Orient" had become an object of philological study. The clear subtext of Arnold's analysis is to reaffirm the cultural subjugation of the Irish and their political assimilation into British nationhood. More than this, "On the Study of Celtic Literature" constitutes an attempt to subvert the liberating implications of Herderian thought: Arnold argues for an English "genius" rooted in a vital, indigenous folk culture, which he labels "Celtic." As for the neighboring island across the sea, the modern Irish might as well not exist. They are elided from Arnold's account in favor of an ancient "Celt" whose sensibility precludes a coherent nationhood. Crucially, it is this rhetorical maneuver—the archaizing of Irish culture—along with his deployment of Shakespeare, that provides the opportunity for discursive resistance and the impetus for Yeats's initial foray into a highly politicized "Shakespace." In four essays from the turn of the century—"The Celtic Element in Literature," "On Magic," "At Stratford-on-Avon," and "Edmund Spenser"—Yeats carefully appropriates this valorizing account of an archaic "Celtic" sensibility, while dismantling the teleological, pseudoempirical framework that orients them toward a British cultural triumphalism.

The first of these essays is "The Celtic Element in Literature" (1897), and here we see the process by which Yeats supplements Arnold's rhetoric to arrive at a different, or at least modified, conclusion. Primarily, this constitutes an epistemological critique:

> When Matthew Arnold wrote, it was not easy to know as much as we know now of folk-song and folk-belief, and I do not think he understood that our "natural magic" is but the ancient religion of the world, the ancient worship of Nature and that troubled ecstasy before her, that certainty of all beautiful places being haunted, which is brought into men's minds. [66]

Here Yeats adopts Arnold's method of citing data as well as doxa to make the claim for the validity of the information he is presenting. In Arnold's case, the argument was underpinned and set in motion by a consideration of new empirical, philological "discoveries": the shared linguistic origin of Teutonic and Celtic languages. Yeats undermines Arnold's authoritative position by suggesting that his knowledge is outmoded, needing to be supplemented by further insights and discoveries concerning "folk song" and "folk belief." So his rhetoric is structured similarly; new information allows us a new understanding. Arnold's logic is weakened by the same maneuver with which it was originally established: "it was not easy to know as much as we now know." The Oxford professor's authority is not called into question; rather he becomes an earnest victim of a limited epistemology: proceeding from a flawed understanding of "folk belief," how could Arnold have possibly reached the correct conclusion? Crucially, Yeats advances his position by supplanting the philological framework of Arnold's essay with a revivalist one, and, as I want to demonstrate further, by replacing a linear teleology with an account of epistemic rupture.

In his initial response to Arnold, then, Yeats proceeds to offer a new interpretation of the data: the "magic" or superstition that Arnold read as specifically Celtic is in fact a characteristic of all "ancient" peoples. His stance is not polemic, but corrective: "Matthew Arnold asks how much of the Celt must one imagine in the ideal man of genius. I prefer to say, how much of the ancient hunters and fishers and of the ecstatic dancers among hills and woods must one imagine in the ideal man of genius?"[67] In this way he makes use of Arnold's literary capital to supplement his own, and then to counter his argument. Notice too that Yeats does not dispute the evidence, merely the conclusion. Validating the same master tropes of barbarity—an aversion to urban settlement, and a proclivity for nature worship—Yeats risks activating and further calcifying stereotypes that had been used since the twelfth century to assert Irish inferiority. However, his "ancient hunters and fishers" are not specifically Irish, and so, rhetorically speaking, his reorientation of the Englishman's work is not radical; it is supplemental. Arnold, according to this argument, was wrong only in his categorization. Thus, "one finds it [natural magic] very certainly in the quotations Arnold makes from English poets to prove a Celtic influence in English poetry . . . in Shakespeare's 'floor of heaven,' 'inlaid with patens of bright gold'; and in his Dido standing 'on the wild sea banks,' 'a willow in her hand,' and waving it in the ritual of the old worship of nature and the spirits of nature."[68] Yeats does not dispute the presence of something Arnold calls "Celtic," which he calls "ancient" in Shakespeare. Indeed, he makes further claims to that end: "Shakespeare found in his Mab, and probably his Puck, and one knows not how much else of his faery kingdom, in Celtic legend."[69] Yeats wants to rewrite the signs of Celticism as signifying a shared, venerable culture of "ancient" wisdom and practices. Crucially, one effect of this line of argument is to sidestep the organizing taxonomy of the nation-state. If the "Celtic" element in literature is intended to signify a natural process of Irish assimilation, resulting in the English "genius" or sensibility, then the "ancient" element in literature, per Yeats, transcends national boundaries. In his primary response, then, Yeats exploits Arnold's use of "Celtic" as a signifier for "archaic," "obsolete," and "pre-Christian" and seizes upon the signified sense, "ancient." And if the imagery of natural magic demonstrates the influence of "ancient" people, rather than "Celtic" people, then Shakespeare's drama no longer typifies the assimilation of the Celt into English letters. Instead, it becomes an example of art belonging to all those who maintain the connection with pre-Christian, pre-urbanized sensibilities. So, Yeats is not only asserting the independent existence of Irish culture, and, by implication, the indigenous cultures of other small, rural, nations; he is also beginning to de-Anglicize Shakespeare.[70] The ramifications of this move for Irish literary capital become clear once we consider the impact of two central aspects of Yeats's thinking: his belief in natural magic, and his vision of the seventeenth century as a moment of seismic, epistemic rupture.[71]

Yeats's neoromantic credo naturally figured him as an opponent to industrialism and positivism, and so, in his essays on Shakespeare and Spenser, Yeats revises another of Arnold's rhetorical appeals: the logic of the march of science. For Arnold, the development of rationalism and sciences such as philology both underpin the claims of English superiority and allow him the tools to demonstrate it. Yeats does not counter the telos here. Rather, he alters the valence, specifically locating the moment of a great epistemic shift in England. Thus, in "At Stratford-on-Avon" (1901) and "Edmund Spenser" (1902), he moves to rewrite the onset of neoclassicism and the Age of Reason as the beginning of a broadly aesthetic and spiritual deterioration in England, the result of which is the disassociation of English and Irish, or more generally, English and ancient folk. Shakespeare, then, belongs to the ancients:

> Shakespeare wrote at a time when solitary great men were gathering to them-
> selves the fire that had once flowed hither and thither among all men, when
> individualism in work and thought and emotion was breaking up the old
> rhythms of life, when the common people, sustained no longer by the myths of
> Christianity and of still older faiths, were sinking into the earth.[72]

This involves Shakespeare, the canonical center of claims to English cultural superiority, in one of Yeats's most common tropes, the curse of Enlightenment thought, material philosophy, and industrialization—perhaps best summed up in his assertion: "Descartes, Locke, and Newton took away the world and gave us excrement instead."[73] Shakespeare, then, produced his art among the last throws of an episteme—"the old rhythms of life"—which was thoroughly replaced in England, but only partially so in Ireland. In his essay on Edmund Spenser, Yeats actually sees the death of this episteme as the primary reason for Shakespeare's greatness: "Thoughts and qualities sometimes come to their perfect expression when they are about to pass away, and Merry England was dying in plays, and in poems, and in strange adventurous men."[74] All this is preparing the ground for Yeats's later attempt to compose a cyclical history of civilization; but here I want to stress the claim he is making about Shakespeare: that "the Bard" is in fact closer to the bards of Ireland than the positivist writers of contemporary England. That this is a radical maneuver should be apparent given Thomas Carlyle's claim sixty years before Yeats that the Stratford peasant was the greatest product of the English nation, more valuable to the English than the Indian Empire.[75] In effect, then, Yeats is rewriting English history as a story of fracture and dislocation rather than continuity, though he never really spells out the reasons for this shift until his later idealist claims of a broadly transcendent cyclicality. But whether a matter of cause or effect, he does characterize this break in terms of the ascendance of Puritanism and the replacement of feudal aristocracy and rural community—"Merry England"— by forms of protocapitalism and the metropolis. As Kiberd sees it, Yeats was "reaching back beyond the imperial mission to a pre-modern, carnivalesque vitality, to those elements which peoples shared before the fall into imperialism and nationalism—elements which survived in Shakespeare's plays, and which seemed to intersect, in suggestive ways, with the folk life of rural Ireland."[76] Irish revivalism in Yeats's hands meant romanticism with an explicitly nationalist agenda, and so the recuperation and dissemination of Irish folk materials, rooted as they were in a nonindustrial, rural locus, naturally entailed recuperating medievalism as an idealized alternative to modernity and its urban sensibilities. In Yeats's early essays, then, we see him supplementing Arnold's claims, reasserting the existence of Arnold's "Celt," denationalizing "him," reorienting "him" as the survivor of a cultural catastrophe, and, in doing so, reversing the signification of Arnold's teleology so that, inasmuch as the Irish still maintain many "ancient" folk traditions and the English do not, the relationship between Ireland and England is no longer one of "Celtic" assimilation into the Celtic-Teutonic synthesis, but of a shared past and a disunited present. Furthermore, as the representative of an older episteme, Shakespeare now belongs to the Irish.

FROM PAGE TO STAGE: DE-ANGLICIZING SHAKESPACE

At one level, the case for contemporary Ireland's affinity for, and proximity to, Shakespeare is the preservation there of feudal codes which were being reiterated in the circulation of legendary material such as the legend of Cuchulain by members of the Irish Literary Revival. These codes of existence include, but are not limited to, "indifference to the State," "scorn of the crowd," and "feudal passion"; they oppose the "big barn-door of common sense."[77] What is notable about Yeats's vision of Ireland, in its focus on peasants, lords, and ladies, is its antimodern archaism: Irish nationhood is rendered an idealized hierarchy, a feudal model with a mythological mode of self-representation. It is easy to see why Yeats would be attracted to Arnold's writing, given the Englishman's crusade against what he regarded as an encroaching bourgeois philistinism. The "scorn of the crowd" Yeats projects onto Shakespeare is an anachronism, a scorn for "the masses," which Kiberd reads as an aspect of anticolonial resistance rather than mere participation in a general critique of modern industrial society: a "revolt against all forms of modernity latent in the more regressive types of nationalism."[78] Shakespeare, like Yeats himself, valorizes both the peasantry and the aristocracy, and the extent to which Yeats emphasizes Shakespeare's affinity for the agrarian poor *and* the landowning class changes in consort with Yeats's disillusionment with Irish nationalism in its more conservative stages. Yeats's Shakespeare is thus a fluid entity, initially associated with "ancient fishers and hunters," and later a voice of aristocratic scorn. In his writings at the turn of the century, Yeats channels a vision, albeit romanticized, of England's "Merry," feudal past, and thus isolates an industrialized England, cutting it off from its store of literary capital.

But what of those "ecstatic dancers in the hills," with whom Shakespeare rubs shoulders in Yeats's response to Arnold? As we have seen, Yeats's early Shakespeare stands for a premodern, rural folk life, and the imagery of natural magic Arnold cites in his essay provides Yeats with evidence that a Shakespearean sensibility operates in rural Ireland, where similar folk beliefs still circulate. Yeats, of course, was an adherent to occult philosophies disseminated via the writings and practices of groups like Madame Blavatsky's Theosophists, and later, Mathers's Hermetic Order of the Golden Dawn. And so there is always an esoteric element to Yeats's Shakespeare. Rather than dismiss Yeats's Neoplatonic weltanschauung, however, I want to see it as a key factor in his appropriation of England's culture hero, and, following Kiberd, as an essential aspect of his peculiar brand of nationalism.[79] Based on two essays published in the London periodical *The Speaker* on May 11 and 18, 1901, "At Stratford-on-Avon" continues the process by which the techniques and aesthetic philosophy of England's national poet are de-Anglicized and co-opted by esoteric, Yeatsian principles: "in his art, as in all the older art of the world, there was much make-believe, and our scenery, too, should remember the time when, as my nurse used to tell me, herons built their nests in old men's beards!"[80] Here he is advocating a new style of stage scenery, more symbolic than the naturalistic sets of Victorian directors like Beerbohm Tree. The playful surprise indicated by the exclamation point and the childish term "make-believe" belies what was, for Yeats, a deeply symbolic and mystical aesthetic philosophy, shared by Shakespeare and "all the older art of the world."[81] Along with the collapse of feudalism, this is what underwrites his opposition to what he sees as the defining aspect of the post-Shakespearean episteme: material positivism, a normative "assumption" which "worked best of all in England where Edmund Spenser's inscription over the gates of his magic city seemed to end 'Do not believe too much.'"[82] In his essay "On Magic," he lays out the occultist tenets of his aesthetic philosophy: "that the borders of our mind are ever shifting, and that many minds can flow into one another . . . and create or reveal a single mind,"[83] that the borders of our memories are similarly fluid, and are in fact one memory, "the memory of Nature herself," and that "this great mind and great memory can be evoked by symbols."[84] Poets and imaginative individuals can, under the right circumstances and by means of symbols, create and control a vision in the minds of their listeners, which itself is drawn from an *anima mundi*—the great memory of the world. Powerful art, in this case, is literally an enchantment, and the features of poetry such as rhyme and rhythm have "arisen, as it seems, out of the sounds the enchanters made to help their imagination to enchant, to charm, to bind with a spell themselves and the passers-by."[85] By this token, "all men, certainly all imaginative men, must be for ever casting forth enchantments, glamours, illusions; and all men, especially tranquil men who have no powerful egotistic life, must be continually passing under their power."[86] Those people who live in modern cities are less capable of participating in the fusion of minds and have more difficult access to the *anima mundi* than those who live in rural solitude: "We cannot doubt," writes Yeats, "that barbaric people receive such influences more visibly and obviously, and in all likelihood more easily and fully than we do, for our life in cities, which deafens or kills the passive meditative life, and our education that enlarges the separated, self-moving mind, have made our souls less sensitive."[87] Here Yeats is using the precepts of his aesthetic philosophy to valorize an agrarian mode of existence that, in his view, exists in more remote parts of Ireland such as the West, and in England's feudal past. To the extent that "Englishness" is aligned in Yeats's thought with a mechanistic worldview, de-Anglicization necessarily means stemming and reversing the influence of industrialism and its attendant positivism. Reporting from a trip to Galway, Yeats notes in "On Magic" how "I myself could find in one district . . . but one man who had not seen what I can but call spirits, and he was in his dotage."[88] Revivalism, for Yeats, was about more than folk literatures; it also meant reviving magical thinking. The belief that such a spiritual reawakening could be achieved through aesthetics is typically taken to indicate a certain naivety on Yeats's part, and perhaps this is so. However, the implications of this faith for Yeats's Shakespeare are significant. For instance, much of Yeats's work for the Irish National Theatre involved the development of "Shakespearean" techniques for a new Irish drama, not merely to appropriate cultural capital, but also as a technology by which the Irish people could be restored to their special status as purveyors and practitioners of natural magic.

In "On the Study of Celtic Literature," Arnold supported his claims that the "Celt" was better off subsumed into the English "genius" with recourse to racist charges of Celtic indolence. As he constructs his Shakespeare, however, Yeats reframes this specific piece of dogma via his esoteric, aesthetic philosophy as a mode of being most conducive to imaginative transformation. Much of this is, of course, borrowed from romantic thought concerning the role of the imagination, but in these essays at the turn of the century, Yeats attributes what he calls "poetic reverie" most often to Shakespeare, noting in "J. M. Synge and the Ireland of His Time," for instance, how Shakespeare used "the slow elaborate structure of blank verse" and a "loosening of his plot" to obtain "time for reverie," giving "his characters the leisure to look at life from without."[89] Poetic reverie, a meditative and introspective stillness with an intensity close to trance, was, for Yeats, the reason for Richard II's superiority over Bolingbroke, and the characteristic feature of Hamlet. Donoghue calls it "Yeats's word for the mind when it is minding its own business, indifferent to the world's."[90] It was abundant until after Shakespeare, and now could be found mostly in Ireland, and then outside Dublin. In fact, as Yeats writes in "Magic," the capacity for unencumbered visionary experience is the privilege of those most removed from the forces of modernity and urbanization; "savages live always on the edge of vision."[91] Yeats is thus reversing the prejudicial view that we see in Spenser's *A View of the Present State of Ireland*, for example, that the city is the center of civility. Instead he privileges the rural margins. This is not an uncommon move in the resistance stage of anticolonialist discourse, and in this specific instance, Kiberd sees the playing out of certain Anglo-Protestant anxieties: the celebration of the land was, therefore, "a familiar strategy of the Protestant Imagination, estranged from the community, yet anxious to identify itself with the new national sentiment."[92] Whatever its place within the intranational complexities of Irish cultural nationalism, this emphasis on the privilege of the isolated, the rural, the superstitious, and the idle separates modern, industrial England from its feudal, agrarian past and connects Shakespeare to the folk artists of contemporary rural Ireland: "if I can unintentionally cast a glamour, an enchantment, over persons of our own time who have lived for years in great cities, there is no reason to doubt that men could cast intentionally a far stronger enchantment, a far stronger glamour, over the more sensitive people of ancient times, or that men can still do so where the older order of life remains unbroken."[93] Indolence reframed as meditative stillness; primitivism refigured as an atemporal mysticism; the "Celtic" element in English letters centralized and privileged: such textual maneuvers demonstrate Yeats's strategy of rhetorical appropriation and subversion in his fin-de-siècle foray into "Shakespace."

DOWDEN, SHAKSPERE, AND THE COSMOPOLITANS

Discourses are housed within institutions. As such, I suggest, Yeats's disagreement with Matthew Arnold needs to be understood as more than an articulation of the Irishman's revivalist principles. In 1901, Yeats visited Stratford to see the Benson cycle of Shakespeare's histories, and the essays he wrote about his experience there—ultimately combined into "At Stratford-on-Avon"—demonstrate his thinking about the necessity for new Irish cultural institutions, and indeed a revived Irish occultism. In "At Stratford," then, Yeats picks up an old quarrel with his father's friend, the Trinity professor Edward Dowden, engaging with Dowden's hermeneutics and again drawing upon the precepts of his religious philosophy. Arguing against the Trinity professor's analysis of Shakespeare and his characters might be read as a kind of anxiety of influence, or even a familial score settling. As Denis Donoghue puts it, "If JBY had two or three reasons for being angry with Dowden, his son had ten."[94] However, as with Arnold, this instance of scholarly erudition signifies more broadly in the context of Yeats's cultural nationalism; Yeats's academic interventions are proxies for a larger struggle to elevate the status of Irish letters and to establish the cultural authority of the Revival. While Yeats's intervention in Arnold's philology should be understood as a straightforwardly nationalist maneuver, his disagreement with Dowden responds to an intranational debate implicating the cultural politics of the Irish Revival, and the not insignificant matter of Irish literature.

This disagreement became public in January 1895, following the reading in Dublin of a lecture by Roden Noel (previously delivered in London) on the poetry of Sir Samuel Ferguson. Dowden's remarks sparked a series of rebuttals and reiterations which were published in the pages of the Dublin *Daily Express*, both making visible and consolidating a division among Irish literati concerning the direction of Irish literature. Although Dowden offered no more of his own opinions in the sallies that followed, his initial remarks had made clear the "cosmopolitan" prescription for Irish literature, a position which was subsequently adopted by John Eglinton and William Larmanie. Representing the "nationalist," or perhaps less generously, "nativist," position were Yeats and George "AE" Russell. Irish writers, argued the cosmopolitans, should remain open to influences from other lands, and this principled position—at least in Dowden's case—found its explicit political correlative in the Trinity don's affirmed Unionism. However, as Kathryn Ludwigson indicates, the "nationalist" versus "cosmopolitan" label tends to elide a more nuanced situation.[95] Regardless of Dowden's political allegiances, Yeats excoriated him in print for a perceived cultural myopia and professional obstructionism, constructing, to a certain degree, a straw man: Dowden the "West Briton," Dowden the Victorian, Dowden the Shakespearean apologist for English imperialism.

Although the so-called Dowden controversy erupted in 1895, Yeats had tested his pose of impassioned acrimony in his November 1886 review of Samuel Ferguson's poetry,[96] taking both Dowden and Trinity College to task for their refusal to consider the literary merits of the Ur-Revivalist. Yeats argued that the Irish professor's position was, in essence, supporting English claims to cultural superiority. This is some of Yeats's most biting polemic, and in many ways he prefigures many of the claims of postcolonial criticism. "It is," for example, a question whether the most distinguished of our critics, Professor Dowden, would not only have more consulted the interests of his country, but more also, in the long run, his own dignity and reputation . . . if he had devoted some of those elaborate pages which he has spent on the much bewritten George Eliot, to a man like the subject of this article. A few pages from him would have made it impossible for a journal like *The Academy* to write in 1880, that Sir Samuel Ferguson should have published his poetry only for his intimate friends, and that it did not even "rise to the low watermark of poetry."[97]

Publishing in the *Dublin University Review*, Yeats at this point does not appear to undermine or circumvent academic authority. His own encomiastic analysis of Ferguson's verse, which makes up the bulk of the article, is supplementary. He positions it as a necessary countermeasure to the academy's deference to English letters. Yeats at this time depended on academic publications for his own visibility. The problem was not that literary reputation was in the hands of academics, but that their preference for canonical English writers was hindering the cultural agenda of the Revival. Dowden, Yeats claims, *should* discuss the poetry of Ferguson and other writers of Irish verse. Instead, he writes about English prose. Academe is recognized as the primary legitimizing force in Irish cultural discourse, and in the interests of patriotism, indeed fairness, it should be more considerate of its critical objects. This is indeed a common concern of modern academics who view their institutions' role in shaping a canon of literature as potentially progressive, as well as historically oppressive.

Of course, a central concern of the Revival in its first flush was the restoration of a body of Irish legends in the cultural consciousness of the Irish people, and this impulse embitters Yeats's response further: "The most cultivated of Irish readers are only anxious to be academic, and to be servile to English notions. If Sir Samuel Ferguson had written of Arthur and Guinevere, they would have received him gladly; that he chose rather to tell of Congal and of desolate and queenly Deirdre, we give him full-hearted thanks; he has restored to our hills and rivers their epic interest."[98] Again, there is no outright condemnation of Irish academia as a whole here; the editorial "we" separates the "most cultivated of Irish readers" from Ferguson's admirers. Nor do we see a watertight syllogism. The "most cultivated" strive to be "academic" *and* "servile to English notions." Yeats is not saying that being an academic necessarily involves fawning to English cultural superiority, just that this is what these individuals are currently doing. However, he is moving inexorably toward a more extreme position:

> If Sir Samuel Ferguson had written to the glory of that, from a moral point of view, more than dubious achievement, British civilization, the critics, probably including Professor Dowden, would have taken care of his reputation. . . . I do not appeal to the professorial classes, who, in Ireland, at least, appear at no

time to have thought of the affairs of their country till they first feared for their emoluments—nor do I appeal to the shoddy society of "West Britonism," but to those young men clustered here and there throughout our land, whom the emotion of Patriotism has lifted into that world of selfless passion in which heroic deeds are possible and heroic poetry credible.[99]

Cowardice and complacency are thus the charges laid at the door of Dowden and his colleagues, while Yeats's rhetoric aligns patriotism and heroic values with revivalist poetics. One must of course acknowledge the passions of youth in Yeats's prose here. However, the ad hominem attacks work to elide much of the complexity in Dowden's cultural politics, not to mention the sincerity of his commitment to humane scholarship.

On the sheer fact of Dowden's opposition to the Revival's literary agenda and concomitant politics, there can be little room for revisionism.[100] Ludwigson has noted how Dowden's peers—including writers championed by Yeats's coterie—were baffled by his support for the Union and his refusal to consider publicly the works of contemporary Irish writers: "For a reason which his friends could not understand, Dowden isolated himself completely from the Irish movement. And the irony of his isolation, to them, was that he not only knew their works but had commended them privately."[101] The reasons for such steadfast public opposition remain opaque, and among his peers, a number of hypotheses were ventured: for John Eglinton, Dowden's geographical position within the Pale prompted him to look longingly across the waters; Ernest August Boyd saw him as a "half-breed Irishman,"[102] shaped by the pressures of a Protestant, Anglo-Irish background. While it can certainly be argued that biographical factors shaped his political outlook, the pressures of cultural hybridity and literary intellectualism—as with Yeats—tend not to resolve themselves into facile political allegiances. Ludwigson, perceptively, identifies a number of factors at work in Dowden's conservative cultural politics, including an adherence to literary cosmopolitanism and a philosophical outlook akin to that of the American Transcendentalists. Dowden's literary criticism, in addition to his overtly political activities, thus constitutes the visible shoots from a profound subterranean rhizome: "Private mythologies of any kind, ones not rooted in the universal experience of mankind, appeared to Dowden to be an escape from the pressure of facts; and this deeply-rooted conviction against the esoteric and provincial precluded Dowden's participation in the revival of Celtic literature to which Yeats and George Russell were to contribute greatly."[103] Ludwigson thus maintains the primacy of Dowden's deeply held belief in universal human experience, in the objective existence of the material world apprehended through human senses, and in the artistic superiority of writers who—like George Eliot—work to bring the creative imagination and scientific fact into a fruitful synthesis. Naturally, argues Ludwigson, given the geographical origins of

Transcendental philosophy, as well as the writers who best exemplified
Dowden's criteria for literary greatness, the Revival's cultural project of
promoting native Irish writers and materials must have irked Dowden. His
opposition to the Revival, then, can be understood on literary and philosophical grounds: "The three basic tendencies of the Movement—the Celtic, the
nationalistic, and the esoteric—were incompatible with his own viewpoint:
Celticism, because of its function as the green banner of nationalism; nationalism, because of its narrow exclusiveness; and subjectivism, because of its
blindness to the truths of science."[104] Moreover, Ludwigson reads Dowden's
Unionism as a translation of his philosophical beliefs and cultural agenda
into the realm of contemporary politics, such that Dowden "became a Unionist not because he believed that the union had brought peace or prosperity to
Ireland, but because he firmly believed that the Separatist party too little
regarded the wholeness of things—it cut itself off too hastily from hereditary
influence and operated apart from the total complexity of structured govern-
ment."[105] Framed in terms of a national conversation about indigenous literature, these strands of Dowden's thought—political, philosophical, and literary—became manifest in his response to the Revival, and in assertions like
this one in 1895 (taken from his introduction to *New Studies in Literature*):
"No folly can be greater than that of fancying that we shall strengthen our
literary position by living exclusively in our own ideas, and showing ourselves inhospitable to the best ideas of other lands."[106] Of course, as a professor of English at the academically conservative Trinity College,[107] the "other
lands" Dowden was particularly attuned to were Anglophone, and the vast
majority of his work was concerned with canonical writers from England:
Shakespeare, Milton, Shelley, and Eliot. It is easy to see how Dowden's
disdain for nativism in literary matters might be read as cultural Anglophilia.

More recently, Andrew Murphy has pointed out a "certain irony"[108] in
Yeats's own evolution into cosmopolitanism in the opening decades of the
twentieth century (an issue I examine in chapter 3), noting that "the movement away from the most rigorous forms of cultural nationalism that we
witness in Yeats's later thinking serves, in part, to bring him closer to the
position that Dowden had mapped out in the *Fortnightly Review* essay the
young Yeats had found so objectionable,"[109] and Murphy concludes his article on Yeats and Dowden with the intriguing suggestion that "had the newly
independent country been more willing to embrace what Yeats's Shakespearian adversary styled the inspiriting shock of strangeness, it is possible that the
poet might have found a more congenial home there."[110] Murphy makes an
astute observation here, but one that perhaps should not be stretched too far.
While Yeats's later work drew upon the literatures of Scandinavia, India,
Arabia, and Japan, for instance, Dowden's putative cosmopolitanism in fact
constituted an Anglo-American axis. Dowden's poet-philosopher of choice
was Walt Whitman, and Ludwigson is particularly compelling in her analysis

of his affinity for the American, noting, for instance, that the "likeness of Whitman's to Dowden's viewpoint resided in their mutual attempt to reconcile modern science, democracy, and industrialism with a concomitant belief in the inherency of divine laws."[111] In essence, then, Dowden objected to Yeats's cultural project on the basis that it "failed to reflect the age . . . failed to absorb into itself science and politics, philosophy and morality."[112] So, since Revival writers promoted a mythical past and spurned scientific positivism, Dowden withheld support.

In advocating a seemingly conservative cultural politics, Dowden, it appears, was in fact pushing for a modern literature which represented the best possible synthesis of scientific thought and idealist philosophy. Fundamentally, the point of departure was a philosophical one: while Dowden, like Whitman, saw the presence of the divine within the material realm, the Kantian romanticism of Yeats and George Russell maintained that the tangible, physical world obstructed access to the ideal, hence their experimentation with visionary techniques to pierce through the veil. In truth, it would seem that there was not a great deal of separation between the two Anglo-Irishmen—Yeats and Dowden—though a generation apart, who rejected the Protestantism of their childhoods in pursuit of religious truth, and who both (latterly, in Yeats's case) opposed the turn toward a narrow nativism in Irish culture. Furthermore, as Terence Brown indicates, Yeats laid more than one obstructionist charge at the feet of his father's friend: "in the autobiography of the poet W. B. Yeats, under the title 'Reveries Over Childhood and Youth,' the unfortunate Dowden is made to bear the responsibility for Victorian Unionist Ireland which, in Yeats's sense of things, put entire generations to sleep with its cultural and political inadequacies, its tiresome evasions, its reactionary torpor."[113] How do we disentangle the network of public, textual, and personal relationships among the three men: Yeats, his father, and Dowden? On the issue of Yeats's autobiography, Brown (following Ian Fletcher) suggests that Dowden may just have been a victim of the young Yeats's habit of antithetical thought, noting how "the structure of 'Reveries,' . . . required the arrangement of characters into revelatory juxtaposition in which Dowden inevitably came off worse in a comparison with 'O'Leary's noble head.'"[114] However, while Yeats may have misrepresented or simplified his opponent's positions, the fact remains that Dowden represented a genuine drag on the momentum of the Revival, and, moreover, worked actively to protect the political status quo. We cannot, therefore, summarily dismiss Yeats's Dowden as wholly a straw man, a foil created by the young poet in order to advance his own cultural agenda.

However, even while acknowledging the reductive quality in Yeats's presentation of Dowden, questions remain as to the nature of the Trinity man's cultural politics. Casting a cold eye on Dowden's life and work, Brown detects a certain psychological anxiety in the professor's so-called

cosmopolitanism, identifying "something verging on the neurotic in his commitment to a universal and therefore somehow sanitized and serene vision of
literary culture over against the offensive demands of the local, with all the
risks they involved of parochialism and misjudgment."[115] Brown suggests
that Dowden seems to have felt a "curious revulsion from something in
Ireland for which a bland style and a cosmopolitan range are the necessary
drapes."[116] Following Brown, perhaps one way to think about the issue is
through the prism of Victorianism and Anglo-Irish identity. Philosophically,
Dowden and Yeats were not miles apart, and, despite the proliferation of
Yeats's occult practices, both men's dissatisfaction with received religion
and subsequent adherence to unorthodox metaphysics situate them equally
within that most Victorian of cultural phenomena: religious skepticism. Further, Brown reads Dowden as a man for whom the "Victorian" sense of
familial duty and the moral demands of respectable bourgeois domesticity
ensconced him within a city and a career that did not fully satisfy him.
Dowden had wanted to become a poet and aspired to a more cosmopolitan
existence than Victorian Dublin afforded. Yet he espoused a dislike for the
sensibility of the neighboring isle. Indeed, the anxious hybridity of the Anglo-Irish in the nineteenth century meant that their literati, no matter how
"nationalist" or "cosmopolitan," were sometimes pressed to excavate alternate allegiances, and this is perhaps evidenced in the construction of ideal
literary canons that did not adhere to the normative boundaries of nation-
state or literary movement. Both Dowden and Yeats, it should be remembered, ultimately constructed their own apolitical world republics of letters.
Put another way, while life in Dublin may have seemed to Dowden a concession to the mundane, he got on with it. Brown reminds us that the Trinity
professorship was not then as prestigious as it might seem to us today, and in
the final telling, he considers Dowden a "slave of Victorian duty,"[117] narrat-
ing the arc of his career as one of remarkable scholarly achievement in the
face of personal dissatisfaction: "So the young man who had aspired to
poetry settled for the life of university don and a reputation as a highly
productive man of letters, publishing widely in the English reviews and
achieving his significant contemporary reputation with his study of Shakespeare."[118] To a certain degree, then, although Dowden was an intellectual
fixture of the Yeatses' circle in Dublin, and though his thinking on art and
spirituality intersected with that of the Yeatses, his "Victorianism"—defined
here both in terms of habitus and faith in scientific progress—made him
available rhetorically to the young revivalist in revolt from the cultural authorities of London and Dublin.[119] Put another way, Dowden's objections to
the insularity of revivalist cultural prescriptions encouraged Yeats to carica-
ture the totality of his outlook as Yeats sought to build his own authority. If
Dowden were the quintessential Victorian academic concerned with an international reputation, then it made sense for him to write about Shakespeare;

and if Yeats wanted to make him a poster child for the stultifying defects of modern science and political Unionism—characterized as "Victorian"—then it also made sense to see Dowden's Shakespeare in such terms. This, indeed, is what we see in "At Stratford-on-Avon," Yeats's only essay that is nominally "about" Shakespeare, which he penned following his visit to Stratford in 1901.

DOWDEN'S SHAKSPERE AND *SHAKSPERE'S* HENRY

The culmination of an enormously popular lecture series at Trinity, Dowden's book on Shakespeare, *Shakspere: A Critical Study of His Mind and Art*, can be seen as the apotheosis of Victorian Shakespeare criticism. Bringing the entire dramatic corpus under the scrutiny of a hermeneutic that emphasized empirical observation, historicism, and biographical inference, the importance of the work lay in the direction it took away from belletristic amateurism of the early nineteenth century, epitomized by Coleridge and Hazlitt. Moreover, its influence was profound and widespread; *Shakspere* went through twelve British editions between 1875 and 1901 and enjoyed critical preeminence second only to its successor, A. C. Bradley's *Shakespearian Tragedy*. The objective of Dowden's criticism, generally speaking, was to assess the degree to which a writer's work registered the philosophical and scientific currents of the time, and as we have seen, Dowden's preference was for texts—like George Eliot's novels—that in his view represented a profound synthesis of empirical observation and metaphysics: the world of the senses and the judgments of the soul. In *Shakspere*, then, Dowden's overarching thesis is that the impact of an evolution in scientific thought in Elizabethan England instigated a new attention to the "facts" of material reality, which, when held in balance with the restive spiritual philosophy of the time, produced Bacon, Hooker, and Shakespeare. As Dowden puts it, "[c]apacity for perceiving, for enjoying, and for reproducing facts, and facts of as great variety as possible,—this was the qualification of a dramatist in the days of Elizabeth."[120] In describing Dowden's method, Ludwigson draws her metaphor appropriately from the scientific realm: "Dowden proceeded in his *Shakspere* as a biologist would treat a living organism: he studied the soil on which the organism grew, and then he carefully examined and analyzed the organism itself."[121] Thus, as historians of Shakespeare reception have indicated, Dowden's hermeneutic fit the times. Gary Taylor suggests that Dowden's vision of Shakespeare as a self-made entrepreneur, a man of material success, "satisfied the mercantile mentality,"[122] while Michael Taylor sees his "resolute fidelity to the fact"[123] as a kind of "spirituality of a sternly Protestant kind."[124] Indeed, it was precisely the adherence of Dowden's thesis to the principles enshrined in a Victorian discourse of science, progress, and "facts" that drew Yeats's ire. In many ways, Yeats's brief, but embittered reading of *Shakspere* represents an assault on the professor's hermeneutic, indeed the whole business of professional, academic criticism. However, within the contours of the Yeats-Dowden dispute and the matter of Ireland's national literature, Yeats's Shakespeare essay offers a glimpse into his occultist cultural nationalism and once more indicates the extent to which invoking Shakespeare meant appropriating (or indeed challenging) his powerful cultural authority.

Though brief, the section of Yeats's essay dealing with contemporary criticism brings this nationalist subtext into full view: "Professor Dowden," writes Yeats, "lived in Ireland, where everything has failed, and he meditated frequently upon the perfection of character which had, he thought, made England successful."[125] Moreover, he claims, Dowden's book epitomizes Shakespeare criticism as a whole, which, over the course of the nineteenth century, "became a vulgar worshipper of success"[126] during a "century of utilitarianism, when nothing seemed important except his utility to the State."[127] In the final tally, Dowden had, it seems, made Shakespeare a materialist and utilitarian, characteristics Yeats reviled and, as we see here, that he associated with an insidious industrial modernity epitomized by English material success. It is for this reason that Yeats could write of Dowden's critical "successors" building upon his assessment of Shakespeare's business acumen such that it "reached its height in a moment of imperialistic enthusiasm."[128] So, without laying the charge of imperial propagandist at the feet of his opponent, Yeats's rhetoric implicates Dowden's Shakespeare firmly within a critical orthodoxy whose tenets had also supposedly justified England's imperial expansion.

Assessing the history plays, Dowden's *Shakspere* elevated the imperialistic Henry V and denigrated Richard II on the basis of their ability to marshal the "facts" of existence and consequently achieve worldly success. Yeats's response, as with his essay on "The Celtic Element in Literature," is to enter into the argument, but to alter the valence of its terms. Whereas with Arnold this meant supplementing their meaning, his approach to Dowden here involves a total inversion. For Dowden, then, Henry is "the man framed for the most noble and joyous mastery of things."[129] He possesses a "noble realisation of fact," and is unquestionably "Shakspere's ideal of manhood in the sphere of practical achievement,—the hero, and central figure . . . of the historical plays."[130] Listing some of the personal traits that make Henry praiseworthy—"freedom from egoism . . . modesty . . . integrity . . . his joyous humour . . . practical piety"[131] —his language aligns a moralistic assessment of character with the precepts of a Transcendentalist view of the material world as permeated with a kind of divine energy. Ultimately, Henry possesses "a true genius for the discovery of the noblest facts," and Dowden argues that he "came into relation with the central and vital forces of the universe, so that, instead of constructing a strong but careful life for himself, life breathed through him, and blossomed into a glorious enthusiasm for existence."[132] Contrarily, Henry V in "At Stratford-on-Avon" is not magisterial, but a coarse manipulator of the hoi-polloi, possessing a "resounding rhetoric that moves men as a leading article does today."[133] He is impressive but animalistic, like a "handsome spirited horse."[134] By contrast, Richard II in *Shakspere* is an effete and ineffective king: he is not interested in the facts of the world, but instead takes an immoral pleasure in their effects upon his emotions and imagination. His mind is intuitive, not intellectual. Henry is masculine; Richard suffers from the "want of true and manly patriotism."[135] Henry is practical, and Richard is "artistic":

> Not alone his intellect, but his feelings, live in the world of phenomena, and altogether fail to lay hold of things as they are; they have no consistency and no continuity. His will is entirely unformed; it possesses no authority and no executive power; he is at the mercy of every chance impulse and transitory mood. He has a kind of artistic relation to life, without being an artist. . . . Instead of comprehending things as they are, and achieving heroic deeds, he satiates his heart with the grace, the tenderness, the beauty, or the pathos of situations.[136]

There is nothing attractive about this figure in *Shakspere*'s scheme. "If only," laments Dowden, "the world were not a real world, to which serious hearts are due, we could find in Richard some wavering, vague attraction."[137] Again, Yeats reverses this judgment (as did Pater), so that Richard becomes a more charismatic figure, a romantic visionary closer in his meditative nature to Yeats's ideal of the occult artist. "Shakespeare," as he sees it, "saw . . . in Richard II the defeat that awaits all, whether they be artist or saint, who find themselves where men ask of them a rough energy, or sweetness of temper, or dreamy dignity, or love of God, or love of His creatures."[138] But this is not far away from Dowden's claim: Richard fails because he is ill suited for the task.

Recently, Andrew Murphy has shown how Yeats, in "At Stratford-on-Avon," actually presents a reductive version of the character-based arguments Dowden makes in *Shakspere*. Thus, while Yeats has Dowden championing Henry V as Shakespeare's ideal of manhood, Murphy astutely reminds us that this was only the case in "the sphere of practical achievement."[139] Murphy continues as follows:

> Dowden's valorizing of Henry thus extends only to the specific sphere of the history plays and he recognizes that, in the greater scheme of things, practical values can only ever have a limited application. . . . Dowden . . . suggests that Shakespeare cultivated the pragmatic side of his character not so much as an end in itself, but rather specifically in order that it might serve as a counterweight against the two potentially excessive (and self-destructive) drives

rooted deep in his own make-up: drives which Dowden identifies as the Ro-
meo obsession and the Hamlet obsession. [140]

Dowden's Shakespeare is thus more carefully nuanced than Yeats allows in
his moment of polemic in the essay. Although in *Shakspere* we might still see
the mind of the critic reflected in the putative psychology of his subject,
Murphy's point remains valid: Dowden and his Shakespeare were more complex than Yeats argued in the pages of his article, whether because of Yeats's
deliberate misreading, or through critical error. Indeed, Yeats's most tren-
chant critique of Dowden's work stands up only through a highly selective
reading of the text. Dowden instead presented a playwright whose art sought
to balance the antithetical qualities of idealism and positive materialism, a
polarized tension that ought to have appealed to Yeats's habit of thinking in
antimonies. Certainly, Yeats, at this juncture in the evolution of his thinking,
was not willing to acknowledge a place for positivism in the art of great
writers (a position which altered in the first decade of the twentieth century). [141] So Murphy's assessment is in line with Yeats's reductive treatment of
Dowden in the 1890s.

In all likelihood, however, on this occasion Yeats probably just reread the
section of *Shakspere* that dealt with the history plays, given that he was in
Stratford to see Benson's history cycle, and that the critical "antithesis" he
notices in Victorian criticism, "which grew in clearness and violence as the
century grew older," [142] concerns only the histories. Indeed, Dowden viewed
the history cycle as fundamental to the development of Shakespeare's "mind
and art," and so, reductive as "At Stratford-on-Avon" might be, Yeats could
still get at the essence of Dowden's position. In the history plays, Dowden
saw a unified opus within the larger corpus of writing. Penned roughly within
the same period of the 1590s, these plays become in *Shakspere* a series of
exercises in the critical analysis of worldly success, and a singular invest-
ment in Shakespeare's moral self-education: "that by his study of history
Shakspere should have built up his own moral nature, and have fortified
himself for the conduct of life, was, we may surmise, to Shakspere the chief
outcome of his toil." [143] Shakespeare's own development thus provides the
model for *Shakspere*'s pedagogical imperative: he learns from his own studies of English history, just as we should. We in turn must learn from the
history plays, reading them as variations upon a single investigative principle:

> [I]n the historical plays we are conscious of a certain limitation, a certain
> measuring of men by positive achievements and results . . . we may recognize
> the one dominant subject of the histories, viz., how a man may fail, and how a
> man may succeed in attaining a practical mastery of the world. . . . The theme
> of the English historical plays is the success and failure of the men to achieve
> noble practical ends. . . . Success in the visible material world, the world of

noble positive action, is the measure of greatness in the English historical plays.[144]

The histories, then, comprise both the central focus of Dowden's study and the proof of his hypotheses. Considered as a single dramatic unit, they become Shakespeare's most successful aesthetic representation of fact: in this case the "facts" of Holinshed's *Chronicles*: "It was not a happy falsifying of the facts of history to which he, as dramatist, aspired, but an imaginative rendering of the very facts themselves."[145] I would therefore suggest that Murphy is mischaracterizing Yeats's work slightly. Dowden's Transcendentalist tendencies supplied him with the idea of a material world suffused with a divine spirit, while Yeats viewed physical matter as a barrier to our experience of the divine. Yeats's reductionism thus precedes his inversion of the two kings in Dowden's scheme by severing the spiritual element from the material. Once Dowden's Shakespeare is understood merely in terms of positive materialism, then through force of metonymy it can be reread as utilitarianism, crass commercialism, and even philistinism. What happens in "At Stratford," rhetorically speaking, is *this* reductive reading. Given the preexisting "Dowden controversy" in regard to Irish literature, *Shakspere*'s focus on the "facts" of *English* history, and the association (encouraged by Yeats's father) of English imperialism and utilitarianism, Dowden is once more framed by Yeats.[146]

Dowden treats the history plays as a single unit presenting the entire spectrum of kingly efficacy, and so Yeats gives us "five plays, that are but one play,"[147] which he felt, as Rupin Desai comments, "contained all the fundamental patterns of political behavior to which human beings were prone."[148] In other words, what we find in "At Stratford-on-Avon" is not a complete reduction of *Shakspere*, but an appropriation. Inevitably, as the refutation of a specific argument, Yeats's comments appear to take on the form of the original thesis as each point is weighed and dismissed in turn. But there is something more happening here. Dowden's vision of the Renaissance as an epistemological shift in England toward positivist materialism, or "fact," finds its correlative in Yeats's essay. Yeats also interpreted the Renaissance as the harbinger of a scientific, industrial modernity. But as far as he was concerned, this was the beginning of the end for English civilization; Yeats's Shakespeare belonged to the older episteme. As Murphy handily argues, "Yeats's Shakespeare looks ruefully backwards; Dowden's looks positively forwards."[149] Again there is the sense that Shakespeare is a kind of honorary Irishman by virtue of his historical position, and because of a certain visionary capability Yeats associates with Richard and the rural Irish.

By mimicking *Shakspere*'s hermeneutic scheme, Yeats thus opens up the polysemous capabilities of Dowden's language. Henry V *is* practical, and Richard *is* effete and poetical, but now those terms signify differently. Referring back to the Yeats-Arnold scheme, we might say that Henry represents the Saxon and Richard the Celt. However, Yeats's enemy is not just a specific reading of Shakespeare's drama, but an entire school of thought and its representatives. The final blow to Dowdenesque biography comes as a rejection of his foundational deductive principles: that we may know the man from his works. We can see this process beginning in the closing paragraphs of "At Stratford-on-Avon" as Yeats proposes an alternate source of knowledge about Shakespeare and his plays. "The Greeks," he explains, "considered that myths are the activities of the Daimons, and that the Daimons shape our characters and our lives."[150] He continues: "I have often had the fancy that there is some one myth for every man, which, if we but knew it, would make us understand all he did and thought. Shakespeare' myth, it may be, describes a wise man who was blind from very wisdom, and an empty man who thrust him from his place, and saw all that could be seen from very emptiness."[151] Yeats is reaching here toward an idealist explanation of personality and artistic creation. The "myth" he depicts here is then located in *Hamlet* in the promotion of Fortinbras, as well as in the story of "that unripened Hamlet,"[152] Richard II. The influence of nonmaterial forces is suggested rather than backed in an unqualified fashion here, but Yeats ends his piece with a reminder of the limitations of Shakespearean biography: "The people of Stratford-on-Avon have remembered little about him. . . . They have remembered a drinking-bout of his, and invented some bad verses for him, and that is about all."[153] Yeats's explanation for this ellipsis, belying the colossal poetic-hero status that Shakespeare had since earned, is cultural and epistemic. The majority of people in Shakespeare's Stratford would not have venerated a poet. "[I]n his day," he claims, "the glory of a poet . . . had ceased, or almost ceased, outside a narrow class."[154] What impressed his countrymen was not euphuistic prowess: "Had he been some hard-drinking, hard-living, loud-blaspheming squire, they would have enlarged his fame by a legend of his dealing with the devil."[155] Several ideas are emerging here. First, the contention that Shakespeare had an imposing personality is being dismissed in the face of a lack of evidence. In fact, the dearth of local legend indicates the opposite: Shakespeare was placid, quiet, and even boring. Second, Yeats wants us to see Shakespeare as somewhat anomalous. He is a poet from outside the narrow poetry-appreciating classes. He is at odds with his environment. Third, and most significant for my argument here, the basis of Dowden's biographical exegesis is being weakened. There is little evidence from his life, Yeats intimates, to support the kind of overarching claims Dowden is drawing out of the dramatist's work. Dowden's position, and that of his school, becomes untenable. These two assertions—that Shakespeare was a quiet man of whom we know relatively little, and that art is not a source of biographical material—develop alongside Yeats's reading and occultist training over the opening decade of the new century as a thorough reworking of the biographical paradigm.

So we have begun to uncover the motivation behind Yeats's opposition to the dominant utilitarian modes of literary scholarship; his disagreement with Dowden's work certainly needs to be understood as more than an apolitical clash of interpretations. Further, I argue, we must not see it as a literary dispute confined to the pages of journals, but rather as a broader move to undermine the academy's position as the bastion of cultural authority in Ireland. His work here not only attempts to establish a new critical interpretation of the history plays, but also marks the direction of the Irish Revival toward the stage, a maneuver which inevitably shifted cultural capital to the theatre—an "Irish" institution which, unlike Trinity College, would promote ancient Irish literary material. His strategy as a whole represents an attack on the ideology of contemporary literary studies; he appropriates the interpretive methodology of character criticism and much of its rhetoric, but revises it to fit his own idealist conception of personality and the relation of art to the artist. Therefore, in pushing for an idealist, esoteric understanding of Shakespeare, Yeats was also establishing the poet-director as the primary authority figure in a new nation's cultural life. These critical interventions presage the Celtic Mysteries and the Irish National Theatre, organs of an occultist and revivalist new Irish nation.

SHAKESPEARE IN THE IRISH NATIONAL DRAMA

"At Stratford-on-Avon" works through an array of topics and themes and is not wholly concerned with Dowden's exegesis and the matter of professional Shakespeare criticism. The essay begins with Yeats-as-tourist, enumerating the various picturesque delights of the town and figuring it as a medieval idyll and alternative to the chaotic modernity of London. Much of the essay addresses the actual performances he witnessed, and significantly, issues of dramaturgy and staging. So, while I have been arguing that Yeats's interventions in two nineteenth-century academic discourses mean that his early Shakespeare has a decidedly Victorian hue, the adjacent sections of "At Stratford-on-Avon" mark the beginning of a new phase in the Irishman's Shakespeare, one that maps onto an emergent paradigm in Shakespeare reception. Yeats's visit to Stratford coincides roughly with his involvement in the Irish Literary Theatre (subsequently the Irish National Theatre Society), and the founding of the Abbey Theatre in 1904 meant that he had the opportunity not only to put into practice the dramaturgical theory he had been developing throughout the last decade of the nineteenth century, but also to begin the process whereby the theatre in Ireland was to usurp the academy as the stronghold of the nation's cultural identity: "The truth is that the Irish people are at that precise stage of their history when imagination, shaped by many stirring events, desires dramatic expression. . . . I always saw that some kind of theatre would be a natural center for a tradition of feeling and thought."[156] Notwithstanding the resilience of Dowdenesque paradigms in the work of the enormously influential A. C. Bradley, for Yeats at least, the stage was to replace the page as the center of a robust intellectual response to received, Victorian modes of thought. [157] Moreover, as Ronald Schuchard has explored in some detail, by the turn of the century Yeats was making frequent pronouncements against the printed word as he worked to restore an oral culture of musical speech and minstrelsy: "Yeats's attendant dream of a revived oral culture, partially inspired by the continuing existence in western Ireland of what he called the 'culture of the cottage,' was conceived in direct opposition to what he called Matthew Arnold's 'culture of scholarship,' an impossible culture for Ireland."[158]

Most of the essays from which I have drawn my evidence for Yeats's revivalist Shakespeare were written during a decade when Yeats's poetic output dropped, while his involvement in Ireland's National Theatre increased. Given the fact that Yeats's reputation as a poet of the *Celtic Twilight* was largely constructed in London, we might see Yeats's early Shakespeare as more than an attempt to appropriate cultural capital, or to weaken English claims to cultural preeminence. Following Casanova's account of the structural inequalities in literary space that limit the artistic agency of writers from the margins, we might see Yeats's visit to Stratford in 1901 as a watershed moment for Yeats's own position in international literary space, marking his commitment to the enlargement of Irish literary capital at the expense of his immediate reputation, founded as it was on the bedrock of critical plaudits from the London literati. Paradoxically, then, writing about Shakespeare— entering "Shakespace"—signaled a reorientation of Yeats's literary identity. Once a composer of critically acclaimed, dreamily aesthetic poetry, Yeats in the 1900s was primarily concerned with a new Irish drama, and with documenting in prose the attempts of his theatre movement to establish itself at the forefront of Irish cultural nationhood. In terms of dramaturgy, at the start of the twentieth century, Yeats stood as an avant-garde figure, elevating the performed sign above the printed word and looking to construct a nation whose central signifying technology was song, gesture, and movement. The idea that the theatre should be elevated over the university as the primary site for producing cultural knowledge represented a dual urge for Yeats. On the one hand, it suggested the potential for de-Anglicizing Irish art and thought. On the other hand, it was crucial in summoning a new Irish nation into being. Yeats drew upon Shakespeare to formulate his conception of the Irish theatre as a counter to the perceived West Britonism of Ireland's cultural elite, and as a means of collecting the Irish within the rubric of a distinctly Yeatsian national culture.

I have argued in this chapter that Yeats's interventions in Victorian literary discourse need to be understood as nationalist phenomena ultimately concerned with cultural authority; in the first case, Yeats entered into Matthew Arnold's philological work on behalf of an Irish cultural nationalism that sought to reframe the racial thinking that relegated the "Celt" to a subordinate position beneath the "Saxon." At stake in this argument was the relative status and visibility of Irish literature. In the case of the Yeats-Dowden dispute, the context was an intranational debate over the goals and strategy of the Irish Literary Revival. In both cases, as we have seen, Yeats worked by a process of engagement and appropriation, entering into preexisting, highly "visible" literary discourse and then supplementing signifieds (in Arnold's case) or reversing them (in Dowden's). By force of metonymy, Shakespeare's cultural authority—constructed primarily by Victorians—was appropriated in order to lend both visibility and credibility to Yeats's Irish cultural project. Indeed, as I hope to have demonstrated, while the net effect of Yeats's work was to de-Anglicize Shakespeare, the real issue at stake was the cultural authority of the Revival. As such, the real irony in the Yeats-Dowden matter is not the eventual proximity of their positions with regard to national literature, but the fundamentally Victorian quality of Yeats's revolt. The story of Yeatsian drama, and thus of Shakespeare in its next stages, constitutes the subject matter of the following chapters; however, the major contours of Shakespeare's construction have been delineated here: the Herderian association with the soul of a vital folk culture, the historical position on the cusp of epistemic rupture, the aesthetic power to draw an audience into a state of reverie, and the valorization of feudal social structures. These factors continue to play a part in Yeats's claims to the Shakespearean inheritance on behalf of a culturally nationalist agenda. Furthermore, I see Yeats's appropriation of Shakespeare as an important chapter in the history of Shakespeare and nationalism more broadly; given the Irishman's later rejection of conservative Irish nativism and his affiliation with international literary modernism, we might see Yeats's Shakespeare as a whole adhering to—perhaps contributing to—the cultural forces by which Shakespeare shed his national and imperial signification and was reconfigured in the twentieth century as a global literary icon.

NOTES

1. W. B. Yeats, *The Collected Works of W. B. Yeats*, vol. 3, *Autobiographies*, ed. Douglas Archibald and William O'Donnell (New York: Scribner, 1999), 54.

2. Ibid.

3. Ibid.

4. W. B. Yeats, "At Stratford-on-Avon," in *The Collected Works of W. B. Yeats*, vol. 4, *Early Essays*, ed. Richard J. Finneran (New York: Scribner, 2007), 78.

5. Adrian Poole, *Shakespeare and the Victorians* (London: Arden, 2004), 2.

6. This point may be more literal than it might seem; Rupin Desai suggests that Yeats may later have regarded Shakespeare as his daimon, or spiritual self. See Rupin Desai, *Yeats's Shakespeare* (Evanston, IL: Northwestern University Press, 1971), 112.

7. Poole, *Shakespeare and the Victorians*, 2.

8. Katheryn Prince, *Shakespeare in the Victorian Periodicals* (London and New York: Routledge, 2008), 9.

9. Michael Taylor, *Shakespeare Criticism in the Twentieth Century* (Oxford: Oxford University Press, 2001), 1.

10. A version of this chapter, focusing on the Yeats-Dowden relationship, but reaching quite different conclusions, has previously been published as "Among the Academics: Yeats, Dowden, and 'West British' Shakespeare in the Irish Literary Revival," *South Carolina Review* 45, no. 2 (Spring 2013): 1–13. I am grateful to Professor Wayne Chapman for permission to reprint here.

11. Poole, *Victorian Shakespeare*, 3.

12. Ibid.

13. Ibid., 3.

14. Ibid., 3, 4, 5.

15. Ibid., 5.

16. Ibid.

17. Ibid., 230.

18. Ibid.

19. In *Shakespeare in the Victorian Periodicals*, Prince does exactly this, drawing upon the work of Andrew Murphy to posit only two phases, "first a rise in Shakespeare's popularity throughout the century tied to improving literacy levels, followed by an attrition late in the century as the availability of alternative reading material or the deadening effect of rote learning stripped Shakespeare of his political resonances." Prince, *Periodicals*, 2.

20. Terence Brown has argued persuasively for the essential Victorianism of the Irish Revival as a whole: "To state the matter in simple terms: pondering the Revival as an expression of Irish Victorianism will lead back to a study of Irish Protestantism not only as one more lamentable attribute of a colonial class which largely sets its face against the emergent nation but as a much more interesting element in a complex of ideas and modes of feeling and action which compromise the Irish Victorian world in which that Revival came to life." Terence Brown, *Ireland's Literature* (Mullingar: Lilliput, 1988), 58.

21. For an overview of the Dowden-Yeats relationship, see Andrew Murphy, "An Irish Catalysis: W. B. Yeats and the Uses of Shakespeare," *Shakespeare Survey* 64 (2011): 209–19.

22. Poole, *Victorian Shakespeare*, 193. Poole elaborates astutely on this point as follows:

> They were particularly interested in the fate of kings and fathers, and in the various kinds of challenge and submission to authority by subjects, servants, wives and children. They also looked outwards to countries, races, and languages other than their own, to the nature of authority carried by England, the English language and their prime literary export Shakespeare, for other European nations, especially France, Germany and Italy. They also looked to all four corners of the empire. To look out was also to look in and to question what England and Englishness was composed of. For all of these enquiries Shakespeare was a key point of reference.

Ibid.

23. Gary Taylor, *Reinventing Shakespeare: A Cultural History from the Restoration to the Present* (New York and Oxford: Oxford University Press, 1989), 167.

24. Ibid., 168.

25. Prince, *Periodicals*, 13.

26. Ibid., 14.

27. Denis Donoghue, "Yeats's Shakespeare: 'There Is a Good Deal of My Father in It.'" *Yeats Annual* 18 (2013): 74.

28. Ibid.

29. Ibid.

30. Quoted in Leon Surette, *The Birth of Modernism: Ezra Pound, T. S. Eliot, W. B. Yeats, and the Occult* (Montreal and Kingston: McGill-Queen's University Press, 1993), 13.

31. George Mills Harper, ed., *Yeats and the Occult* (Toronto: Macmillan, 1975).

32. R. F. Foster, "Protestant Magic: W. B. Yeats and the Spell of Irish History," *Proceedings of the British Academy* 75 (1989): 243–66.

33. W. B. Yeats, *Early Essays*, 39.

34. Ibid., 33.

35. Surette, *Birth of Modernism*, 13.

36. William H. O'Donnell, "Yeats as Adept and Artist: *The Speckled Bird*, *The Secret Rose*, and *The Wind among the Reeds*," in *Yeats and the Occult*, ed. George Mills Harper (Toronto: Macmillan, 1975), 57.

37. Surette, *Birth of Modernism*, 31.

38. Ibid.

39. Yeats's idealized Irish peasant, so central to his writing in the 1890s, proves somewhat problematic for postcolonial theorists. See Stephen Regan, "W. B. Yeats: Irish Nationalism and Post-Colonial Theory," in *Nordic Irish Studies* 5 (2006): 87–99. As Regan writes, "The English stereotype of the Irish peasant as ignorant and savage is replaced by a more dignified and appealing image," but "Yeats's rehabilitation of the peasantry as the source of Irish wisdom and value is so idealistic and exclusive as to hinder rather than promote the cause of national unity" (92). "That version of Irish life," he continues, "is also one that effectively predates sectarian conflict. What the peasant appears to practice is not Catholicism but a form of occult spirituality close to Yeats's own" (92). I argue here that this idealized construction of the Irish peasantry is precisely the maneuver that allows Yeats to claim an "Irish" sensibility at work in Shakespeare's drama.

40. Surette, *Birth of Modernism*, 14.

41. Ibid., 31.

42. J. W. Jackson, "Ethnology and Phrenology as an Aid to the Biographer," *Anthropological Review and Journal* 2 (1864): 126–40.

43. Richard Halpern, *Shakespeare among the Moderns* (Ithaca, NY: Cornell University Press, 1997), 21.

44. Ibid., 20.

45. Ibid., 21.

46. This point is not a new one. Philip L. Marcus writes that, "while Arnold's definition of the 'Celtic note' gained wide acceptance, it permitted such broad interpretation that the Irish transformed features he considered defects into virtues." See Philip L. Marcus, *Yeats and the Beginning of the Irish Renaissance* (Ithaca, NY, and London: Cornell University Press, 1970), 2.

47. Declan Kiberd, *Inventing Ireland: The Literature of the Modern Nation* (London: Vintage, 1995), 318.

48. Yeats's rhetorical strategy has been noted by Robert Welch: "While always aware of how much he owed to English . . . [Yeats] also wanted to bring into play a counter-text or set of counter-texts expressive of his own Irishness and of Ireland itself, arguing all the time that such elements were not merely nationalist but that they connected to the mother-lode, from which all master-spirits drew." Robert Welch, "A Literary Causerie," in *W. B. Yeats: Writings on Irish Folklore, Legend and Myth*, ed. Robert Welch (London: Penguin, 1993): xxx. I owe this observation to David Gardiner, "'To Go There as a Poet Merely': Spenser, Dowden, and Yeats," *New Hibernia Review* 1, no. 2 (1997): 127.

49. Kiberd, *Inventing Ireland*, 32.

50. Matthew Arnold, "On the Study of Celtic Literature," in *The Complete Prose Works of Matthew Arnold*, vol. 3, *Lectures and Essays in Criticism*, ed. R. H. Super (Ann Arbor: University of Michigan Press, 1962), 337.

51. Ibid.

52. Ibid., 334.

53. Ibid.

54. Ibid., 355.

55. Ibid., 341–42.

56. Ibid., 341.
57. Ibid., 338.
58. Ibid., 344.
59. Ibid., 345.
60. Ibid.
61. Ibid., 346.
62. Ibid., 347.
63. Ibid.
64. Ibid.
65. Ibid., 361.
66. W. B. Yeats, *Early Essays*, 130.
67. Ibid., 136.
68. Ibid., 130.
69. Ibid., 137.
70. Cf. John Butler Yeats in *Essays Irish and American* (Dublin, 1918): "I can say to myself 'Here among these [Irish] peasants is the one spot among English-speaking people where Shakespeare would have found himself a happy guest,'" quoted in *Shakespeare and Ireland: History, Politics, Culture,* ed. Mark Thornton Burnett and Ramona Wray (New York: St. Martin's, 1997), 110. Interestingly, Yeats's move here reverses the ethnographic thrust of Spenser's *View,* which Bruce McLeod sees "displacing contemporary Ireland onto ancient Britain and comparing both to the 'mightie empire' of *his* England." Bruce McLeod, *The Geography of Empire in English Literature, 1580–1745* (Cambridge and New York: Cambridge University Press, 1999), 47.
71. See Desai, *Yeats's Shakespeare.* As Desai discusses in his chapter "*Shakespeare* in Yeats's History Book," Yeats's view of Shakespeare was not one of absolute "bardolatry," nor did his impression of the Renaissance remain static; rather, "His changing attitudes towards Shakespeare and the Renaissance reflect the stages through which he passed from his early work to his *Last Poems*" (53–54). However, though Yeats did alter his opinions of the Renaissance as a whole, it was always regarded as a moment of epistemic change, later codified in the large cyclical structures of gyres in *A Vision* (1922). It was "the age in which the rationalistic mind displaced the imagination and poured contempt on ancient myth" (46). Shakespeare was consistently situated by Yeats at the end of the older cycle. In "Yeats and the English Renaissance," McAlindon identifies 1904 as the year in which Yeats's previously "ambiguous" attitude toward the English Renaissance lost its pejorative undertones, becoming central to his "aristocratic myth," a reactionary aversion to "mass" politics and overtly Catholic, revolutionary politics. This hardening of attitudes is the subject of chapter 3 of this book. For McAlindon's argument in full, see "Yeats and the English Renaissance," *PMLA* 82, no. 2 (1967): 157–69.
72. W. B. Yeats, *Early Essays*, 82.
73. W. B. Yeats, "Pages from a Diary in 1930," in *The Collected Works of W. B. Yeats,* vol. 10, *Later Articles and Reviews,* ed. Colton Johnson (New York: Scribner, 2000), 325.
74. W. B. Yeats, *Early Essays*, 263.
75. On Tuesday, May 12, 1840, Carlyle delivered a lecture on "The Hero as Poet: Dante; Shakespeare," and asked his audience, "which million of Englishmen, would we not give up rather than the Stratford Peasant?" "Indian Empire, or no Indian Empire," he exhorted, "we cannot do without Shakespeare!" Thomas Carlyle, *On Heroes, Hero-Worship and the Heroic in History* (1841), notes and intro. Michael K. Goldberg (Berkeley: University of California Press, 1993), 96.
76. Kiberd, *Inventing Ireland*, 274.
77. W. B. Yeats, *Early Essays*, 265.
78. Kiberd, *Inventing Ireland*, 298.
79. Historically, Yeatsians have been squeamish in dealing with Yeats's occult pursuits. Fortunately, this trend has been corrected in recent decades, perhaps most fruitfully by postcolonial critics who see the occult as a tertium quid between Yeats's allegiances to England, to Ireland, and to the Anglo-Irish within Ireland. Certainly this is Kiberd's reading. Regan also notes how Yeats's interest in Druidic and other pre-Christian cultures allowed him cognitively

to "bypass the sectarian conflicts of his own time" and "to reconcile his nationalist and universalist ideals." Regan, "W. B. Yeats," 94. Indeed, this idea constitutes a central thesis of this study. As with his cultural allegiances, so with his Shakespeare: Shakespeare is a de-Anglicized and highly mysticized Shakespeare.

80. W. B. Yeats, *Early Essays*, 73.
81. Ibid.
82. W. B. Yeats, *Essays and Introductions* (New York: Macmillan, 1961), 401.
83. W. B. Yeats, *Early Essays*, 25.
84. Ibid.
85. Ibid., 35.
86. Ibid., 33.
87. Ibid., 34.
88. Ibid.
89. Ibid., 240.
90. Donoghue, "Yeats's Shakespeare," 91.
91. Ibid., 34.
92. Kiberd, *Inventing Ireland*, 107.
93. W. B. Yeats, *Early Essays*, 34.
94. Donoghue, "Yeats's Shakespeare," 77.
95. Ludwigson writes that the "basic difference between the Dowden and the Renaissance supporters is somewhat blurred by its being cast at that time as a 'Nationalist-cosmopolitan' controversy. Dowden, Eglinton, Larminie, and others, who represented the 'cosmopolitan' side of the controversy, could not be described either as anti-Irish or as pro-British; they considered themselves to be 'Anglo-Irish,' men who respected nationalism as 'a perfectly natural and genuine sentiment,' but who felt that it did not take into account the facts in modern Ireland, whose culture was deeply rooted in English, as well as Irish soil." Further, Ludwigson identifies in the *Express* articles "three aspects which correspond to the three basic tendencies of the movement itself: nationalism versus cosmopolitanism, Nationalists versus Unionists, esoteric idealism versus objective idealism." See Ludwigson, *Edward Dowden* (New York: Twayne, 1973), 142, 141.
96. The first version of the article was published in *The Irish Fireside*, and the second version was published in *The Dublin University Review* in November 1886. Both are published in *The Complete Works of W. B. Yeats*, vol. 9, *Early Articles and Reviews*, ed. John P. Frayne and Madeleine Marcheterre, 3–27 (New York: Scribner, 2004).
97. Ibid., 11.
98. Ibid., 12.
99. Ibid., 11, 27.
100. Katheryn Ludwigson makes this point succinctly: "In the late 1880s until his death, Dowden lectured at various patriotic meetings in favor of maintaining the political alliance of Ireland with England, attended Unionist demonstrations, assisted as secretary of the Liberal Union, founded a Unionist Club, worked 'for some months on nothing by Unionist work' in the Irish office, led the Unionist Alliance, and even requested from Swinburne a Unionist song." Ludwigson, *Edward Dowden*, 45.
101. Ibid., 44.
102. Ibid., 128–29.
103. Ibid., 44.
104. Ibid., 129.
105. Ibid., 45.
106. Ibid., 47.
107. On the fundamentally "Victorian" character of Trinity at this time, see Terence Brown, "Edward Dowden: Irish Victorian," in *Ireland's Literature* (Mullingar: Lilliput, 1988), 29–45.
108. Murphy, "An Irish Catalysis," 219.
109. Ibid.
110. Ibid.
111. Ludwigson, *Edward Dowden*, 118.
112. Ibid., 147.

113. Brown, *Ireland's Literature*, 29.

114. Ibid., 30.

115. Ibid., 43.

116. Ibid.

117. Ibid., 41.

118. Ibid., 34–35.

119. In terms of his "Victorian" characteristics, Brown comments that "in many respects Dowden was the Trinity don of the period in whom the currents of the Victorian age ran most freely," and also aligns him with "that characteristic Victorian figure, the popular lecturer, who combined sensibility with secular uplift for a middle-class audience anxious for spiritual sustenance of an easily digestible kind in the absence of secure religious faith." Brown, *Ireland's Literature*, 31, 39–40.

120. Edward Dowden, *Shakspere: A Study of His Mind and Art* (New York: Harper, 1918), 9.

121. Ludwigson, *Edward Dowden*, 24.

122. Gary Taylor, *Reinventing Shakespeare*, 215.

123. Michael Taylor, *Twentieth Century*, 5.

124. Ibid.

125. W. B. Yeats, *Early Essays*, 78. Gardiner summarizes Dowden's position vis-à-vis the English literary canon as follows: "Dowden taught English literature at a time when Irish literature was . . . trying to get an audience. Consequently, throughout his career at Trinity College, Dublin, Dowden withheld his support from Irish writers and Revivalists. In Dowden's work, Ireland was always a sort of backwater to the 'one noble river' of English culture." David Gardiner, "To Go There as a Poet," 117.

126. W. B. Yeats, *Early Essays*, 78.

127. Ibid., 77.

128. Ibid., 79.

129. Dowden, *Shakspere*, 169.

130. Ibid., 213, 210.

131. Ibid., 215.

132. Ibid., 213.

133. W. B. Yeats, *Early Essays*, 81.

134. Ibid.

135. Dowden, *Shakspere*, 199.

136. Ibid., 194.

137. Ibid., 201.

138. W. B. Yeats, *Early Essays*, 79.

139. Murphy, "An Irish Catalysis," 212.

140. Ibid., 212–13.

141. In his essay on the topic of Yeats and Dowden's Shakespeare, Andrew Murphy makes the following observation:

> Dowden would have approved the change taking place in Yeats during the first decade of the twentieth century, a change which Yeats's father, however, forcefully opposed. The poet son seemingly had expressed to his father a doubt concerning the complete subjectivity of the creative experience and had admitted an attraction to a view of organic harmony of the subjective and objective, such as Goethe and Dowden held. Yeats's father protested in a letter to his son: "The English admiration for strong will, etc., is really part of the gospel of materialism and money-making and Empire-building. . . . You would be a *philosophe* and you are really a poet. The men whom Nietzsche's theory fits are only great men of a sort, a sort of Yahoo greatness. The struggle is how to get rid of them. . . . You are haunted by the Goethe idea, interpreted by Dowden, that a man must be a complete man. It is a chimera, a man can only be a specialist."

See Murphy, "An Irish Catalysis," 138.

142. W. B. Yeats, *Early Essays*, 78.

143. Dowden, *Shakspere*, 163.
144. Ibid., 166, 169, 280.
145. Ibid., 276.
146. For more on the balance of the concrete and the spiritual that Dowden found in Shakespeare, as well as a fascinating account of the revisions Dowden had made to his manuscript, see Ludwigson, *Edward Dowden*, 113–15.
147. W. B. Yeats, *Early Essays*, 82.
148. Desai, *Yeats's Shakespeare*, 16.
149. Murphy, "An Irish Catalysis," 215.
150. W. B. Yeats, *Early Essays*, 82.
151. Ibid.
152. Ibid., 81.
153. Ibid., 82.
154. Ibid., 82–83.
155. Ibid., 82.
156. W. B. Yeats, *Explorations*, selected by Mrs. W. B. Yeats (New York: Macmillan, 1962), 74, 210.
157. And in this Yeats was not alone; he later had a powerful ally in Harley Granville-Barker, the prolific director and writer whose fight for a national theatre provides a useful correlative to Yeats's own struggle in Dublin. As Dennis Kennedy surmises, "Harley Granville-Barker was everywhere that drama mattered in England in the first sixteen years of the century, but nowhere was his power of thought and action more evident than in his fight for a national theatre." See Dennis Kennedy, *Looking at Shakespeare: A Visual History of Twentieth-Century Performance* (Cambridge and New York: Cambridge University Press, 2001), 190. Granville-Barker was a giant influence on Yeats's dramatic philosophy, both in terms of his dramaturgy and his emphasis on Shakespeare as a creature of the theatre. It is easy to see why Yeats regarded him as sponsoring an intellectual revolt in Shakespeare studies. Granville-Barker's well-received *Prefaces* comprise a sweeping refutation of one hundred years of scholarship: "Nineteenth-century scholarship suffered from a surfeit of Shakespeare as philosopher, Shakespeare as mystic, as cryptogrammatic historian, as this and that, and as somebody else altogether. And the nineteenth century theatre suffered from the nineteenth century. Till at last it has seemed but common sense to return to Shakespeare as playwright." Harley Granville-Barker, *Prefaces to Shakespeare* (London: Sidgwick and Jackson, 1927), 22. In place of "Shakspere" the observer of fact, Granville-Barker posits Shakespeare the actor-director. As such, his corpus becomes less a kind of spiritual autobiography than a record of his dramaturgy.
158. Ronald Schuchard, *The Last Minstrels: Yeats and the Revival of the Bardic Arts* (Oxford and New York: Oxford University Press, 2008), 192. By 1905, Yeats was claiming that Shakespeare could not have achieved literary prowess had his father known how to read and write. Schuchard, *Last Minstrels*, 192.

Chapter Two

The Birth of a Nation

Shakespeare in the Irish Dramatic Movement

The Gods have returned to Eri and have centered themselves in the sacred mountains and blow the fires through the country. They have been seen by several in vision. They will awaken the magical instinct everywhere, and the universal heart of the people will turn to the old Druidic beliefs.
—W. B. Yeats, letter to George Russell, June 1896

In March 1901, Yeats visited Stratford-upon-Avon in order to see the Benson Shakespeare cycle of history plays, and to garner ideas for the Irish Literary Theatre. His encomiastic response is recorded in two essays that he wrote for *The Speaker*, which he later combined and published in *Ideas of Good and Evil* as "At Stratford-on-Avon." Read simply as a piece of journalism, the essay is relatively unremarkable. Primarily, it reiterates a key Yeatsian pre-scription for dramatic art: it should eschew realism in favor of a ritualistic, poetic drama of symbol and suggestion. Fully contextualized, the piece be-comes far more significant. It is here, at the turn of the century, that we meet Yeats's Shakespeare fully fledged: an appropriation of Shakespeare into the framework of an idiosyncratic occult nationalism. In the preceding chapter I narrated the public emergence of Yeats's Shakespeare, partly an inheritance from his father and partly the product of his own esoteric aesthetic ideals. Rhetorically speaking, Yeats deployed Shakespeare to elevate the status of indigenous Irish writers, and as we have seen, this meant intervening in two literary-critical conversations fraught with ideological baggage in the context of Irish cultural nationalism. The first—mediated through Matthew Arnold's pronouncements on the nature of the "Celt"—argued for Shakespeare's radical distance from the sensibility of modern, industrialized people. By empha-sizing an epistemological distance between contemporary English modes of

67

thought and feeling and an "ancient" predilection for magical thinking, Yeats's rhetoric decoupled England and its most potent cultural icon. Shakespeare, Yeats implied, belonged to the Irish. Yeats's second maneuver was more directly aimed at Dowden and his authority. Exculpating Richard II from charges of idleness and worldly failure, Yeats inverted the dominant reading of Shakespeare's histories—housed in character criticism—by isolating and excoriating what he saw as an imperialistic, utilitarian subtext. Yeats deposed Henry V, Dowden's favorite, and promoted the unlikely Richard on the basis of his capacity for "poetic reverie." Richard became a dreamy aesthete, and thus, in Yeats's scheme, a "Celt." Again, what distinguished the "Celt" in Yeats's rhetoric was, in part, an ability to pierce the hylic thickness of material reality and to access a higher plane of existence: Richard the seer replaced Henry the doer in the pantheon of Shakespeare's most significant characters. Yeats thus constructed an occult hermeneutic as the basis for evaluating Shakespeare's characters, and in the service of Irish literary nationalism. In doing so, he furnished us with one of the more bizarre instances of Shakespearean appropriation in English letters.

Taken together, as I have argued, these interventions effectively de-Anglicized Shakespeare with recourse to Yeats's religious philosophy. Moreover, Yeats's Shakespeare provides valuable insight into the Anglo-Irishman's management of his own cultural hybridity, as well as an example of literary-resource acquisition by a small nation seeking independence and self-definition. As Pascale Casanova writes of the Literary Revival, "The distinctive quality of the Irish case resides in the fact that over a fairly short period a literary space emerged and a literary heritage was created in an exemplary way."[1] By the turn of the century, Shakespeare had become fully implicated in Yeats's most influential literary-nationalist project: the development of an avant-garde theatre in Dublin. From 1898 to 1904, when the Abbey Theatre was purchased to permanently house the Irish National Theatre, Yeats worked tirelessly toward the goal of creating a national repertoire housed in a theatre that would rival the centers of European dramatic production, and whose ultimate function was nothing less than the bringing into being of the new Irish nation. Rebecca Steinberger reminds us that "the purpose of the Abbey was, in a sense, to correct and alter the portraits of Irish characters on the dramatic stage and free the drama from formulaic anglicized styles,"[2] so it might seem somewhat paradoxical that a dramatic endeavor intended to banish the stage Irishman and "English" modes of representation might look to Shakespeare—England's most potent cultural icon—for inspiration. As we have seen, however, Shakespeare in Yeats's thinking was not straightforwardly "English," but instead the voice of a preindustrial folk culture whose drama operated through feudal codes and heroic values historically on the cusp of eradication.

Yeats's contributions to periodicals such as *Samhain* during these years make frequent reference to Shakespeare as he seeks to outline a dramaturgy suitable for nation building, as well as for promoting Ireland's cultural status among European nations. It is in this sense that Yeats's Shakespeare evolves during these years into a key touchstone for a Yeatsian aesthetic program at once nationalist and occultist, and while Yeats's theatrical recourse to Shakespearian precedent has received scholarly attention, less frequently considered is Shakespeare's prominence within Yeats's esoteric nationalism during this important period. Yeats's use of Shakespeare during this time—both in crafting his plays and in propagandizing the precepts of a new Irish drama— constitutes a fascinating view of emerging trends in Shakespearean stagecraft refracted through an occult lens. For this reason, Yeats's Shakespeare deserves the attention of literary historians concerned with both Irish literary nationalism and Shakespeare reception. The new Irish drama developed by Yeats and his coterie was intended to be more than a program for disseminating Irish legendary and folkloric materials, and more than an organ for national self-expression. A detailed examination of Yeats's Shakespeare during this period reveals Yeats's belief that a ritualistic, symbolic, and poetic drama could literally transform an audience, restoring visionary contact with an ideal realm. In other words, the singular purpose of Yeatsian dramaturgy was to reconcile religion to art by infusing dramatic technique with occult technology.[3] Yeats not only aspired to create a new Irish repertoire that would restore to the people a lost art of poetic drama, and a concomitant passion for balladry and musical speech, but he also prescribed a dramaturgy analogous to the ritual magic of an occult society, such that plays produced and performed by a poet-priesthood might prove capable of summoning into being a unified Irish nation of saints and heroes. Yeats's turn-of-the-century activities clearly demonstrate that the basis for this sacred theatre was to be a combination of occultist ritual and avant-garde theatrical techniques. Curiously, Yeats's visit to Stratford in 1901 has not been fully examined in the context of this esoteric nationalism. Parsing Yeats's references to Shakespeare in his essays written during the first decade of the twentieth century, a picture emerges of a nationalist poet-playwright responding to paradigm shifts in stagecraft while contemplating the theatre's role in disseminating an idealized version of the nation's heroic past. As such, the desire to recover a more authentic presentation of Shakespeare's plays, manifested, for example, in the work of the Elizabethan Stage Society, found its correlative in the efforts by Yeats and his coterie to bring back a variety of archaic Irish cultural practices and to make the past live again in the present.

FROM THE CELTIC MYSTERIES TO A MYSTICAL THEATRE

In the last few years of the nineteenth century, Yeats turned his energies to two major projects that were intended to shape the cultural life and aesthetic sensibilities of the emerging Irish nation: the first, the "Celtic Mysteries," derived from the Neoplatonic principles and ritualistic practices of occultist organizations, particularly the Order of the Golden Dawn; the second, the Irish Literary Theatre (later the Irish National Theatre Society), was to prove a much greater success, despite Yeats's later pronouncements that it had failed to popularize poetic drama and a difficult, symbolist art. From Richard Ellmann onward, Yeats's biographers have connected the dots between these two ambitious projects: "Yeats's endeavors to found an order and to found an Irish theatre came about the same time," writes Ellmann, "and the synchronization is significant. Occultism or . . . spiritual ideas, underlie all his early plays and his theories of what the national theatre should be."[4] Similarly, concludes R. F. Foster, "The theatre would provide a common symbolism and a common meditation. Crucially, in WBY's personal quest the theatre would slowly replace the Celtic Rites on which he had worked with Gonne."[5] In *Yeats's Nations*, Marjorie Howes reiterates this thinking: "The line from the Celtic Mysteries to the early Irish theatre runs remarkably straight. . . . Yeats's Irish theatre relied heavily on ritual and symbol and sought to produce a meditative, visionary experience for the audience."[6] On this, critical consensus is clear: Yeats crafted ritualistic, symbolical plays with purported transformational capabilities whose legitimacy derived from the practices of the Golden Dawn and whose power was to be harnessed for nationalist purposes. The intersection of religion and the arts thus underpinned Yeats's literary nationalism, and he maintained the need for a clerisy, or class of literary priests, to lead the new Irish nation toward a revived spirituality. As John Eglinton surmised, "if he could have his way, I think he would make of the whole profession of literature one vast secret order, training its novices in the occult sciences and instructing them in a system of symbolic images, somewhat as they seem to have done in the bardic colleges of ancient Ireland."[7] Recently, Ronald Schuchard has covered much of this terrain in his careful study of Yeats's attempts to restore the bardic arts, although he sees 1906 as the year when Yeats ultimately launched his project to revive a denuded oral culture in Ireland:

> A century later we can begin to see that Yeats's experiments in minstrelsy and his statements about the printing press that so bemused and baffled the public in the first five years of the twentieth century, were the recurring signs of a long-planned attempt to establish . . . a "spiritual democracy." This would be effected in part by developing the Abbey into a unique "theatre of speech," one that would not only redress the cultural imbalance brought by the book but

restore personal utterance to dramatic, narrative, and lyric poetry for all the people.[8]

Before examining in detail the function of Shakespeare within this nexus of interests, I want to briefly redraw this line from the Celtic Mysteries to the "mystery" theatre.

Yeats's attempts to devise rituals for a "Celtic" society of hermetic knowledge date from around 1896. Over the following five or six years, Yeats identified a ruined castle that was to become its headquarters—the "Castle of Heroes" at Lough Key—and with the help of MacGregor Mathers and Maud Gonne he constructed rituals like those of the Golden Dawn that would lead adepts through a series of levels within the Order toward the eventual goal of spiritual rebirth through knowledge of the operations of a nonmaterial reality. Drawing upon Cabbalistic hermeticism, adepts would pursue spiritual knowledge—gnosis—through the study of druidic lore, and by participating in visionary exercises of the type familiar to Yeats from his years with the Golden Dawn, producing visions by concentrating on symbolic shapes and colors, for instance. That the Celtic Mysteries was to be a fundamentally nationalist organization is made clear by Ellmann:

> The doctrines would be the same as those of Theosophy and the Golden Dawn, but associated here specifically with Ireland. They "would unite the radical truths of Christianity to those of a more ancient world." To the "Castle of the Heroes" would come the finest men and women of Ireland for spiritual inspiration, fortified by the supernatural powers which the Irish mystical order had concentrated, to act, in Florence Farr's words, as living links "between the supernatural and terrestrial natures."[9]

Again, Yeats's pursuit of the Celtic Mysteries is well-known critical territory, and interested readers should turn first to *The Man and the Masks* for an authoritative account of its history. For my purposes, I want to furnish context for the fin-de-siècle construction of Yeats's Shakespeare. Of key importance to my own work here is the nature of the Mysteries as both a community of scholar-adepts and a series of meditative technologies that connected ritual, symbol, and transcendental visionary experience. I turn once more to Ellmann for an overview of the organization's bizarre synthesis of scholarship and ritual magic:

> On the inner truth of the rite depended the order's spiritual sanctions, and Yeats and Maud Gonne devoted themselves with great ardor to its construction. They read John Rhys's *Celtic Heathendom* and various other works in order to fill in the background of pre-Christian Ireland; they worked out parallels between the Irish gods and Graeco-Roman ones. But beyond this haphazard scholarship was their use of symbolic meditation. They would impel their imaginations to dwell on the ancient divinities, who would often obligingly

seem to take definite shape and to enlighten them on various aspects of the
other world. Yeats called this method of meditation "vision," but perhaps
deliberate revery would be a more accurate and acceptable designation. [10]

As we have seen in the first chapter of this book, a capacity for "poetic
reverie" is what elevated Shakespeare's Richard II over the efficient, imperialistic Henry V, the basis of Yeats's critical attacks on Edward Dowden's
Shakspere. Symbolic meditation constituted a means of communicating with
the dead, receiving visions of the past and future, and, perhaps most significantly in terms of Yeats's nationalism, a technology for countering the utilitarian, positivistic modes of thought which, in his mind, distinguished the
English, urban bourgeoisie, and modernity more generally. In Yeats's overtly
nationalist writing, the modernizing of Irish culture was therefore typically
couched in the elegiac rhetoric of loss, and channeled through vituperative
broadsides against the agents of bourgeois materialism: the newspapers,
"politics," and commercial art. The function of the Celtic Mysteries was to
be nothing less than a turning back of the clock and the restoration of a
preindustrial culture whose occultist aesthetics would unite stratified social
classes. Like the Golden Dawn, the Celtic Mysteries was to be a secret
society, granting access only to an elite, and so, in order that an entire nation
might be restored to its ancient religious sensibility, a technology was required to transfer knowledge from the adepts to the people in the same way
that priests used the ritual of the mass. That the chronology of the Celtic
Mysteries matched that of the new Irish dramatic movement makes clear that
a ritualistic, symbolic drama was to provide exactly this function, and although his work on the rites of the new order ended abruptly in 1902, Yeats's
drama developed from these principles. In 1899, in the pages of *Beltaine*, a
periodical of the Irish dramatic movement, Yeats expounded on the sacred
nature of the new drama, and on the sacerdotal function of his coterie: "In the
first day, it is the art of the people; and in the second day, like the drama
acted in old times in the hidden places of temples, it is the preparation of a
Priesthood. It may be, though the world is not old enough to show us any
example, that this Priesthood will spread their Religion everywhere, and
make their Art the Art of the People." [11] Such thinking was by no mean
peculiar to Yeats or the Order of the Golden Dawn. In *The Birth of Modernism*, for instance, Leon Surette explains how "accounts of secret history"
typically privilege "small groups or coteries of extraordinary individuals that
from time to time achieve positions of power and influence." [12] "When occult
secret history is adopted by poets, painters, and musicians," he continues,
"creative artists become the elite group that carries on the sacred and secret
tradition." [13]

Yeats's desire to construct the Celtic Mysteries must have gained further
impetus from the eruption of interpersonal conflict within the Order of the

Golden Dawn in London at the turn of the century. The various squabbles and doctrinal controversies are now well documented and form the plot of Yeats's abandoned semiautobiographical novel, *The Speckled Bird*, as well as prompting, in March 1901, one of his earliest overtly occultist prose pieces: "Is the Order of R. R. et A. C. to Remain a Magical Order?" Again, this is pretty well-worn critical terrain, as is the fact that Yeats ended up siding with Annie Horniman in the Order's disputes; Horniman, of course, was to become the Abbey's wealthy patron, purchasing the old Mechanic's Institute in Dublin in 1904. The point here is that "At Stratford-on-Avon" was written at a time when Yeats was dealing with a crisis in one society (the Golden Dawn), constructing mystical rituals for another (the Celtic Mysteries), and vaunting an ambitious theatrical project in Dublin; reading the essay in this context thus reveals the centrality of Shakespeare to Yeats's spiritualist drama. Moreover, the essay's opening segments depict Stratford as an ideal Yeatsian community: a revivalist locus of coterie culture and adeptship. In Stratford, in 1901, Yeats saw a priest class in training, studying sacred rituals and then participating in them via the performance of the Shakespearian history cycle. Stratford therefore offered Yeats a model for Irish theatre as a national cultural institution that might initiate Irish adepts to lead the sacred nation into being, and, perhaps, as a means of thinking through the problematic signification of his own Anglo-Irish hybridity. Having Celticized Shakespeare, Yeats now fashioned Stratford as an archaic tertium quid between the bourgeois, imperialist metropolis and its quasi-colonial periphery in the rural margins.[14]

AT STRATFORD-UPON-AVON

In its longer form, "At Stratford-on-Avon" consists of six sections, three of which are concerned with Shakespeare's characters and were published in the second of two essays for *The Speaker*. Having examined in some detail the longer essay's character criticism in the previous chapter, here I want to focus primarily on the initial essay, in which Yeats describes his activities while staying at Stratford and offers a review of the Benson cycle of history plays: *King John, Richard II, 2 Henry IV, Henry V, 2 Henry VI,* and *Richard III,* "played in their right order, with all the links that bind play to play unbroken."[15] The sequence, writes Yeats, "has moved me as [the theatre] has never done before,"[16] and this emotional impact derives from two factors: "partly because of a spirit in the place, and partly because of the way play supports play."[17] Before turning to the plays themselves, a "strange procession of kings and queens,"[18] I would like to consider Yeats's sense of a "spirit in the place," an important part of the essay that has hitherto gone unremarked. "At Stratford" is essentially a utopian piece: Yeats represents the town as an ideal community, a literary commune of like-minded individuals bound together by class and mutual intellectual sensibility, Shakespearean adepts learning from masters. The essay's primary rhetorical strategy is the establishment of a series of antitheses: urban versus rural, low culture versus high, utilitarianism versus idealism, and modernity versus the preindustrial past. Second-person pronouns invite the reader to share in the opinion of the narrator as he then privileges one side of each binary. The essay begins by pitting an archaic rural idyll against the metropolis, with the tropes and tone of a Victorian travelogue, enthusing in archaic picturesque over the soft materiality of the place: its "quiet streets, where gabled and red-tiled houses remember the Middle Ages," its "theatre that has been made not to make money, but for the pleasure of making it," and its "green garden by a river side."[19] Yeats's Stratford is a temporal oasis where the nasty, troublesome aspects of modern life have been effaced—its theatre is noncommercial, and its gentle rusticity contrasts the hustle and bustle of the city, represented metonymically by "hurrying cabs and ringing pavements."[20] Yeats emphasizes Stratford's tranquility, which is recognized as a precondition for meditation: "All day [the traveler] does not hear or see an incongruous or noisy thing, but spends hours reading the plays, and the wise and foolish things men have said of them, in the library of the theatre," he informs us, and "[i]t is certainly one's fault if one opens a newspaper."[21] Stratford is rendered the hermetic province of an intellectual leisure class, and all is organized around Shakespeare: "there is no need to talk of anything but the play in the inn-parlour, under oak beams blackened by time and showing the mark of the adze that shaped them."[22] Throughout this section of the essay, Stratford is positioned as London's antithesis in terms of its appearance (rustic), its commercial activity (absent), and its aesthetic predisposition (nonpopular). Instead of riding in London's "hurrying cabs," the visitor to Stratford "rows by reedy banks and by old farm-houses, and by old churches among great trees."[23] The sense here is that Yeats has in fact traveled back in time as he has moved away from London, and his enthusiasm for the Shakespeare Festival counterpoises antipathy for the capital's bourgeois, commercial aesthetics: "In London, we hear something that we like some twice or thrice in a winter, and among people who are thinking the while of a music-hall singer or of a member of parliament."[24] London, in fact, possesses an "evil prestige" which Stratford "may help to break," and lest Yeats has not made his point entirely clear, he asserts that "a bitter hatred of London is becoming a mark of those that love the arts, and all that have this hatred should help anything that looks like a beginning of a centre of art elsewhere."[25] Clearly Yeats has his Dublin enterprise in mind.[26]

    Much of "At Stratford" is, therefore, an attack upon a familiar object of Yeatsian contempt—a commercial philistinism in the arts—and so a thinly veiled promotion of the new Irish Literary Theatre, whose object was to produce a challenging, self-consciously literary repertoire. The Shakespeare Festival obviously furnished Yeats with ideas for his own theatre; thus, for instance, his remarks in "At Stratford" that "[t]o them [the theatre and library] will be added a school where speech, and gesture, and fencing . . . will be taught"[27] find their correlative in the first edition of *Samhain*, also written in 1901, when Yeats proposes that "the Technical board" should "give a small annual sum of money to a school of acting which would teach fencing and declamation, and gesture and the like."[28] Again, however, such parallels have not gone unnoticed by critics. Of greater import to my argument here is the description of Stratford as a locus for collective intellectual enterprise; read in the context of Yeats's occult activities during these years, "At Stratford" identifies a revivalist enterprise underway in Shakespeare's birthplace, and tropes the town's visitors as pilgrims visiting an almost monastic, quasi-occultist community where Shakespearian "adepts" pour over sacred texts in the library before witnessing Shakespearian rituals. The actors at Stratford are, for instance, "slowly recovering the lost tradition by musical speech,"[29] while Yeats's rhetorical georgics invoke archaic symbols of a preindustrial age that seems to have remained intact in England's provinces: "tinted glass . . . reedy banks . . . old churches . . . great trees."[30] Again, I am arguing for this manner of signification within the context of Yeats's occultist and aesthetic enterprises at this time, and this essay offers the clearest instance of Yeats appropriating Shakespearean cultural capital to bolster his Irish literary-nationalist endeavors. Writing about the disruptions in the Golden Dawn at this time, R. F. Foster draws a parallel between the secret society and an academic body: "Much as the study-programme of the Order supplied his need for an academic structure, the squabbles among the adepts resembled controversies within a university department: dealing with hierarchies of authority, curricula, workloads and methods of examination."[31] This is an astute observation, and I have argued in the previous chapter for an understanding of Yeats's interest in societies—literary and occult—as part of a nationalist project of wresting cultural authority from academe in general, and Trinity College in particular. In line with this thinking, Andrew Murphy, in his reading of "At Stratford," detects an attitude of "studied casualness" and "critical *sprezzatura*"[32] in Yeats's tone as he narrates his time spent reading Shakespeare criticism in the library—"I have turned over many books in the library"[33]—betokening an "attempt to set up a strong contrast between himself and the Trinity professor [Dowden]."[34] However, I am arguing here for another interpretation of Yeats's Shakespeare essay, one that foregrounds Stratford's materiality and cultural enterprise, rather than the dispute with Edward Dowden. As such, the library-theatre nexus at Stratford represents an ideal synthesis of ritual art and religious study approximating the Celtic Mysteries and its concomitant Irish Literary Theatre, its adepts training to enter the priesthood of Shakespearean mysteries. That fact that

Yeats locates such an ideal at the symbolic center of English cultural heritage offers a caveat against facile or reductive assessments of Yeats's cultural nationalism. As elsewhere in his prose, the binary of urban versus rural proves a more compelling geographical scheme for espousing nationalist sentiment than political antagonism between London and Dublin.

Studying at Stratford thus fulfills Yeats's personal requirement for a passive, meditative life and an alternative educational institution; in terms of his nationalist enterprise of training a new Irish priesthood equipped with a ritualistic, transformational art, "At Stratford" reveals the Irishman thinking carefully along utopian lines about the potential for a national drama housed in a revivalist scholarly community as the center of national cultural life, and he closes the first section of his essay by suggesting that art and religion could be reconciled in conditions like those found at Stratford: "the arts would grow serious as the Ten Commandments."[35] But the essay's hostility to London needs to be understood as more than an aesthete's shot at commercial theatre, or as a simple gesture of nationalistic protest. As Yeats makes clear, a clamorous city life has detrimental repercussions for visionary capabilities: "In London," he writes, "the first man one meets puts any high dream out of one's head, for he will talk to one of something at once vapid and exciting. . . . But here he gives back one's dream like a mirror."[36] This suggestion of intersubjectivity is not mere metaphor. Adepts within the Golden Dawn—and the Celtic Mysteries—routinely entered collective trances by meditating on certain symbols. The ability of multiple people to simultaneously share a dream or vision is a fundamental belief of Yeats, set out in his essay, "Magic" (written the year before his Stratford visit), as the first tenet of his "magical" beliefs: "That the borders of our mind are ever shifting, and that many minds can flow into one another."[37] This remained a core conviction for Yeats; at the end of his life in 1938, for instance, he recalled how a dream about dead bodies had passed through his sisters' house from the mind of one dreamer to the next.[38] So, the emphasis Yeats places on Stratford's tranquility, as opposed to the noise and bustle of London, makes it a location conducive for meditation, and thus for the mind's reception of visions from beyond the veil. In "Magic," Yeats explains how "life in cities, which deafens or kills the passive meditative life, and our education that enlarges the separated, self-moving mind, have made our souls less sensitive [to enchantment]."[39] In this context it becomes clear that Yeats is advancing an occult hermeneutic with regard to Shakespeare's drama. With sleepy Stratford preparing the audience for visionary experience, the ritualistic histories on stage possess the capability for inducing trance-like states, and, provided that the audience is suitably prepared—having studied in the Shakespeare library, for instance—and of a unified sensibility, the plays can in fact induce states of intersubjectivity and a collective visionary experience. This is the fundamental technology of Yeatsian theatre, and the basis for his belief that, given the right preparation and circumstances, a symbolist Irish drama with a ritualistic stagecraft and an archaic, national content might unify Ireland. Moreover, this is what Yeats saw in Shakespeare, although in his view the links between a symbolic, "religious" drama and a unified audience were disintegrating as Shakespeare wrote his plays. "Unity of being" is the phrase Yeats would use when imagining the ideal fusion of religious art and a unified social imaginary, and typically the social structure best suited to such a cultural arrangement was hierarchical and elitist, hence his attraction to the structure of hermetic societies, within which the adept must move vertically through levels of initiation in pursuit of gnosis and spiritual power. Notwithstanding his later attraction to "Byzantium" as an ideal, Yeats at this time deploys ancient Greece most readily as a historical precedent. But he also points frequently to Elizabethan England. "We know that the songs of the Thames boatmen," he would later write, "in the age of Queen Elizabeth had the same relation to the great masterpieces [as Gaelic folk songs to the new Irish drama]."[40]

Clearly, in the context of an Irish cultural nationalism, and as Ireland inched toward independence, this is a politically fraught appropriation of England's chief cultural icon and its "golden age." The signifying power of Shakespeare the English culture hero must explain why, in the first issue of *Samhain* (1901), Yeats seems to hedge, declaring that the repertoire of the new Irish drama has "far greater need of the severe discipline of French and Scandinavian drama than of Shakespeare's luxuriance,"[41] and that Irish writers should "study the dramatic masterpieces of the world," but avoid Shakespeare, since, "being the only great dramatist known to Irish writers," they have "cast their work too much on the English model."[42] In the same essay, Yeats asserts, "Let us learn construction from the masters, and dialogue from ourselves,"[43] but while this formula seems entirely appropriate for a de-Anglicized drama, he then approvingly quotes a letter from "a relation of mine" (his father), who provides the following analogy:

> It is natural to an Irishman to write plays; he has an inborn love of dialogue and sound about him, of a dialogue as lively, gallant, and passionate as in the times of great Eliza. In these days an Englishman's dialogue is that of an amateur—that is to say, it is never spontaneous. I mean in *real life*. Compare it with an Irishman's, above all a poor Irishman's, reckless abandonment and naturalness, or compare it with the only fragment that has come down to us of Shakespeare's own conversation.[44]

Shakespeare is an ambivalent signifier in the discourse of Irish literary nationalism, and particularly in Yeats's prescriptions for Irish drama. But here once more we find one of the primary rhetorical purposes of Shakespeare: a strategy of mediation between Yeatsian cultural politics and a competing mode of Irish nationalism demanding overt propaganda on the stage and a

thorough de-Anglicization of Irish cultural life in general. Writing and speaking only in English, and with strong literary and familial ties to England,
Yeats fends off accusations of West Britonism by deploying Shakespeare's
cultural status as a literary genius, while simultaneously forging connections
between preindustrial, Elizabethan England and an Irish agrarian society that
he promotes as the model and inspiration for a future Irish nation. It is a bold
and bizarre maneuver: Shakespeare is both culturally elite and the voice of
the people. Here, for instance, is Yeats appropriating Shakespeare's moral
authority in 1903 to defend *The Hour-Glass* against charges in D. P. Moran's
The Leader that he "did not care whether a play was moral or immoral":
"The plays of Shakespeare had to be performed on the south side of the
Thames because the Corporation of London considered all plays immoral."[45]
The critic's voice is aligned with the Puritan authorities of sixteenth-century
London, Yeats's drama with Shakespeare's, and London again signifies a
pernicious hostility to high art with an obvious resonance in the context of
Irish nationalism. And in an issue of *Beltaine* from 1899, Yeats defends his
prescriptions for poetic drama by asserting that the "audiences of Sophocles
and of Shakespeare and of Calderón were not unlike the audiences I have
heard listening in Irish cabins to songs in Gaelic about 'an old poet telling his
sins,' and about 'the five young men who were drowned last year' . . . or to
some tale of Oisin."[46] So, a perceived sociocultural affiliation among the
rural poor of Ireland's West and the Elizabethan English underpins the construction of Shakespeare as a model for Irish revivalism. Moreover, since
Yeats's nationalism was also fundamentally bound up with his religious
philosophy, this affiliation is both strengthened by, and in turn strengthens,
the claim that Shakespeare's audience and the rural Irish maintained bonds
with the unseen world. A Shakespearean drama was necessarily a symbolic
one, and since symbols were the basis for visionary experience, a Shakespearean drama was also a visionary one.

A VERY STRANGE PROCESSION

I want to return to Yeats's Stratford visit of 1901, when he saw *King John*,
Richard II, *2 Henry IV*, *Henry V*, *2 Henry VI*, and *Richard III* "played in their
right order, with all the links that bind play to play unbroken."[47] For the
visiting Irishman, Shakespeare's history plays were one "unbroken" series;
they comprised a single unit, a dramatic ceremony, "five plays that are but
one play,"[48] a "strange procession of kings and queens, of warring nobles, or
insurgent crowds, of courtiers, and of people of the gutter."[49] Later in this
essay, Yeats begins the process of counterinterpretation whereby he famously inverted the critical orthodoxy concerning the protagonists of several of
Shakespeare's most famous, and most ideologically imperialist, history

plays. But here I want to focus on Yeats's description of these plays as a single "strange procession," and the effect of that spectacle on his imagination. He remarks that this sight was "full of an unearthly energy," which caused him to feel "as I have sometimes felt on grey days on the Galway shore, when a faint mist has hung over the grey sea and the grey stones, as if the world might suddenly vanish and leave nothing behind."[50] In other words, the spectacle of the play, rather than the language or specifics of action, has brought the spectator Yeats close to trance, just as the spectacle of the grey Galway shore had done before. Galway for Yeats is always a *topos hibernia* and *topos mystica*. "Ireland is always Connacht to my imagination," he would later write, "for there more than elsewhere is the folk tradition that is the loftiest thing that has come down to us within the ring of Ireland."[51] Both of these "spectacles" are united as symbols—always more than mere literary devices—provoking the same imaginative response. As Yeats comments in his essay on "Magic," "I cannot now think symbols less than the greatest of all powers whether they are used consciously by the masters of magic, or half unconsciously by their successors, the poet, the musician and the artist."[52] Rhetorically, then, Yeats aligns the archaic pageantry of Shakespearean chronicle history with the transformative power of the Irish landscape. Through his occult doctrine, Shakespeare's histories are emptied of their specific content and context, which would unmistakably mark them as part of an English history, and the remainder acts as a great ritual. "The people my mind's eye has seen have too much of the extravagance of dreams," he continues, "to seem more than a dream, and yet all else has grown dim before them."[53] Of course, the "mind's eye" is not a conventional metaphor for the imagination in Yeats's discourse: Yeats is suggesting a visionary experience.

The second section of "At Stratford" deals straightforwardly with stage and set design, advocating theatres "in the shape of a half-closed fan, like Wagner's,"[54] and "[d]ecorative [i.e., nonnaturalistic] scene-painting."[55] Again, the passage reads on one level as simply an endorsement of avant-garde stagecraft, making particular mention of Gordon Craig's scenery, for instance, and by itself this section of the essay provides an interesting overview of contemporary trends in staging Shakespeare: Victorian pictorialism is rejected in favor of abstraction, for instance. However, in the context of an occultist aesthetics, the short review becomes much more significant. All of Yeats's prescriptions for stagecraft are ultimately concerned with the audience's experience of the play-ritual; if, as I have been arguing, the first part of the essay depicts Stratford as an ideal Yeatsian fusion of mystery theatre and hermetic academy—his vision for an Irish national theatre—this second section shows us the technologies with which the new Irish priest class would reforge the links between its audience and the unseen world. Yeats's ideal nation was to be achieved through other means than circulating the

poetry of Samuel Ferguson, for instance, and what Yeats saw in the spectacle
of Shakespeare's histories in 1901 was not just good drama or high culture,
but the exposition of a "universal symbol" of English history, delivered by
means of the dramatic-occult technology he wished to import onto the Dublin stage: ritualized pageantry, metrical speech, the high rhetoric of the archaic aristocracy, visual nonrealism, and folkloric or legendary themes.

"I do not think there is anything I disliked in Stratford," muses the visiting Irishman, "but the shape of the theatre."[56] Yeats takes issue with the half-
round Shakespeare Memorial Theatre, which in his view is unsuitable for
contemporary dramatic art. Whereas Elizabethan drama was primarily ora-
torical—"the players were content to speak their lines on a platform, as if
they were speakers at a public meeting"[57] —contemporary drama is "the art
of making a succession of pictures," and therefore a more appropriate space
would be "the shape of a half-closed fan, like Wagner's theatre."[58] The
advantage of this shape is that it permits the entire audience to see the stage
from essentially the same vantage point: "pictures could be composed for
eyes at a small number of points of view, instead of for eyes at many points
of view."[59] By thus controlling the audience's perspective, spectators would
enjoy a collective spectacle, focusing on a nonnaturalistic set: "we could
make our pictures with robes that contrasted with great masses of colour in
the back cloth and such severe or decorative forms of hills and trees and
houses that would not overwhelm, as our naturalistic scenery does, the idealistic art of the poet."[60] Again, Yeats's prescriptions for a poetic drama with
an abstract stage set are well known, as is the method practiced by Yeats's
occultist coterie of inducing visions by concentrating on symbolic shapes and
colors: Maud Gonne was at this time busy devising such special colors for
the Celtic Mysteries. In Stratford, then, Yeats saw the potential for a drama
capable of producing a collective symbolic meditation, and it is seemingly
only the shape of the Memorial Theatre that prevented such a phenomenon
during Yeats's visit. This section of "At Stratford" is therefore concerned
primarily with advancing an avant-garde stagecraft capable of generating a
visionary aesthetic experience, and Gordon Craig is singled out for particular
praise: Yeats had witnessed his production of *Dido and Aeneas* for the Pur-
cell Society on March 26, immediately prior to his Stratford visit, and "despite some marring of his effects by the half-round shape of the theatre, it
was the first beautiful scenery our stage has seen."[61] Yeats's encomium is
unfettered here, and he proceeds to praise Craig for creating "an ideal country where everything was possible, even speaking in verse, or speaking in
music, or the expression of the whole life in a dance."[62] Of course, Yeats had
precisely such a poetic drama in mind for the Irish theatre, and again he
draws from an esoteric religious philosophy to inform his dramaturgy: "the
whole life" might seem on one level to refer to the totality of the human
experience, a liberal-humanist critical commonplace for Shakespeare's cor-

pus, but Yeats could equally mean the "daimon" here, a term referring to the totality of an individual's existence throughout time—the reincarnated soul's complete sequence. As we shall see, Yeats brings up this concept in reference to Shakespeare at the end of "At Stratford."

Having valorized Craig's anti-illusionist stage sets, Yeats returns to Shakespeare's drama to advance his argument. He admits that there is some merit to the revival of archaic stagecraft epitomized by William Poel's Elizabethan Stage Society (though he does not mention Poel specifically)—a return to "the platform and the curtain"[63] —but he then turns back to his cherished ideal of symbolic set design. His argument here is as follows: "we can only get rid of the sense of unreality, which most of us feel when we listen to the conventional speech of Shakespeare, by making scenery as conventional";[64] in other words, an anti-illusionist scenery is called for because Shakespeare's language is "conventional," in the sense that it is governed by an archaic rhetoric and nonnaturalistic poetic and dramatic codes. A "conventional" scenery for a "conventional" speech: Yeats is pushing for productions of Shakespeare that, like Craig's *Dido and Aeneas*, create "an ideal country," and for Yeats this has to mean the "unseen" country, a higher plane of reality beyond the sensory realm. He proceeds to elaborate on this point:

> Time after time [Shakespeare's] people use at some moment of deep emotion an elaborate metaphor, or do some improbable thing which breaks an emotion of reality we have imposed upon him by an art that is not his, nor in the spirit of his. It is also an essential part of his method to give slight or obscure motives of many actions that our attention may dwell on what is of chief importance, and we set these cloudy actions among solid-looking houses, and what we hope are solid-looking trees, and illusion comes to an end, slain by our desire to increase it.[65]

An anachronistic imposition of Victorian mimetic standards thus constitutes the main problem with contemporary Shakespeare productions: the world of Shakespeare's drama is an ideal one, following its own codes of behavior and signification. Shakespeare occludes character motivation in order that the audience should focus on "what is of chief importance," and a few sentences later, Yeats elaborates on what is truly significant in Shakespeare's plays: "It brings us near to the archetypal ideas themselves, and away from nature, which is but their looking-glass."[66] What Yeats sees in Shakespeare's drama, then, is a ritualistic and anti-illusionist art with the capacity to deliver its audience into the higher realm of archetypal reality; Yeats's only negative criticism of Benson's staging is his omission of "the scene in *Richard III* where the ghosts walk, as Shakespeare wrote it,"[67] since it betokens a capitulation to contemporary standards of mimetic realism, but "had his scenery been as simple as Mr. Gordon Craig's purple back cloth that made Dido and Aeneas seem wandering on the edge of eternity, he would have found noth-

ing absurd in pitching the tents of Richard and Richmond side by side."[68]
Yeats cannot countenance an artificial return to Elizabethan staging, but he
also firmly rejects Victorian pictorialism. His third way, epitomized by
Craig's bold, abstract color schemes, situates Shakespeare firmly within the
dramatic strictures of avant-garde theatre. More than this, it is promoted on
the basis of an occultist hermeneutics. With the revivalist coterie as a new
Irish priest class, the Irish mystery theatre would stage nationalist, archetypal
dramatic rituals, and in doing so it would strengthen the links between the
Irish people and a preindustrial, "Celtic" sensibility. Again, by drawing upon
Shakespeare for a model, Yeats performs a complex and esoteric appropriation of the Englishman's cultural capital, lending artistic credibility to the
new Irish drama and cementing literary connections across the Irish Sea.

MYSTICAL DRAMA AND THE FALLACY OF SINGULAR MEANING

In *Yeats: The Man and the* Masks, Richard Ellmann relates an account of a
collective vision experienced by "a group of enthusiastic Celts"[69] under
Yeats's tutelage in 1897. Having concentrated on the appropriate symbols
and following a series of suggestive prompts, the group was led by Yeats in a
"Celtic ceremony of initiation" and was then "transported . . . to a mountain-
ous district where we found ourselves before an ancient well."[70] Led by
Yeats and Florence Farr, the adepts looked into the well and saw there "the
world of form . . . the plane of Art."[71] Then, "we returned as we came to the
path through the wood where the guardian waited to guide us," and the group
"absorbed light" from the mysterious guardian's "throne" so that "when at
last we mounted through the Lethe-like waters we brought with us still the
light from the throne."[72] At this point, however, the collective vision begins
to diverge: "Two of our number had not brought enough of this light with
them and when we reached the well they noted the leafless ash-trees and the
chill and cheerless aspect of the scene which was not so to the rest."[73] Before
the vision dissipates, however, unity is restored, and "we all waited together
till the ash-tree budded again and the scene assumed warmth and life."[74] This
is a fascinating account on a number of levels, hinting at the careful control
of the vision by Yeats, who initiates, guides, and ends it. It also reveals a
tendency for multiple adepts to share a vision, but then to experience subtle
variations: for some members of the group, the final scene appears "lifeless,"
and they have to wait until the scene once more becomes unified, presumably
with the prompting of Yeats or Farr. Similarly, in his essay "Magic," Yeats
recounts two such collective visions. "At the time," he reflects, "these two
visions meant little more to me . . . than a proof of the supremacy of the
imagination, of the power of many minds to become one, overpowering one

another by spoken words and by unspoken thought till they have become a single intense, unhesitating energy."[75] However, while the visions were shared, the power to direct the event lay with one powerful individual: "One mind was doubtless the master, I thought, but all the minds gave a little, creating or revealing for a moment what I must call a supernatural artist."[76] These are the kinds of collective experience that Yeats hoped to translate into the theatre, but while the small coterie of adepts here proves pliable, theatrical audiences were a much greater challenge. In miniature, this was the problem that was to dog Yeats throughout the first decade or so of the twentieth century: how to control an audience's collective transformation through the dissemination of aesthetic affect. As a locus for cultural production, the theatre is a useful alternative to the university. As a means of constructing a new nation, of instilling a shared set of values in a people, theatrical productions are flawed vehicles, since they are as prone to multiple interpretations as written works of art. Poststructuralist theorists have argued successfully for the fundamental polysemy of the sign, such that the instability of meaning is now a critical commonplace. This was certainly not the case during the early decades of the twentieth century, and the modernist Shakespeare was subject to frequent attempts to excavate totalizing patterns of meaning. G. Wilson Knight's "spatializing hermeneutics," for example, provide a fascinating corollary, particularly given Knight's own spiritualism (see chapter 4). Yeats's involvement with the theatre at this time is therefore characterized by his sometimes exasperated attempts to provide for a unified audience response to his work. His experiments with various dramaturgical techniques as he tried to control the signifying capabilities of each performance, and his frustration when unable to do so—in his response to the *Playboy* riots, for example—were generally voiced in accusations of willful misinterpretation and critical myopia. As far as Yeats was concerned, the stage *could* yield a controlled and singular signification in the hands of an expert director-producer. And in his attempts to fill that role, he developed an intricate and impressive knowledge of multiple aspects of theatrical production, from set design to acting style. James Flannery notes to this end how "the plays of Yeats, which were created out of a world of the imagination, required not only an original scenic style but a means of actually realizing that style in terms of the money, materials, and manpower available. Yeats himself met this challenge by becoming a serious student of the techniques, as well as the principles, of set design, set painting, and construction."[77] This conflict of meaning control between the director and the audience was not capable of resolution and ultimately pushed Yeats toward exclusive modes of theatrical representation like the Japanese Noh.

Flannery points out in his study of the Abbey Theatre that the poet-playwright maintained the vision of a totalizing dramatic signification despite fluctuations in his technology: "In more than fifty years' involvement with the theatre, Yeats's ideas did shift, but it was a shifting in methods to achieve an end rather than a change in the end itself."[78] I am primarily interested here in the first decade after Yeats's visit to Stratford, when his commitment to theatre was absolute and the output of his lyric poetry correspondingly low. Generally speaking, his experiments with staging plays at the Abbey focused on the actor's voice, the actor's movement, and stage scenery, in that order of importance. In a 1904 edition of *Samhain* entitled "The Play, the Player, and the Scene," he expresses the desire for innovative staging but then qualifies the statement in terms of its relative importance: "we must have a new kind of scenic art. I have been the advocate of the poetry as against the actor, but I am the advocate of the actor as against the scenery."[79] The scenery was important for Yeats only in the way it encouraged the audience to focus on the actor. "A forest," for instance, "should be represented by a pattern and not by a forest painting."[80] Although he softened toward realistic sets like the interior of peasant households in the course of the Abbey's early development—this a response to the successes of some of Lady Gregory's and Synge's plays—Yeats felt strongly that symbolic patterns and colors were more useful to his aesthetic in pointing up the relationship between actor and environment. "The actor," Flannery explains, "was not seen as a three-dimensional, flesh-and-blood figure. Instead, he was but another element in the overall stage pattern—a symbol of human perfection rather than a reflection of life as it existed in the stalls and pit of the theatre."[81] The set should therefore contribute to a sense of alien presence in the actor, an otherness that would alter the subjectivity of the audience. Mostly, Yeats attempted to do this by using colors in order to contrast or harmonize the actor with the backdrop. Flannery's study of Yeats's theatre is again useful here. He sees the year 1902 marking a movement away from ritualistic pattern in Yeats's visual arts, toward a preference for two or three colors as the dominant visual motif. Ultimately, the difficult conditions at the Abbey, including a constant shortage of money, meant the need for scenery that could be assembled, dismantled, and reused easily. In 1910, Yeats finally resolved this problem by employing screens developed by Gordon Craig. These were large panels that could be slid into grooves and arranged to create the three-dimensional space that the Abbey so badly required. For Yeats, they represented a triumph of stage engineering, creating the effect he desired at low cost. Most importantly, they focused attention onto the actors, who, in turn, focused on the delivery of their lines.

Yeats wanted his actors to remain still; slow movements and stylized gestures contributed to the eeriness of the performance, again creating the sense of otherness he deemed suitable for the presentation of ancient Irish legend and folk material. The language was to do the play's work: "That we may throw emphasis on the words in poetical drama, above all where the words are remote from real life as well as in themselves exacting and difficult, the actors must move, for the most part, slowly and quietly, and not very much, and there should be something in their movements decorative and rhythmical as if they were paintings on a frieze."[82] Given the contemporary trend in Shakespeare production toward a renewed archaism, an effort to revive the authentic experience of Shakespeare's drama, an interest in the artistic possibilities of metrical speech connected Yeats's work directly to the innovative revivalism of the Elizabethan Stage Society. Indeed, Michael Taylor sees the legacy of William Poel lingering in the technique of today's Shakespearean actors: specifically "his conviction that the speaking of Shakespeare's verse needs an 'exaggerated naturalness' and 'tuned tones,' as though Hamlet's naturalistic-sounding advice to the Players were to be stiffened with a touch of Marlovian declamation."[83] The focus was the utterance, but that could not work without stillness. That this kind of performance was to some degree effective, and certainly a departure from normative styles, is registered by the *Times Literary Supplement*, in a review of May 8, 1903. Invited to perform in London for the first time at the Queen's Gate Hall, the players of the Irish Theatre Society acted five short plays, including three by Yeats: *The Hour Glass, Cathleen Ni Houlihan*, and *A Pot of Broth*. "First and foremost," comments A. B. Walkley, "there is the pleasure of the ear."[84] He continues:

> This, of course, is an accidental pleasure; we mean that it has nothing to do with the aesthetic aims of the Society, nothing to do with the dramatic theories or poetic gifts of its President, Mr. W. B. Yeats, nothing to do with art at all; it results from the nature of things, from the simple fact that Irish speakers are addressing English listeners. It is none the less a very exquisite pleasure. We had never realised the musical possibilities of our language until we heard the Irish people speak it.[85]

Walkley is wrong. Aside from the Irish accents, Yeats wanted his actors to speak musically, and his ideal actor should have an "acute sensitivity to the vocal properties inherent in every word."[86] In 1901, he was working with the actress Florence Farr—a fellow member of the Golden Dawn—on a technique called "cantillating," whereby verse was spoken as if to the accompaniment of music. In his experiments with Farr he used a psaltery—a lute-like instrument tuned to quarter tones to imitate speech. This was a difficult trick to master. The actress had to sustain stressed syllables and pitch each word or syllable at a certain note. Again, this work had both an aesthetic and nationalistic purpose: "There is no doubt," writes Flannery, "that in their minds the method they chose was also intended to capture some of the religious aura of bardic art."[87] In *The Last Minstrels*, Ronald Schuchard carefully charts the progress of the Yeats-Farr project, itself part of a grand vision of the restoration to Ireland of an ancient bardic culture:

Yeats knew that the fractured harmony between poetry and musical speech had scarcely held together beyond the seventeenth century. Nonetheless, as the poet's relation to his culture and the common man was one of his abiding interests as a young poet, he had become a student of bardic traditions wherever he found them: the Irish *File*, the English bards, the rhapsodists of ancient Greece, the minstrels of Europe and India. [88]

To this list, I suggest, we might add the Bard of the Elizabethan stage. Such was the importance of the intoned word to Yeats that by 1904 he had created a form of poetic drama that, according to Flannery, required "five different styles of vocal utterance: peasant dialect . . . a declamatory kind of prose . . . iambic pentameter . . . an impassioned lyric verse . . . and the pitched incantory verse style."[89] The point here is that A. B. Walkley was wrong to discount the influence of Yeats's art in the players' performance at the Queen's Gate. However, his observation is fascinating:

> We are listening to English spoken with watchful care and slightly timorous hesitation, as though it were a learned language. . . . These Irish people *sing* our language—and always in a minor key. It becomes in very fact "most musical, most melancholy." Rarely, very rarely, the chant disintegrates into a whine. But, for the most part, the English ear is mildly surprised an entirely charmed. Talk of *lingua Toscana in bocca Romana!*[90]

Besides the whine, this is exactly the effect that Yeats wanted to achieve—a strange and musical utterance that dominates the performance as its central feature, unencumbered by the techniques of normative, realistic stage production. The audience is startled and transformed by the unusual, unearthly quality of the spoken word. It begins to experience poetic reverie. And this, in part, is a result of a stylized, restrained acting manner, coupled with a sparsely decorated stage:

> As a rule [the actors] stand stock-still. The speaker of the moment is the only one who is allowed a little gesture. . . . The listeners do not distract one's attention by fussy "stage business," they just stay where they are and listen. . . . And in their demeanour generally they have the artless impulsiveness of children. . . . Add that the scenery is of Elizabethan simplicity—performance is a sight for sore eyes.[91]

This is the kind of effective staging of his drama that Yeats was to struggle with at the Abbey. Despite the infantilizing of the Irish actors—a frequent trope of colonialist discourse—Walkley appreciates the contribution made to the performance by the lack of movement. Yeats would also have been happy to have his stage compared to Shakespeare's. However, no amount of prescriptive, occultist technology—audience perspective, abstract colors, versifying, statuesque actors—can create a singular, unified response to a complex dramatic work, and this is made clear in Walkley's review. Although he praises the production for its novelty, Walkley appears to be enchanted merely by accents. It is not the "aesthetic aims of the Society" that make this performance special; rather it is the "simple fact that Irish speakers are addressing English listeners."[92] It is the "nature of things," by which Walkley means the scrambling of fixed national categories: "Talk of *lingua Toscana in bocca Romana!*"[93] The reviewer here misinterprets the frisson he experiences. Seemingly unaware of the irony of his Latin phrasing, he mistakes linguistic appropriation and hybridity for a saturnalian inversion of categorical difference. Despite Walkley's claims, this too was central to Yeats's cultural project; Yeats required an idiom that was neither modern English (redolent of newspapers and nationalist oratory) nor Gaeilge (which he did not speak and had a limited audience). The strangeness of Shakespeare's language on the modern stage found its correlative in the linguistic performance of the Irish players, such that a revived Hibernian English was being produced: "we have looked for the centre of our art where the players of the time of Shakespeare . . . found theirs—in speech, whether it be the perfect mimicry of two countrymen of the roads, or that idealised speech poets have imagined for what we think but do not say."[94] As Declan Kiberd indicates, this language signified the clash of cultures, but not the subordination of one to the other. Thus the literature produced by Yeats and his coterie "arose not among the Irish speakers of the west nor among the drawing-rooms of a self-enclosed gentry, but from the impact of one civilization (Gaelic) upon another (English)."[95] Walkley's error can perhaps be understood as a signature of his time and place, but it ably demonstrates a flaw at the center of Yeats's efforts to create a ritualistic drama capable of producing a singular audience response. He might control the shape of the theatre, the design of the sets, the movement and musical speech of the actors, but he couldn't control the audience in the same way that he could guide a visionary journey of like-minded dreamers.

A STATELY PROGRESS: PRESCRIPTIONS FOR A UNIFIED IRELAND

In order to transform Ireland through collective participation in the nation's sacred rituals, the new Irish arts would have to reach audiences beyond Dublin. This fact explains Yeats's call for the establishment of multiple theatre societies throughout the country, as well as various loci for the performance of poetry in the minstrel tradition. Schuchard thus reminds us of Yeats's ambitious project to revive Ireland's oral culture, and to do so by reestablishing the ancient "'processional order,' which derived from the *priscus magi.*"[96] "In the new manifestation of the order," writes Schuchard,

"Yeats would have the poet-priest employ the ancient arts of this tradition to speak through legend and symbol to all levels of culture, on the stage though players trained in passionate speech, in the countryside through minstrels trained in the arts of reciting lyrical and narrative poetry."[97] In a 1904 issue of *Samhain*, entitled "The Dramatic Movement," for instance, we find the following statement: "We can hardly do all we hope unless there are many more of these little societies to be centres of dramatic art and of the allied arts."[98] It would be of little use to Ireland if the new mystery drama was to reach only the citizens of its capital, and so, "[i]f we are to push our work into the small towns and villages, local dramatic clubs must take the place of the old stock companies."[99] Yeats continues as follows: "A good-sized town should be able to give us a large enough audience for our whole, or nearly our whole, company to go there; but the need for us is greater in those small towns where the poorest kind of farce and melodrama have gone and Shakespearean drama has not gone, and it is here that we will find it hardest to get intelligent audiences."[100] Here once more we see the dual signifying capabilities of Shakespeare as both a metonym for high art and a technology for popular cultural transformation. "Shakespearean drama" has not gone to certain small towns, so the residents of these places are unprepared for the work of Yeats and his coterie—they cannot supply "intelligent audiences." Part of Yeats's evident enjoyment of his time at Stratford is the sense of camaraderie he feels in the company of "our friends . . . who care for the arts [and] have few new friendships among those that do not,"[101] and herein lies the problem for a Yeatsian drama of occult transformation: producing a unified visionary experience required not only a unified dramaturgy; it necessitated a unitary sensibility of people "who care for the arts." Just as adepts in a secret society must advance along the various levels of gnosis through esoteric study and initiation rites in order that they might share a vision, Irish audiences must be trained, and Shakespeare's plays constitute a part of that training. This problem of audience sensibility underlies Yeats's increasing frustration with the reception of his work. While Yeats clearly enjoyed stirring up hostile critics as a means of promoting his drama, negative criticism invariably pointed up the flaw in his theatrical project, namely its reliance for its affective capabilities on a unified audience response. But who was to be transformed? The rural folk of Ireland's West and their old, aristocratic "betters" were already, in Yeats's view, suitably prepared for initiation into the new Irish nation, and indeed were already assimilated into the stratified but "organic" social body constituting the nascent, ideal Yeatsian nation. It was, of course, the urban bourgeoisie, with their "English" utilitarianism, popular-commercial aesthetics, and taste for headlines and scandals that Yeats regarded as the enemy of his drama and yet hoped to train up. Throughout his writings, Yeats spun the story of the Irish National Theatre as a negotiation for Irish self-representation between a mandarin and the masses, and certainly he could not have demanded a diet of literary drama for the new nation without pitting himself against the perceived forces of crass, bourgeois philistinism. In this sense, the success of Yeats's theatre would always be paradoxical: without the agents of middle-class taste to rail against, his theatrical endeavors might not have been elevated via the critical infamy of nationalist writers like D. P. Moran in *The Leader*. On the other hand, the Irish National Theatre was supposed to transcend narrow class interests with recourse to mystical technologies, uniting the nation in a shared visionary experience. This paradox—a reliance upon, and determination to transcend, social difference—informs the tautology at the center of Yeats's 1919 essay, "A People's Theatre," which I will turn to in the next chapter. Here I want to complete the picture I have been outlining of a nexus of literary, nationalist, and occultist ideas, finding their expression in Yeats's references to Shakespeare.

The Celtic Mysteries was to be an occult collective as well as a school for Ireland's intellectual priesthood. Reincarnated as the Irish National Theatre Society, the ritualistic function remained; the idea was for a coterie of artists to instill a collective will, a shared spiritual-aesthetic ethos, and an awareness of collectivity under the aegis of the Irish nation. As we have seen, Yeats had recourse to a set of esoteric religious beliefs to furnish him with the dramaturgic principles for this arrangement, but his underlying conception of the affective process itself was likely influenced by contemporary political ideas concerning the power of mobs. As Marjorie Howes puts it, "Yeats viewed the theatre as a potential means of mobilizing and 'nationalizing' the masses, something he recognized any successful nationalism in the age of mass politics must do."[102] Evidence of this claim is readily apparent in most of Yeats's writings on the theatre. Most frequently it is figured in terms of cultivating the tastes of the Irish bourgeoisie for difficult—that is, nonrealist—art, and the dissemination of a body of Irish folkloric material, along with its symbolic freight. This, of course, was to transcend the petty squabbling of "newspaper" politics: "It is possible, however, that we may have to deal with passing issues until we have re-created the imaginative tradition of Ireland, and filled the popular imagination again with saints and heroes."[103] Indeed, that kind of action would result from the audience's immersion in the work of a society which "has no propaganda but that of good art."[104] Howes points out that "[f]or Yeats, the theatre as occult ritual could inspire audiences to practical work in the public sphere precisely because it accessed the intersubjective unconscious, instinct and the emotions."[105] In her fascinating chapter on this aspect of Yeatsian drama, Howes uncovers the period's interest in the psychology of crowds to account for this rationale. As she sees it, Yeats was building on ideas that had been circulating since the advent of mass politics in the nineteenth century, and which had found their most influential voice in Gustave Le Bon, whose *La Psychologie des foules* (1895) became something of a handbook for the governing classes. Crowd theory commonly held that the individual within a crowd would lose subjectivity, or rather that their subjectivity would fuse with those around them into a single mind, not unlike how Yeats understood the process of a collective trance. For most crowd theorists, then, this group mind could be controlled by a leader through what was essentially mass hypnosis, hence the perceived threat of radical, charismatic folk leaders such as Maud Gonne to the authorities. Such theorists tended to differentiate between temporary, popular, and other threatening "mobs," and the more permanent, positive group mentality of the "nation"— thus between official and unofficial forms of mass hypnosis. Howes goes on to locate in Yeats's writing a general anxiety along these lines: a desire to forge the nation constantly fraught by a fear of the mob. Certainly, Yeats's writings on the theatre abound with reiterations of the Irish theatre's beneficial potential, and scorn for the critics of its plays, who are rarely named but are generally seen as a mob comprising members of the institutions that regulate the opinions of the chattering classes: "how can one, as many would have us, arouse the mob, and in this matter the pulpit and the newspaper are but voices of the mob, against the English theatre in Ireland upon moral grounds?"[106] Yeats is pushing for an understanding of "great" art as nonpolemical, nonproselytizing, but imbued with transformative potential at a "nonpolitical" level. This is, of course, a fallacy. The riots that followed the first performance of Synge's *Playboy of the Western World*, for instance, are figured in Yeats's accounts as a struggle over the leadership of the pliable mob. In "On Those That Hated *The Playboy of the Western World*, 1907," the hostile detractors are "Eunuchs" who "ran through Hell and met / On every crowded street to stare / Upon great Juan riding by."[107] Visualized as street flotsam, then, the objects of scorn are castrated, powerless, but held in thrall by spectacle. Note also the class valence of that spectacle. The horse-borne "great Juan" rides disinterested past the pedestrian classes: the plebeians. Yeats's opinions of the crowd were thus at best ambivalent, and this too is reflected in the longer version of "At Stratford-on-Avon," which ends by drawing a historical analogue: "in [Shakespeare's] day the glory of a Poet, like that of all other imaginative powers, had ceased, or almost ceased, outside a narrow class."[108] "The Puritanism that drove the theatres into Surrey," he continues, "was but part of an inexplicable movement that was trampling out the minds of all but some few thousands born to cultivated ease."[109] Just as hermetic adepts kept alive a secret history of spiritual knowledge across the ages, so too has a "narrow" class maintained "imaginative powers": this is the class capable of reforging the connection between art and religion, ritual and vision. As I examine in the next chapter, Yeats's definition of the ideal audience became increasingly exclusive as the years passed, to the point where he ultimately called for "an unpopular theatre and an audience like a secret society where admission is by favour and never to many."[110]

Another poem, "Paudeen," written in 1913 when Yeats was moving toward increasingly nonpopulist forms of drama, provides a useful measure of the class prejudice with which the poet-adept circumscribed the visionary experience. It opens with a familiar deprecation of the shopkeeping classes of Dublin. Paudeen, a diminutive of Patrick, and thus a tawdry, shabby namesake of Ireland's patron saint, is seen "in his shop" with his "fumbling wits" and "obscure spite."[111] The speaker, "[i]ndignant" in the face of this urban mediocrity, stumbles "blind / Among the stones and thorn-trees" until "a curlew cried and in the luminous wind / A curlew answered."[112] Here the strange luminosity of the wind is explained literally in terms of the "morning light," and metaphorically as the force of an epiphanic vision:

> A curlew answered; and suddenly thereupon I thought
> That on the lonely height where all are in God's eye,
> There cannot be, confusion of our sound forgot,
> A single soul that lacks a sweet crystalline cry.[113]

The speaker bears witness to a visionary transformation brought on by the cry and response of the curlew, and the poem's topography moves from the cramped interiority of a Dublin shop toward an evocation of the sublime. He concludes that even old Paudeen in his shop has a soul with a "sweet crystalline cry," but that cry is deafened by the "confusion of our sound." The sheer materiality of existence, and especially urban existence, works to dull the speaker's awareness of Paudeen's soul and the possibility of its transcendence. But it is the speaker who is transformed, not "our old Paudeen."[114] As the possessive pronoun suggests, Paudeen is not the subject of the poem but the occasion for the poet's spiritual metamorphosis. What I want to locate here is the key relationship between subject, object, and transformative technology. What the poem tells us is that *even* the lower middle classes in Dublin are potentially transformable, though they cannot transform themselves. It is a member of the Irish "clerisy"—the poet-occult aristocracy—who receives the sudden transcendence of vision, the spectacle of a god's-eye view. Paudeen's own transformation is omitted here, but its potential is implied. However, since the transformative technology of natural symbols such as curlew cries at dawn are available only to the leisure and rural laboring classes, what forces are made available to the shopkeeper, to the newspaper writer, to the urban bourgeoisie? Since, in Yeats's opinion, the life of crowded cities dulled the mind's visionary capabilities, Dublin's middle classes thus presented a dual problem to his occult-theatrical initiative: they had neither the taste for avant-garde aesthetics nor the kind of premodern sensibility upon which Yeats saw his symbolist drama working appropriately. The solution that Yeats seems to reach, both in his writings for the Irish Dramatic Movement and in his later prose, is that a visionary experience may not be available to the masses in the purely mystical sense, but that a lesser emotional effect could be achieved through a spectacle of archaic, aristocratic power. In other words, while the shopkeeping classes are excluded from the transformative capabilities of symbolic meditation, they might be assimilated into the ideal Yeatsian nation by a kind of mute acceptance of their position and the guidance of their social and intellectual superiors. Like the plebeians overcome by the sheer majesty of "great Juan riding by," the emotional impact of a symbolic drama staging archaic heroic ideals—the death of Cuchulain, for instance—and promoting a hierarchical class ideology would at least silence the naysayers, and perhaps prepare them for initiation into the spiritual life of the new nation. We see this in Yeats's exegesis of Shakespeare's histories in "At Stratford," for instance. For Yeats, these staged displays of state power are nonpolitical—"politics" being the domain of the chattering classes—but powerfully spectacular: "Shakespeare cared little for the State, the source of all our judgments, apart from its shows and splendours, its turmoils and battles, its flamings-out of the uncivilised heart."[115] Despite the apparent acknowledgment of the state's role in constructing "our judgments," Shakespeare here is interested in the trappings of power, not its articulation as policy; and for Yeats, these displays are symbolic, ritualistic, and highly affective. So, once more, Yeats had recourse to a powerful cultural touchstone; if the middle classes could not be transformed immediately, they could be prepared for a future assimilation through the "Shakespearean" spectacle of a heroic feudal past.

A DIET OF SHAKESPEAREAN HISTORY

Though he was probably unaware of it, Yeats had a connection with a figure he would probably have placed at a highly objective phase in *A Vision*: John Churchill, Duke of Marlborough, the man responsible for advancing English power in Europe through a series of military victories against the French in the early eighteenth century. Both men claimed that their entire knowledge of English history came from Shakespeare's history plays.[116] In fact, Yeats later proposed a similar form of schooling for his own son, Michael. In "Pages from a Diary in 1930," published in *Explorations*, he remarks how "[w]hen my [occult] instructors began their exposition of the Great Year all the history I knew was what I remembered of English and Classical history from school days, or had learned since from the plays of Shakespeare or the novels of Dumas."[117] Rather than seeing this as a flaw, he recommends a similar pedagogy to Michael's tutor: "Do not teach him a word of history. I shall take him to Shakespeare's history plays, if a commercialised theatre permit, and give him all the historical novels of Dumas, and if he cannot pick up the rest he is a fool."[118] Like father, like son—Yeats's prescription of Shakespearean history points up his own distaste for normative approaches to the teleological understanding of historical process. By 1925, Yeats had con-structed a metaphysical account of civilizational change that not only claimed a transcendent signified, a sort of occult *primum mobile*, but also posited a set of cyclical processes as the determining power in temporal change. Earlier, in fact, in his 1901 essay, "Magic," Yeats predicted his own later systematizing, as he called for a new approach to the study of historical change that saw history as a reaction to discrete occult events occurring through the minds of the sensitive: "If all who have described events like this have not dreamed, we should rewrite our histories, for all men, certainly all imaginative men, must be for ever casting forth enchantments, glamours, illusions; and all men, especially tranquil men who have no powerful egotis-tic life, must be continually passing under their power."[119] Again: "May we not learn some day to rewrite our histories, when they touch upon such things?"[120] and "[o]ur history speaks of opinions and discoveries, but in ancient times when, as I think, men had their eyes ever upon those doors, history spoke of commandments and revelations."[121] Yeats here is not only pushing for an assimilation of an occultist "secret" history into the historio-graphical mainstream, he is also commenting on the use of history.

"History" was not a litany of dates and battles to be digested by the young. Yeats's comments on Shakespeare's history plays reveal what he regards as the purpose of representing history on the stage or in the class-room: to venerate the heroic ideals central to his occultism, his art, and his conception of the nation. The fact that Shakespeare manipulated historical sources to produce his drama was not only irrelevant; it was precisely the point. What mattered in history were not the objective facts and figures, the economics or politics, but the overall pattern of the rise and fall of heroic values, as well as the self-awareness that followed from witnessing a specta-cle of miraculous, aristocratic power. It was an archetypal, spiritual history that Shakespeare had captured in the form of a great ritual: "The five plays, that are but one play, have, when played one after another, something extrav-agant and superhuman, something almost mythological," writes Yeats in "At Stratford-on-Avon."[122] And he continues: "These nobles with their indiffer-ence to death and their immense energy seem at times no nearer the common stature of men than do the Gods and the heroes of Greek plays."[123] An aestheticized history becomes "almost mythological," and it is exactly this Shakespearean quasi-mythological spectacle that Yeats sought in his dramat-ic presentation of Irish legends: "Had there been no Renaissance and no Italian influence to bring in the stories of other lands, English history would, it may be, have become as important to the English imagination as the Greek myths to the Greek imagination."[124] Again, we see here the impact of what Casanova terms "the Herder effect" as Yeats draws a line from ancient Greece, through Shakespeare, and into the emerging Irish cultural space, eliding Roman and French literary precedents. Moreover, as Leon Surette indicates, the reduction of historical materials to mythological patterns, and then to broader metaphysical operations, constitutes a significant interpretive technique within the occult tradition: "It was the standard hermeneutic of Hellenistic Neoplatonism, which read Mediterranean mythology as a vast allegory, which—if properly understood—revealed the nature of the divine."[125] History-as-mythology: Yeats's exegesis of Shakespeare's history plays—and indeed his tragedies—reveals his thinking about the possibility of using drama to unify the Irish social strata, and if the bourgeoisie were incapable of visionary experience, they might still be assimilated into the sacred cultural life of the nation at a more rudimentary level by internalizing the "heroic" ideals of the cultural and social elites.

A short essay of 1903, "Emotion of Multitude," suggests a similar dual functioning of a ritualistic, "historical" drama. "I have been thinking a good deal about plays lately," Yeats begins, "and I have been wondering why I dislike the clear and logical construction which seems necessary if one is to succeed on the Modern Stage."[126] His answer is that contemporary drama derives its construction from France, and it therefore "has everything of high literature except the emotion of multitude."[127] While Greek drama obtained this "emotion" "from its chorus," "Shakespearian Drama gets the emotion of multitude out of the sub-plot which copies the main plot, much as the shadow upon the wall copies one's body in the firelight."[128] Using *King Lear* and *Hamlet* as his examples, Yeats deploys a critical commonplace—parallelism in Shakespeare's plot construction—in order to account for what he regards as the archetypal quality of Shakespearean drama: "very commonly the sub-plot is the main plot working itself out in more ordinary men and women, and so doubly calling up before us the image of multitude."[129] In typical Yeatsian fashion, the essay moves quickly to mysticize this exegesis, drawing upon Neoplatonic principles that posit the material world as the shadow of an ideal realm:

> Indeed all the great Masters have understood, that there cannot be great art without the little limited life of the fable, which is always better the simpler it is, and the rich, far-wandering, many imaged life of the half-seen world beyond it. There are some who understand that the simple unmysterious things living as in a clear noonlight are of the nature of the sun, and that vague, many-imaged things have in them the strength of the moon.[130]

This is Yeats's Shakespeare, an appropriation of Shakespearean criticism into the framework of an occultist cultural nationalism. In terms of my argument here, I want to connect this little piece to Yeats's thinking about the "problem" of the petit-bourgeois theatregoer. Shakespeare's double plot construction was usually explained at this time as an appeal to a dual audience. Elizabethan drama, so the thinking went, offered high rhetoric and royal pomp to its gallants, and bawdy clowning to its groundlings. In this way,

Yeats is drawing his mystery-critical hypothesis from a sociological commentary on the divided status of theatregoers in Shakespeare's London. While this simplistic division has been challenged more recently, the high/low binary underpins a culturally elitist understanding of Shakespeare's "universal" appeal. Moreover, I contend, it corresponds to Yeatsian dramatic prescriptions; the cultural elite and the "mob" might both be affected by the revivalist drama, in different but complementary ways. Those living in the "noonlight" might not achieve the kind of ecstatic experience Yeats claimed his drama to be capable of, but in a diluted form, they might still join in an emotionally transformative response.

Locating the affective power of Shakespeare's histories in their proximity to myth and hostility to social realism presents something of a problem when it comes to Shakespeare's most popular history: *1 Henry IV*. "At Stratford-on-Avon" makes no mention of the play, since it was not performed as part of the Benson Cycle, owing no doubt to its anomalous, seriocomic nature. Certainly, given the play's naturalistic tavern scenes, its subversive collapsing of social difference, and Falstaff's ironic commentary on the nature of honor, Yeats would have found it difficult to interpret the sequence as a universal, symbolic myth transcending the material realm and betokening aristocratic ideals had it been staged. As I hope to have shown, Yeats's Shakespearean hermeneutics were informed by class prejudice; in his own compositions, archaic settings denied bourgeois self-representation, and since the historical characters were drawn from a legendary past—the shared mythic corpus of a nation—they also allowed for an exclusivist representation of Ireland. Yeats's *The Countess Cathleen*, for example, focuses on a rural class which was guided by an older, landed class. The urban middle classes were not to be prepared for nationhood with images of themselves. Like modern critics today, Yeats located the symbolic potential of Shakespeare's historical characters in the rituals and metonyms of their power: their high rhetoric and its metrics, the theatrical pageantry of court and state occasion, and the honor codes of a warrior aristocracy. However, as today's critics also point out, Shakespeare's texts resist a singular, unifying interpretation. To view the dramatis personae of Shakespeare's history plays as essentially a parade of nonillusionary symbols is to ignore the most popular character in his entire canon: the eminently "realistic" Falstaff. So Yeats had to think through the problem of the anomalous knight, and he did so through several strategies. The first involved raising the status of Falstaff's dialogue. Thus he notes in a 1903 issue of *Samhain* ("The Reform of the Theatre"), "The speeches of Falstaff are as perfect in their style as the soliloquies of Hamlet."[131] Yeats is able to recuperate Falstaffian speech by comparison to the parts of Shakespeare that were then, as now, considered illustrative of his genius: Hamlet's soliloquies. Yeats then proceeds with recourse to an old rhetorical ideal of matching style, subject, and speaker: "One must be able to make a king of Faery or an old countryman or a modern lover speak that language which is his and nobody else's, and speak it with so much emotional subtlety that the hearer may find it hard to know whether it is the thought or the word that has moved him, or whether these could be separated at all."[132] Falstaff's speech is thus capable of "moving" through its "emotional subtlety," just as the more noble characters move with lyricism and passionate intensity—that is, highly metaphorical, symbolic language.

Within this passage is a key to Yeats's second strategy; Falstaff was occasionally turned into Yeats's second Irish ideal, the rural peasant: "when I think of free-spoken Falstaff I know of no audience but the tinkers of the roadside that could encourage the artist to an equal comedy."[133] With the slightly ambiguous phrasing here, the tinkers are seen as both the model for Shakespeare's character and the kind of audience for whom he was fashioned. Falstaff's wit and bawdy are folk characteristics, in spite of Yeats's acknowledgment elsewhere of the Oldcastle controversy: "he made Sir John Falstaff out of a praiseworthy old Lollard preacher."[134] Thus the fat knight can be assimilated into the representational project as a member of the Irish rural poor, who, thought Yeats, practiced an older, magical way of life. The last tactic was again part of Yeats's general concern with "realism," which "is created for the common people . . . and is the delight to-day of all those whose minds, educated alone by school-masters and newspapers, are without the memory of beauty and emotional subtlety."[135] Mirroring neoclassical attitudes to Shakespeare, then, Yeats figures the realistic, comic, elements of Shakespearean drama as disruptions of dramatic unity: low material designed to "please the common citizen standing on the rushes of the floor."[136] As the dual use of the term "emotional subtlety" here and above shows, Yeats deployed Falstaff as an example of Shakespearean brilliance, and as a critique of his technique. These positions could in fact be reconciled by blaming the audience—Shakespeare *had* to pander to popular taste, though when he did so he still displayed his characteristic genius. Ultimately, as the sometimes contradictory rhetorical maneuvers indicate, Falstaff was too problematic to fit the nonillusory spectacle of power that was Yeats's vision of Shakespeare's history plays. Yeats's attempts to transform the fat knight into an Irish tinker suggest that the stage Irishman could not be banished entirely from the social imaginary; moreover, they indicate the ideologically fraught hermeneutics with which Yeats tried to shoehorn the "low," comic elements of Shakespearean history into his own, elitist prescriptions for a transformative national drama. Just as Shakespeare seemingly wrote for two audiences at the Globe, so too would the Abbey's repertoire work on two levels: a visionary experience for the cultivated, and an awe-inspiring spectacle for the masses. "Shakespeare's groundlings," Yeats would later write, bemoaning popular distaste for his drama, "watched the stage in terrified sympathy."[137]

THE BARD AND THE NATION (ONCE AGAIN)

In the course of the Parnell Memorial Lecture at Cambridge University in 1998, Denis Donoghue laid out what he saw as Yeats's contribution to, and understanding of, the evolution of the Irish people from a race to a nation, and then ultimately to a modern state. Taking as a point of departure Matthew Arnold's assertion that "the Celts, and specifically the Irish and the Welsh, had for centuries been a race but not a nation,"[138] Donoghue looks to Yeats as a key player in the formation of the Irish nation through its cultural revival. In doing so, he rightly indicates the fluidity of Yeats's use of the words "race" and "nation":

> [H]e did not maintain a strict distinction between race and nation. The word "race" occurred to him when he scanned the far horizon of myth and legend, and when he consulted the evidence drawn from Celtic anthropology, folklore, and archaeology. . . . The word "nation" occurred to Yeats when he thought of a people being impelled toward self-expression and self-transformation. . . . The poet was its representative voice, the bard.[139]

While it is certainly true that Yeats did not police the boundaries of his terminology, he did employ his concepts of "race" and "nation" in a manner that accounts in large part for his somewhat naive—or more generously, "ambitious"—aspirations for the new Irish theatre, as well as Shakespeare's role within it. In the editions of *Samhain* covering the development of the Irish National Theatre, spanning the years 1901 to 1908, Yeats uses the word "race" eight times. Two of those are references to the "human" race, and two are specific to the "Irish" race; the rest refer to various generic or abstract conceptions of race as a group of people not necessarily tied to or emanating from a specific geographical locale. For example:

> I do not think it a national prejudice that makes me believe we are harder, a more masterful race than the comfortable English of our time, and that this comes from an essential nearness to reality of those few scattered people who have the right to call themselves the Irish race. It is only in the exceptions, in the few minds where the flame has burnt, as it were, pure, that one can see the permanent character of a race.[140]

To some degree, with his talk of "the permanent character of a race," Yeats here seems to be pushing for a conventionally modern attitude to race as a set of inherent, essential characteristics that are hereditarily determining, and both caused by and inscribed in pathological difference. The "we" here stands in contrast to the "comfortable English of our time." But Yeats's "race" here is not exclusive in the conventional sense of modern race; notice the modifiers "comfortable" and "of our time." The people who can call themselves the "Irish race" are a "few scattered people." For Yeats, this primarily means the rural folk of Ireland's West, who were seen by Yeats and his revival coterie as retaining the folk memory of a stock of ancient legends lost to the city dwellers and bourgeoisie. This is not mere nativism: the "reality" which confers upon them membership of an Irish "race" is an idealized access to the supramaterial realm, and as such is available to the nonrural with appropriate training. Immediately prior to this passage, Yeats explains how this "race" comprises the base for a theatrical audience: "I would not be trying to form an Irish National Theatre if I did not believe that there existed in Ireland, whether in the minds of a few people or of a great number I do not know, an energy of thought about life itself, a vivid sensitiveness as to the reality of things, powerful enough to overcome all those phantoms of the night."[141] This sentence, typical of Yeats's prose in its movement from the concrete to the abstract, helps us understand Yeats's concept of "race" as a fundamentally nonmaterial category: "racial" characteristics are located in the mind, not inscribed in the body, and manifest themselves in a certain "energy of thought."

Another example, this time from an essay of 1910, proves illustrative. In "J. M. Synge and the Ireland of His Time," Yeats notes how great writers can in fact affect material history by tapping into "race": "Synge, like all of the great kin, sought for the race, not through the eyes or in history, or even in the future, but where those monks found God, in the depths of the mind, and in all art like his, although it does not command—indeed because it does not—may lie the roots of far-branching events."[142] This passage is consistent with Yeats's reactions to the public clamor for didactic nationalist drama, against which he commonly responded with a Neoplatonic cry for the transcendence of great art. Thus the power of Synge's drama is that it "does not command," and the race that he searches for is not to be found in the reality of material things, in the visible world, but again, "in the depths of the mind." Yeats then writes of a "nobleness of emotion" common to a race, of which "great poets . . . have dreamed in solitude," great poets who "to this day in Europe are creating indestructibly spiritual races, like those religion has created in the East."[143] Clearly, "race" here signifies a much greater fluidity in terms of its potential membership; it is a spiritual, not a biological collective. In the same essay, then, Yeats distinguishes between great art, which is concerned with the immaterial, and the "popular and picturesque," a "condescension to knave or dolt."[144] Unsurprisingly, it is the art of the disinterested which stands for the eternal, idealized race:

> Only by the substantiation of the soul . . . whether in literature or in sanctity, can we come upon those agreements, those separations from all else, that fasten men together lastingly; for while a popular and picturesque Burns and Scott can but create a province, and our Irish cries and grammars serve some

passing need, Homer, Shakespeare, Dante, Goethe and all who travel in their
road define races and create everlasting loyalties.[145]

Again, we see race here figured as a shared spiritual philosophy, whose
defining aesthetic product is "great"—that is, disinterested and lyrical-mythi-
cal—art. Here also, in embryonic form, are the beginnings of Yeats's historical system. Homer, Shakespeare, and Dante are all figures who come later to
illustrate the eternal flux of cyclical civilizations, sitting at key moments in
the change from "primary" to "antithetical" periods of history. The races of
"everlasting loyalties" are in many ways the antithesis of the temporary-
sounding "Irish cries . . . of passing need." What we are beginning to see is a
picture of "race" as opposed to "nation": the "race" Yeats visualizes in connection with Irish nationhood transcends time, but in modern Ireland it includes Protestant, Anglo-Irish literati such as himself—visitors to Stratford
we might say—and the rural laboring classes, particularly in the West: poet-
landowners and visionary folk tenants.[146]

Returning to his Parnell Memorial Lecture, Donoghue sees the nation, for
Yeats, as "a people being impelled toward self-expression and self-transformation."[147] This is an astute definition in a number of ways. First, it lays
stress on the singular nature of the national collective. The nation is "a
people," who have a "self" that can be expressed and transformed. Second,
the impetus for such expression and transformation seems to be coming from
the top down; this "people" is "impelled." Yeats in fact uses the word "nation" thirteen times in the *Samhain* publications during the 1900s, and these
instances handily illustrate Yeats's conception of a nation as a stratified but
organic collective whose emergence relies both on esoteric, immaterial
forces, and on the work of a bard. Thus, writes Yeats in 1904, "if it is a Spirit
from beyond the world that decides when a nation shall awake into imaginative energy, and no philosopher has ever found what brings the moment, it
cannot be for us to judge,"[148] and "[w]e call certain minds creative because
they are among the moulders of their nation and are not made upon its
mould."[149] The disparity between the two accounts hardly needs glossing. In
the first, the nation is a sleeping entity that is awoken into life by an immaterial "Spirit." In the second, the metaphor shifts to the human artificer who,
like a sculptor, moulds a shape from plastic material. But in both cases,
nation building is the result of transcendent forces: the "moulders of the
nation" are themselves not a part of "its mould." Here we see a philosophical
basis for the sacerdotal function Yeats ascribes to the artist, as well as the
reason why a nationalist drama needed to avoid speaking directly to the
political and social issues of the day: national art—that is to say, art that is
capable of "awakening" the nation—cannot be created from the same mould
as the nation itself; in other words, national artists must draw from the past.
This, of course, is the basis of Yeats's revivalist aesthetics. The nation is

something that exists in potential, but it must be shaped by certain "creative minds" at the appropriate moment in history. Such thinking was typical of occultist accounts of historical change, which tended to champion individual agency: "once in a while, enlightened individuals achieve positions of power and influence, and the results are momentous."[150] Further, this Yeatsian conception of the nation mirrors his esoteric philosophy of human life: the earthly, material body situated in the present time was only a part of the individual's full existence, its "daimon." In the fifth section of "At Stratford-on-Avon," we see this principle applied to Shakespeare:

> The Greeks, a certain scholar has told me, considered that myths are the activities of the Daimons, and that the Daimons shape our character and our lives. I have often had the fancy that there is some one Myth for every man, which, if we but knew it, would make us understand all that he did and thought. Shakespeare's Myth, it may be, describes a man who was blind from very wisdom, and an empty man who thrust him from his place, and saw all that could be seen from very emptiness.[151]

What follows is the characterological exegesis of Richard II and Henry V, which I have examined at length in the previous chapter. What I want to highlight here, though, is the way in which Yeats fuses two analogous processes: the reemergence of the archetypal "myth" in the work of great artists, and the reemergence of individual human life comprising the totality of the "Daimon." Yeats's pronouncements on the mystical life of the nation thus find a correlative in the cyclicality of the individual soul and the recurrence of the artist's primary theme. As blades of grass emerge annually from subterranean rhizomes, so too must the nation periodically take material form from an unseen current or root: its race. There are in fact some tantalizing hints in Yeats's prose that he might have considered Shakespeare to be a part of his daimon, just as he later did during his bizarre epistolary relationship with early modern African ethnographer Leo Africanus, whose spirit he initially contacted via séance in 1912.[152] Rupin Desai, for one, draws attention to Yeats's depiction of Shakespeare as a quiet, shy individual who (like Yeats) put his energy into his artistic creations. Moreover, at least one Irish symbolist was making crazier claims about Shakespeare at this time: while tracking down an obscure reference in a letter from Yeats to Lady Gregory, dated January 13, 1903, Ronald Schuchard unearthed "The Shrine," a "short-lived quarterly edited in Stratford-upon-Avon by the Irish-born R. H. Fitzpatrick, [which] was dedicated to the belief that Shakespeare had been the Second Coming of Christ, but that the world was only now ready to receive this momentous news."[153]

Yeats had not fully worked out his theory of historical cyclicality—the rise and fall of "primary" and "antithetical" civilizations—when he visited Stratford in 1901, but as I have shown in the previous chapter, he did conceive of the late Renaissance in Europe as a moment of epistemic rupture followed by the decay of a mystical sensibility and the rise of a culturally catastrophic modernity identified as industrial, utilitarian, and scientific. This, again, was the conceptual framework for his de-Anglicizing of Shakespeare. With this in mind, it becomes clearer why, at the turn of the century, his head full of mystical rites and intimations of a national spiritual reawakening, Yeats would look to Shakespeare in particular. Both writers, it seemed, belonged to the same "ancient" race, if not the same daimon. Correspondingly, the new Irish nation would emerge from the same rhizome that had produced Elizabethan England. Such magical thinking allowed Yeats to mediate his own national hybridity and appropriate cultural capital for his dramatic endeavors. Furthermore, as I argue in chapter 4, implicating Shakespeare in a mystical definition of "race" contributed significantly to the twentieth-century process by which Shakespeare was freed from a narrow racial signification—Anglo-Saxon—and became an international possession; as we shall see, the story of Yeats's Shakespeare is also a part of the development of an autonomous "Shakespace." Yeats's religious philosophy must also have granted a certain millenarian appeal to the Shakespearean mystery theatre: as *A Vision* was later to confirm, Yeats's National Theatre was an idea whose time had come, and the Irish dramatic aesthetic was to be the technology whereby artist-adepts of the Irish race would initiate audiences into the mystical rites of nationhood through the ritualistic presentation of legendary materials. "A nation should be like an audience in some great theatre," he would later write, "watching the sacred drama of its own history; every spectator finding self and neighbour there, finding all the world there, as we find the sun in the bright spot under the burning glass."[154] The gyres were turning, the time was right for a cultural renaissance, and the means were becoming available for awakening the nation into an awareness of, and communion with, its own culture.

Examining Yeats's interest in the Benson history cycle and his contemporaneous forays into Shakespearean criticism tells us a good deal about how the revivalist conceived of the ideal nation and the role of a national theatre as its central cultural institution. Of course, Yeats's dramatic compositions met with mixed reviews, and it quickly became apparent that archaic, revivalist drama, replete with an occultist stagecraft, was not to inspire a national, mystical reawakening; neither would it placate the demands of middle-class theatregoers for more entertaining fare. By 1903, writes Ellmann, Yeats's mystery theatre was moving in a different direction: "The theatre audience, to which he was more responsive than he pretended, needed more substantial fare, and in 1903 John Synge, with his *Shadow of the Glen*, diverted the movement from Yeats's half-religious intentions. Yeats, without renouncing his own position, accommodated himself."[155] Certainly, the overtly "Shakespearean" quality of Yeats's plays—see *On Baile's Strand*, for instance—

dissipated after a few years of experimentation, and while Yeats continued to invoke Shakespeare in editions of *Samhain* and *Beltaine*, direct references drop rapidly from his discourse after about 1911. But Shakespeare was deployed in a number of ways in the service of Irish literary nationalism, and while the period 1901–1904 marks the heyday of his influence on Yeats's mystery theatre, by no means did he vanish from the Irishman's discourse following the professionalizing of the Irish National Theatre Society and the passing of the baton to Synge. Shakespeare remained a metonym for apolitical, challenging "high" art in Yeats's theatrical propaganda, though his use as an instrument for mystical nation building certainly diminished. As I intend to show in the next chapter, Yeats's disillusionment with the cultural life of the new nation, beginning in the 1900s, but increasing after the political upheavals of 1916–1922, altered Yeats's Shakespeare: virtually disappearing from his prose in the early to mid-1920s, he reemerges after Yeats's senatorial career as a reactionary, aristocratic figure, deployed fitfully in post hoc defenses of the revivalist cultural program, and as a high-culture warrior and scourge of the philistine masses.

NOTES

1. Pascale Casanova, *The World Republic of Letters*, trans. M. B. DeBevoise (Cambridge, MA: Harvard University Press, 2007), 304.

2. Rebecca Steinberger, *Shakespeare and Twentieth-Century Irish Drama: Conceptualizing Identity and Staging Boundaries* (Aldershot and Burlington: Ashgate, 2008), 33.

3. In "The Autumn of the Body," (1898) published in *Ideas of Good and Evil*, Yeats remarks that "[t]he arts are . . . about to take upon their shoulders the burdens that have fallen from the shoulders of priests, and to lead us back upon our journey by filling our thoughts with the essence of things, and not with things." W. B. Yeats, *Essays and Introductions* (New York: Macmillan, 1961), 193.

4. Richard Ellmann, *Yeats: The Man and the Masks* (London: Norton, 2000), 128.

5. R. F. Foster, *W. B. Yeats: A Life*, vol. 1, *The Apprentice Mage: 1865–1914* (New York and Oxford: Oxford University Press, 1998), 213.

6. Marjorie Howes, *Yeats's Nations: Gender, Class, and Irishness* (New York: Cambridge University Press, 1996), 70.

7. William Kirkpatrick Magee, *Irish Literary Portraits* (London: Macmillan, 1935), 65. Cited in Kathryn R. Ludwigson, *Edward Dowden* (New York: Twayne, 1973), 131.

8. Ronald Schuchard, *The Last Minstrels: Yeats and the Revival of the Bardic Arts* (Oxford: Oxford University Press, 2008), 190.

9. Ellmann, *The Man and the Masks*, 121–22.

10. Ibid., 123.

11. Cited in Ellmann, *The Man and the Masks*, 130.

12. Leon Surette, *The Birth of Modernism: Ezra Pound, T. S. Eliot, W. B. Yeats, and the Occult* (Montreal and Kingston: McGill-Queen's University Press, 1993), 51.

13. Ibid., 51.

14. I follow Richard English in using the term "quasi-colonial" to refer to the Irish experience of English rule. English, *Irish Freedom: The History of Nationalism in Ireland* (London: Macmillan, 2006), 125. (See introduction, n. 15.)

15. W. B. Yeats, *The Collected Works of W. B. Yeats*, vol. 4, *Early Essays*, ed. Richard J. Finneran and George Bornstein (New York: Scribner, 2007), 73.

16. Ibid.

17. Ibid.
18. Ibid.
19. Ibid.
20. Ibid.
21. Ibid.
22. Ibid.
23. Ibid.
24. Ibid., 74.
25. Ibid.
26. McAlindon reads "At Stratford" as an articulation of Yeats's "aristocratic myth" that was to become more directly articulated after 1904 or so, in response to an emergent popular Catholic nationalism and his own sense of alienation from Ireland's developing national culture. For McAlindon, the descriptions of Stratford primarily signify the influence of William Morris on Yeats's thought at this time, who also "loathed the modern . . . world and lamented the disastrous effects of its puritan morality, utilitarianism, and rationalism upon the arts." T. McAlindon, "Yeats and the English Renaissance," *PMLA* 82, no. 2 (1967): 158. McAlindon therefore surmises that Yeats, like Morris, saw the English Middle Ages as a cultural ideal. Of course Yeats does specifically reference Morris in the essay. However, McAlindon pays no attention to Yeats's occult life at this time, and so, I argue, while he correctly identifies a major source of Yeats's utopian thinking, he misses the larger context of the essay: Stratford as a locus for the study of hermetic texts and the practice of ritual magic.
27. W. B. Yeats, *Early Essays*, 74.
28. W. B. Yeats, *The Collected Works of W. B. Yeats*, vol. 8, *The Irish Dramatic Movement*, ed. Richard J. Finneran and Mary FitzGerald (New York: Scribner, 2003), 5.
29. W. B. Yeats, *Early Essays*, 74.
30. Ibid.
31. Foster, *Apprentice Mage*, 241.
32. Andrew Murphy, "An Irish Catalysis: W. B. Yeats and the Uses of Shakespeare," *Shakespeare Survey* 64 (2011): 211.
33. W. B. Yeats, *Early Essays*, 78.
34. Murphy, "An Irish Catalysis," 211.
35. Ibid., 75.
36. Ibid., 74.
37. Ibid., 25.
38. W. B. Yeats, *The Collected Works of W. B. Yeats*, vol. 5, *Later Essays*, ed. William H. O'Donnell (New York: Scribner, 1994), 248.
39. W. B. Yeats, *Early Essays*, 34.
40. W. B. Yeats, *Irish Dramatic Movement*, 130.
41. Ibid., 8.
42. Ibid., 6–7.
43. Ibid., 7.
44. Ibid., 8–9.
45. Ibid., 29.
46. Ibid., 148.
47. W. B. Yeats, *Early Essays*, 73.
48. Ibid., 82.
49. Ibid., 73.
50. Ibid., 74.
51. W. B. Yeats, *Irish Dramatic Movement*, 115.
52. W. B. Yeats, *Early Essays*, 39.
53. Ibid., 74.
54. Ibid., 75.
55. Ibid., 75–76.
56. Ibid., 75.
57. Ibid.
58. Ibid.

59. Ibid.
60. Ibid.
61. Ibid., 76.
62. Ibid.
63. Ibid.
64. Ibid.
65. Ibid.
66. Ibid., 77.
67. Ibid., 76–77.
68. Ibid., 77.
69. Ellmann, *Man and the Masks*, 123.
70. Cited in Ellmann, *Man and the Masks*, 124.
71. Ellmann, *Man and the Masks*, ibid.
72. Ibid.
73. Ibid., 124–25.
74. Ibid., 125.
75. W. B. Yeats, *Early Essays*, 30.
76. Ibid., 31.
77. James W. Flannery, *W. B. Yeats and the Idea of a Theatre: The Early Abbey Theatre in Theory and in Practice* (New Haven, CT: Yale University Press, 1976), 259.
78. Ibid., 190.
79. W. B. Yeats, *Explorations*, selected by Mrs. W. B. Yeats (New York: Macmillan, 1962), 177.
80. W. B. Yeats, *The Letters of W. B. Yeats*, ed. Allen Wade (London, Methuen: 1962), 309.
81. Flannery, *Yeats and the Idea of a Theatre*, 242.
82. W. B. Yeats, *Explorations*, 177.
83. Michael Taylor, *Shakespeare Criticism in the Twentieth Century* (Oxford: Oxford University Press, 2001), 132.
84. A. B. Walkley, "The Irish National Theatre," *Times Literary Supplement* 69 (May 8, 1903): 146.
85. Ibid.
86. Flannery, *Idea of a Theatre*, 192.
87. Ibid., 196.
88. Schuchard, *The Last Minstrels*, 3.
89. Flannery, *Idea of a Theatre*, 199. Ronald Schuchard has now furnished us with the definitive account of Yeats's work with Farr on reviving musical speech:

> Yeats was keenly aware that the experience of poetry had become a private experience for a literate and educated elite, no longer accessible to or part of the imaginative life of the common man. Undaunted, he was committed to reversing the modern shift of poetry from the ear to the eye; it was essential to his visions of cultural revival in Ireland . . . for the next twenty years Yeats and Farr would collaborate in their efforts to return musical speech to lyrical, narrative, and dramatic verse in a modern revival of the minstrel tradition.

Schuchard, *The Last Minstrels*, 14, 20.
90. Walkley, "Irish National Theatre," 45.
91. Ibid., 46.
92. Ibid.
93. Ibid., 45.
94. W. B. Yeats, *Explorations*, 212.
95. Declan Kiberd, *Inventing Ireland: The Literature of the Modern Nation* (London: Vintage, 1995), 162.
96. Schuchard, *The Last Minstrels*, 193.
97. Ibid.
98. W. B. Yeats, *Irish Dramatic Movement*, 42.

99. Ibid.

100. Ibid.

101. W. B. Yeats, *Early Essays*, 75.

102. Howes, *Yeats's Nations*, 67.

103. W. B. Yeats, *Explorations*, 79.

104. W. B. Yeats, *Irish Dramatic Movement*, 22.

105. Howes, *Yeats's Nations*, 89.

106. W. B. Yeats, *Irish Dramatic Movement*, 29.

107. W. B. Yeats, *The Poems*, ed. Daniel Albright (London: David Campbell, 1992), 162.

108. W. B. Yeats, *Early Essays*, 83.

109. Ibid.

110. W. B. Yeats, *Later Essays*, 255.

111. W. B. Yeats, *The Poems*, 161.

112. Ibid.

113. Ibid.

114. Ibid.

115. Ibid., 80.

116. Bryan Bevan, *Marlborough the Man* (London: Robert Hale, 1975), 15. Gary Taylor makes note of Marlborough's claim in *Reinventing Shakespeare: A Cultural History from the Restoration to the Present* (New York: Oxford University Press, 1991), 66.

117. W. B. Yeats, *Explorations*, 291.

118. Ibid., 321.

119. W. B. Yeats, *Early Essays*, 33.

120. Ibid., 35.

121. Ibid.

122. Ibid., 82.

123. Ibid.

124. Ibid.

125. Surette, *Birth of Modernism*, 27.

126. W. B. Yeats, *Early Essays*, 159.

127. Ibid.

128. Ibid.

129. Ibid.

130. Ibid., 160.

131. W. B. Yeats, *Irish Dramatic Movement*, 26.

132. Ibid., 26–27.

133. Ibid., 58.

134. Ibid., 55.

135. This is from his essay "Certain Noble Plays of Japan," in W. B. Yeats, *Essays and Introductions*, 227.

136. Ibid.

137. W. B. Yeats, *Later Essays*, 246.

138. Denis Donoghue, "Three Presences: Yeats, Eliot, Pound," *Hudson Review* 62, no. 4 (2010): 226.

139. Ibid., 231–32.

140. W. B. Yeats, *Irish Dramatic Movement*, 147.

141. Ibid.

142. W. B. Yeats, *Essays and Introductions*, 341.

143. Ibid., 342.

144. Ibid., 341.

145. Ibid.

146. Summarizing Yeats's nationalism in his essay, "W. B. Yeats: Irish Nationalism and Post-Colonial Theory," Stephen Regan writes how Yeats "entertains a fantasy of aristocratic power and breeding that goes all the way back to the Italian renaissance culture he had read about and admired in Castiglione's *Book of the Courtier*, shortly before he visited Italy with Lady Gregory in 1907." Stephen Regan, "W. B. Yeats: Irish Nationalism and Post-Colonial

Theory," *Nordic Irish Studies* 5 (2006): 98. "What might be said about Yeats with more confidence," he continues, "is that he endeavoured to create a number of powerful and enduring myths of Irishness that might shape a new national consciousness. The Ireland that he envisaged was a nation with a distinctive cultural and spiritual identity, an imagined community free of sectarian differences." Ibid. As I hope to demonstrate here, Shakespeare's ritualistic drama and symbolic, musical verse contributed significantly to his vision of Ireland's "cultural and spiritual identity" and to the means by which he hoped to shape a new national culture.

147. Donoghue, "Three Presences," 226.

148. W. B. Yeats, *Explorations*, 145.

149. Ibid., 158.

150. Surette, *Birth of Modernism*, 39.

151. W. B. Yeats, *Early Essays*, 80–81.

152. On this relationship, see Oliver Hennessey, "Talking with the Dead: Leo Africanus, Esoteric Yeats, and Early Modern Imperialism," *English Literary History* 71, no. 4 (2004): 1019–38.

153. Ronald Schuchard, "Yeats's Letters, Eliot's Lectures: Towards a New Focus on Annotation," *Text* 6 (1994): 302. In his essay, Schuchard narrates this discovery, which he made by connecting the letter's reference to "my Shrine" to a fascinating anecdote in an unpublished fragment of AE's autobiography. AE recalls a meeting of the Brotherhood of the Three Kings, during which "Yeats began to speak . . . about myself that I was a magnet who gathered about him all the wild characters of Ireland. Then he told them the story of Fitzpatrick. Now said Yeats feeling he too was a magnet 'If there was such a man in London he would be bound to be here.' A figure rose up, at the end of the room. 'I am he.' It was Fitzpatrick." Schuchard, "Yeats's Letters," 302. Schuchard includes an entry from the first number of *The Shrine* (May 1902), in which Fitzpatrick prophesizes a Shakespearean spiritual reawakening: "this re-extension of the human mind . . . will lead to a fuller comprehension of Shakespeare. For he, too, was a symbolist in his dawn before the dawn." R. H. Fitzpatrick, *The Shrine* 1 (May 1902): 2–3. Cited in Schuchard, "Yeats's Letters," 302.

154. W. B. Yeats, "Commentary on Three Songs," *Poetry* 45, no. 3 (December 1934): 133.

155. Richard Ellmann, *Man and the Masks*, 133–34.

Chapter Three

Disappointment, Degeneration, and Despair

Yeats's Late Shakespeare

Between W. B. Yeats's efforts to craft an organic national community through the Abbey Theatre and his interment "'Neath Ben Bulben's Buttoks," Ireland became a dominion of the British Empire, and finally, in 1937, an independent, sovereign state. Yeats won the Nobel Prize for literature and was appointed senator in the Irish Free State, serving from 1922 to 1928. In the cultural realm, modernism became the dominant aesthetic paradigm among the avant-garde, eschewing Victorian poetics; T. S. Eliot published *The Waste Land* in London, Joyce published *Ulysses* in Paris, and, in 1916, Yeats signed with Macmillan, making his lyric verse widely available outside Ireland in affordable, mass-produced editions for the first time since the late 1890s. Yeats's literary reputation was made; he married and became a father. The Abbey, with an annuity from the Cosgrave government, was enjoying some success. From 1922, Yeats was an internationally acclaimed poet, a statesman, and a prominent literary figure in Ireland's cultural life. After 1922, also, Yeats's Shakespeare virtually disappeared from view. Yeats's increasingly elitist brand of cultural nationalism had not won the day post-Treaty.[1] Ireland was not the organic community that Yeats had worked toward at the opening of the twentieth century, nor had he and his coterie of Protestant literati established ownership of a new national culture. Dublin was excluded from the cosmopolitan network of modernist activity. Irish artists during the 1920s faced division, approbation, and increasingly alarmist calls for censorship from a powerful Jansenist clergy, beginning with the Dail's introduction of legislation to censor films in 1923, and culminating in

107

the successful passing of the 1929 Censorship of Publications Bill. The Abbey was staging manifestly political productions, against its continuing claims of neutrality, and tilting ever more in the direction of what was popular: social realist drama. In short, Irish nationalists had achieved many of their political ambitions; Irish cultural life, however, was not what Yeats had prescribed.

Yeats did not stop discussing Shakespeare during the final decades of his life, but he did slow down. His Shakespeare did not die out, but he did change. Accounting for this change allows us to further excavate Yeats's construction of Shakespeare and his function within Yeats's cultural nationalism. As we have seen, Shakespeare figured prominently in the Irishman's occultist prescriptions for the cultural life of the new nation, particularly in the years following his visit to Stratford-upon-Avon in 1901. As such, changes in Yeats's Shakespeare signal shifts in Yeats's nationalist stance— his aspirations and prescriptions for Irish national culture—mediated via his religious philosophy. Ever the bricoleur, Yeats poached from the thought of his day to suit his interests: early Shakespeare was, then, an appropriation and subversion of Victorian racial ideology, best understood in terms of early revivalist goals for the de-Anglicization of Irish culture and the enlarging of Irish literary space. The Shakespeare of the early twentieth century was initially a bulwark against so-called imperialist, positivist ideologies inherent in the character critique of Bradley and Dowden, then an antirealist creator of verse drama, and a poet mage whose ritualistic displays of aristocratic power offered a model for the ideal Yeatsian nation: organic, stratified, and hostile to post-Enlightenment modes of thought and action. Furthermore, Yeats's imaginative archaisms—his interest in Renaissance culture and his study of the hermetic tradition—permitted him to cognitively finesse Ireland's sectarian strife.[2] Late Yeats's Shakespeare, as we shall see, responded to several connected factors: public cultural life in a nascent Irish state, anxiety concerning mass culture and politics, and concomitant developments in Yeats's esoteric practices away from the ritual magic of hermetic societies and toward the pursuit of a gnostic, metahistorical system. In 1922 Yeats also left the Golden Dawn. Taken together, these factors point to the local failure of Yeats's highbrow cultural nationalism—and a hardening of his dislike for the tastes of a rising Catholic middle class—more than the influence of external factors, such as the shock of the Great War, Poundian poetics, or Eliot's refiguring of the literary tradition. In short, then, we can identify three primary modes of Shakespeare appropriation by Yeats: de-Anglicization, nation building, and a later, reactionary phase responding to the sociocultural life of the Irish state post-Treaty. For many years, the model of adeptship within a hermetic society underpinned his prescriptions for an Irish national culture. If we are to take seriously Yeats's religious philosophy, as I believe we must, then we must also take seriously the idea that Yeats's increasing disillusionment with Irish culture and society stemmed at least in part from his view that what made the Irish nation special was a folk sensibility which, if cultivated correctly by a class of benevolent magi, could restore lost connections between the living and the dead, and that this intuitive capacity was facing extinction at the hands of clerics, politicians, and the popular press. One striking change in Yeatsian occultism during the last twenty or so years of his life is a drift from the order to the individual, from a society of truth seekers to a personal visionary quest (with no small help from his wife).[3] Late Shakespeare therefore registers a loss of faith, not in the existence of a world beyond the material one, but in the power of small societies of like-minded individuals to effect change en masse, and to do so via suggestion, symbolism, and ritual.

I have also maintained that Yeats's appropriations of Shakespeare in the context of the Literary Revival should be considered attempts to enlarge Irish literary space, given the cultural and nationalist signifying capabilities of Shakespeare, his iconic status and attendant cultural capital. As Pascale Casanova argues, "the accumulation of literary resources is necessarily rooted in the political history of states."[4] Changes in Yeats's Shakespeare therefore responded also to the shifting structural relations between Ireland and England, and among European nations more generally, in the realm of literary-capital acquisition and deployment at the end of the nineteenth and the beginning of the twentieth centuries. As such, Yeats's appropriation of Shakespeare contributed to the process by which Shakespeare was liberated from an Anglo-Germanic signifying status, denationalized, and globalized. To borrow from Pascale Casanova's model of an autonomous literary space—the "world republic of letters"—we might say that "Shakespace" gradually achieved its own autonomy in the twentieth century, eventually freed from straightforwardly chauvinist racial and nationalist significations.[5] As I want to demonstrate in this chapter, Yeats's late Shakespeare responds primarily to his dissatisfaction with the direction of the new Irish nation-state.

Ultimately, Shakespeare was a product of periodical culture. Between 1885 and 1903, Yeats contributed to periodicals 347 times.[6] His contributions dropped sharply after 1903, after which he contributed to periodicals 192 times until his death in 1939.[7] The periodical culture in which Yeats operated at the turn of the century represented the formative arena for the development of Shakespeare as a cultural nationalist figure associated primarily with Yeats's work for the National Theatre. The diminution of Shakespeare in later years most readily responds to a decreasing involvement with the Abbey Theatre, and therefore to a decreasing contribution to periodicals. By 1919, Yeats could articulate both disappointment with the Abbey's artistic trajectory and a certain satisfaction with the commercial success of what he referred to as a "People's Theatre," a veritably Irish cultural institution. That being said, if we count the number of direct references to Shakespeare

in his prose, we see a relatively uniform pattern through 1911, followed by a
tapering-off period until 1919, with a spike in that year.[8] The period 1901 to
1919 contains the greatest number of references, with 1919 marking a qual-
itative change: eleven of the thirteen direct references to Shakespeare in 1919
come from two pieces published in the *Irish Statesman* bemoaning the direction of Ireland's cultural life and restating the original goals of the Irish
National Theatre movement.[9] The 1920s, therefore, represent a watershed in
Yeats's writing on Shakespeare, with only sixteen direct references, compared to forty-eight from 1900 to 1909, thirty-three from 1910 to 1919, and
thirty-three from 1930 until the poet's death. Moreover, of those sixteen
references, only one appears in a periodical—*The Dublin Magazine*—while
nine are found in *Autobiographies*, and five come from the first edition of *A
Vision*. We might therefore infer that this decade of civil strife and direct
involvement in Irish politics represents a time of introspection and self-
fashioning for the poet as he reflected on his career and the chaos preceding
and following Ireland's evolving political emancipation. When Yeats's
Shakespeare reemerges in the public sphere in the 1930s, he has changed,
perhaps not utterly, but demonstrably all the same.

So what does Yeats's late Shakespeare look like? The significant texts
here are *A Vision* (1925 and 1937) and *On the Boiler* (1938), as well as a
number of essays and articles written during these years that reference
Shakespeare, although in a changing context: "If I Were Four-and-Twenty"
and "A Theatre of the People" provide significant evidence for a shift in the
tenor of Yeats's rhetorical deployment of Shakespeare. The Shakespeare of *A
Vision* recycles a number of familiar topoi from Yeats's thought, particularly
in the case of his historical significance as an artist situated on the cusp of
epistemic rupture. However, as I intend to demonstrate, he is distanced from
the earlier context of a revivified Irish folk sensibility and a salvific project to
restore an organic community of saints and scholars. The Shakespeare of *A
Vision* has been dislocated from the urgency of pre-Treaty Ireland, implicated instead in the entirely idealized, abstracted, and eternal movement of the
gyres. In *A Vision*, Yeats presents a portrait of Shakespeare as a visionary
artist out of sync with his age, a figure bearing no little resemblance to Yeats
himself. Moreover, with the publication of the second edition of *A Vision* in
1937, Yeats distances himself from his own system, a move that is indicative
both of the failure of Yeatsian cultural nationalism in post-Treaty Ireland and
of the Irishman's retreat from public life. Finally, *On the Boiler*, a tub-
thumping diatribe against contemporary Irish and mass culture, renders
Shakespeare a reactionary, vituperative agent put to rhetorical use against a
variety of political, cultural, and epistemological enemies. It is, of course,
mainly in this text that critics locate evidence of Yeats's intellectual involvement with eugenics. However, I argue that this does not counter my claim
that Yeats moves Shakespeare away from overtly racial discourse. Instead it

reveals reactionary anxiety concerning the destratification of Irish society, the ascendance of the Catholic middle class, and the decline of Anglo-Irish influence, another sign of Yeats's disappointment with the social structure and cultural tastes of post-Treaty Ireland. Yeats wanted a nation, but he got a state. As Ezra Pound noted sardonically after the Easter Rising, "[Yeats] don't like Republics. He likes queens, preferably dead ones."[10]

Examining Yeats's deployment of Shakespeare during the 1920s and 1930s reveals both continuity and change, and although it might seem somewhat arbitrary to draw a line between Yeats's Shakespeare of the 1920s and that of the 1930s, there are, I believe, distinctions of tone and tenor, responding, I think, to local factors: politicized criticism of plays at the Abbey, legislation restricting artistic freedom of production and consumption and imposing Jansenist social prescriptions, a popular taste for realism in art, urbanization, and democracy, the latter understood by Yeats as a tyranny of bourgeois philistinism. These factors can perhaps be organized under the rubric of an official Irish national identity, legislated, policed, and legitimized by the clergy and the press, and fundamentally at odds with Yeats's cultural nationalism, never a straightforward antipathy to England, but complicated by sectarian and classist allegiances, not to mention literary rivalries. Yeats's Shakespeare changes during the last two decades of Yeats's life, I maintain, in response to these local factors. In Yeats's prose of the 1920s we find much the same Shakespeare that Yeats constructed in his writings of the first two decades of the twentieth century, but tinged with regret for the direction of the Abbey and its audience. As I have argued in the previous chapters, a theatrical audience was one of the primary metaphors by which Yeats imagined the nation (and in fact more than mere metaphor, given certain occultist preoccupations). And so we find in Yeats's prose during this time disappointment with popular taste, tempered with nostalgia for an earlier stage of revivalist aspirations and a grudging acknowledgment of the Abbey's success. The Revival had succeeded in enlarging Irish literary space in large part via the establishment of this cultural institution, along with a national dramatic repertoire. However, Yeats did not have the national culture he had desired, one possessed of a shared sensibility: "unity of being," a fusion of intellect and emotion. In this period, Yeats's Shakespeare primarily registers disappointment, and in the final years of his life, disappointment becomes despair. The Shakespeare of *On the Boiler* (1938) is thus a haughty, scornful aristocrat, a Nietzschean Übermensch and purveyor of authoritarian values.

Of course it is also during these years that Yeats wrote *A Vision*, his occult manifesto and the product of visionary experiments with automatic writing following his marriage to George Hyde-Lees in 1917. Until relatively recently, this text had received scant attention, and its largely embarrassed critical reception hinged around its utility in helping to decipher the esoteric symbolism of Yeats's lyric poetry. Like Declan Kiberd, however, who sees *A Vision* as Yeats's attempt to articulate "a spiritual foundation for the new nation-state,"[11] I want to argue for the significance of this work in terms of Yeats's cultural nationalism. Shakespeare features prominently in both editions of the text, and is used to validate the theory of personality types in the section entitled "The Great Wheel," and the cyclicality of history in "Dove or Swan." I have argued that Shakespeare provides a focal point for a nexus of Yeatsian concerns about art, nationality, and religious philosophy, and it is in this context that the two versions of *A Vision* supply evidence for Shakespeare's shifting valence. I have characterized the shift in tone from the 1920s to the 1930s as a move from disappointment to despair; the first edition of *A Vision*, I argue, demonstrates how Yeats's occult philosophy furnished him with solace and optimism for the future: against the encroaching philistinism of modernity is set the movement of the gyres, which ultimately promises of change of direction. As we shall see, Yeats identified more forcefully than ever with Shakespeare's position at a moment of epistemic rupture and decay; however, while Yeats's early Shakespeare had initially emerged from the ideal of an organic community possessing unity of being, now he was an artist diverging significantly from the prevailing characteristics of his age. The first edition of *A Vision* therefore removes Shakespeare from a local, revivalist project into an abstract realm of metaphysical cyclicality. Changes to the second edition of the text, I contend, reveal a deep pessimism via an additional layer of abstraction. To put it another way, Yeats in the 1920s had recourse to his occult philosophy to deflect profound anxieties about the advent of modernity in general and the direction of Ireland specifically. Shortly before his death, Yeats lost his faith in the regenerative principle of the gyres and shifted to an embittered posturing. His late Shakespeare embodies this change.

A NATION ONCE AGAIN: CULTURAL AND POLITICAL NATIONALISMS

Despite Yeats's direct involvement in the politics of the new Irish nation from 1922 to 1928, it is important to understand his nationalism as "cultural" rather than "political." As Michael Boss notes, "Yeats's politics might be described as a politics of felt identity. For it was the national identity of the Irish as a feeling for the land that he was concerned with; not conventional politics. It may also be described as a cultural politics, for the purpose of national politics, for Yeats, was to help recuperating an original, authentic and unitary Irish nation."[12] A "cultural politics" is a useful term for understanding Yeats's revivalism and his work for the Senate during the 1920s, and, as we have seen, Yeats's work for the Irish stage was intended to bring about an "authentic and unitary" nation possessed of a shared aesthetic sensibility that both differentiated the Irish from their "objective" English neighbors and cemented social bonds between Ireland's social classes. The key term in Yeats's prose is "unity of being," a concept he deploys readily in his prescriptions for the ideal theatrical audience and the ideal Irish nation. "Unity of being" primarily signifies a fusion of emotion and intellect and therefore a synthesis of antimonies, and Yeats famously located several periods of history during which entire communities evidenced such unity: the Athens of Sophocles, Byzantium around 500 AD, and the Italian Renaissance. Shakespeare and his Elizabethan audience, according to this system, represented the final flowering of this sensibility, after which Western Europe began its steady descent into the stultifying epistemologies of empirical science and philosophical positivism. While certain artists and thinkers possessed unity of being after this epistemic rupture, such individuals were disconnected from their nations, and so thinking about unity of being inevitably meant theorizing techniques for restoring the broken connections between communities' folk culture and their poets. As we have seen, Yeats turned to the stage as a means of reforging these links: disseminating mythology and folklore via symbolic dramatic ritual—as Shakespeare had once done—was the Abbey's function within Yeats's revivalism, and for an explanation of the actual mechanism by which Irish drama was to restore the Irish nation to its premodern unity, Yeats had recourse to ritual magic. The key point here is that Yeatsian cultural nationalism had a fundamentally sociocultural goal, not an explicitly political one: unity of being signified both a mystical capacity for an intuitive experience of reality beyond mere sensory impression and the socioeconomic conditions enabling it. Though he always supported Home Rule, the idea that Yeats was pushing for independence and national sovereignty throughout his career is a product of revisionist history, some of which was practiced by Yeats upon himself. This is a point made by R. F. Foster, who notes how Yeats remained silent on the issue of allegiance during the Great War, and similarly so concerning sovereign status for Ireland until after the 1916 Easter Rising, at which point he masterfully wrote himself back into national, political celebrity through such poems as "Easter, 1916." In terms of this specific, hugely celebrated poem, for instance, Foster comments on how, "in the mood of 1916," it was read as "republicanism, pure and simple,"[13] despite its complex meaning and initial circulation as a "samizdat"[14] among trusted friends. In fact, writes Foster, "Yeats's public statements were distinctly un-republican. He attacked the 'oppression' of the military, criticized censorship, but also stressed the advisability of granting dominion status and said that Ulster should not be coerced."[15] Yeats was no revolutionary firebrand, and certainly no statist.

Certainly the history of nationalism in Ireland is complex and multifaceted. It is for this reason that Richard English encourages us to think in terms of plural Irish nationalisms and to discount reductive historiography: "In practice," writes English, "the historical development of Irish nationalism has been contingent and jagged and varied rather than inevitable and smooth and uniform; any teleology identified has been very much that of nationalist faith, rather than that born from coldly factual observation."[16] A "cultural politics" of "felt identity" thus defines Yeats's work for the Irish Revival; but Irish nationalism—like all nationalisms—was a contested site of competing claims to legitimacy and rival models of national identity. As Ireland staggered toward independence, the Anglo-Irish revivalism of Yeats and his coterie—a Protestant-inclusive cultural nationalism—increasingly lost ground to an official political nationalism that pushed for a dominant Catholic, bourgeois identity. Perhaps this was inevitable. Postcolonial theorists have identified exactly such a trend in the struggles of small nations seeking and achieving independence from foreign rule. John Hutchinson, for instance, (following Elie Kedourie) argues for a certain inevitability: "in terms of its own communitarian goals, cultural nationalism is a failure, and . . . it regularly shifts into a state politics to institutionalize its program in the social order. In doing so, it paves the way for its supersession by political nationalism."[17] Political nationalism, like cultural nationalism, derives from Enlightenment thought, and is therefore a response to the process of modernization. However, it differs in its objectives. Political nationalism proposes that the collective is bound by the rational will of individuals to subsume their identity to the group through reasoned, willed participation in a political entity; "[t]heir ideal," notes Hutchinson, "is a civic *polity* of educated citizens united by common laws and mores like the *polis* of classical antiquity."[18] What distinguishes cultural nationalism, per se, is its turn to history and nature to distinguish and circumscribe the members of the collective. In other words, while political nationalism draws its organizing force from the ethics of reason, cultural nationalism looks to the past in order to conceive of the state as "the product of [a civilization's] unique history, culture, and geographical profile."[19] In this way, cultural nationalism reads the nation as existing prior to its organization as a state, an idea that permeates Yeats's writing. It promotes the idea of nations as organic entities, rather than political units, "living personalities, whose individuality must be cherished by their members in all their manifestations."[20] Further, Hutchinson reads the advent of cultural nationalism in the eighteenth century as a response to a crisis: "the erosion of traditional identities and status orders by the modernization process as mediated by a reforming state."[21] He defines the "modernization process" as "those changes that occur in economic, cultural, political and military institutions when scientific principles are applied to solve problems of social and natural life."[22]

What is emerging from this account is the degree to which Yeats's work for the Revival, despite its esoterica, falls in line with mainstream cultural nationalist thought; the nation in Yeats's writing is always conceived of as an organic entity, composed of different classes and status groups bound togeth-er by a shared culture, and opposed to the exogenous forces of moderniza-tion. The role of revivalist writers like Yeats was to inculcate the collective with "lost" cultural material, much as the occultist student seeks to recover a secret history of gnosis dating from antiquity. By this reading, Irish revival-ism should not be mistaken for a retrograde flight from all aspects of modern life; rather, we should understand the proclivity for the folk element in reviv-alist doctrine as part of a progressive goal; thus "the past is to be used not in order to return to some antique order but rather to re-establish the nation at a new and higher level."[23] In light of Yeats's involvement with the Irish Na-tional Theatre, his membership and valorization of occult groups like the Golden Dawn, his establishment of journals like *Samhain*, and the dissemina-tion of his aesthetic and occultist philosophies through published articles and essays, it seems difficult not to characterize his work in the opening decades of the twentieth century in terms of the goals and techniques of cultural nationalism, as theorized by Hutchinson:

> The aim of cultural nationalists is . . . the moral regeneration of the historic community, or, in other words, the re-creation of their distinctive national civilization. . . . Typically cultural nationalists establish informal and decen-tralized clusters of cultural societies and journals, designed to inspire a sponta-neous love of community in its different members by educating them to their common heritage of splendor and suffering. They engage in naming rituals, celebrate national cultural uniqueness and reject foreign practices, in order to identify the community to itself, embed this identity in everyday life and differentiate it against other communities.[24]

Even prior to the 1916 Rising, the literary revivalism of the earlier years— Yeats's revivalism—had been losing out to a popular aesthetics grounded in a political nationalism that posited the formation of a sovereign, Catholic state as its primary goal and called for the policing of indigenous literary output to ensure the adequate representation of this official identity without competition. The most serious challenge to Yeats's revivalism, therefore, was a competing mode of Irish nationalism.

In this way, what we see happening throughout Yeats's work for the Senate in the 1920s is the consistent articulation of the organicist goals of cultural nationalism within an overtly political framework. This we can dis-cern in his frequent calls for "unity," up and against the Cosgrave govern-ment's increasing identification of Irish commonality in one religious group (Catholic), one dominant class (bourgeois professionals), and one dominant political philosophy (de-Anglicized political nationalism). It is in light of the failure of cultural nationalism that Protestant, Anglo-Irish figures such as Burke, Berkeley, and Swift come to replace Shakespeare as the writers most

frequently invoked in Yeatsian discourse to articulate frustrations with Ireland's sociocultural trajectory. During the 1920s, then, the disappearance of
Shakespeare from local periodicals registers the increasing obsolescence of
Yeats's cultural politics within a changing political context, rather than the
radicalization of Yeats's thought.

SHAKESPEARE AND UNITY OF BEING: 1919–1928

From about 1919 onward, Yeats's references to Shakespeare in his prose
respond to the processes I have just outlined whereby a cultural nationalism
increasingly lost ground to a provincial political nationalism which pushed in
the press and the pulpit for standards of cultural production and consumption
that reinforced this prescription for national identity. Yeats's work for the
Senate between 1922 and 1928 demonstrates a keen awareness of the perils
of representative democracy in such terms, and a championing of minority
rights, specifically the Anglo-Irish aristocratic and artistic communities. In
his prose contributions to periodicals we find a series of defenses of revivalist goals, primarily those associated with the Abbey Theatre and its audience.
As discussed above, the concept of unity of being provides the crucial rhetorical link between a Yeatsian nationalist aesthetic and a sense of distress at the
insularity of social legislation: the divorce controversy of 1925, the Censorship of Publications Bill (1929), and the push for a thorough linguistic de-
Anglicization by making Gaeilge compulsory in schools. Where we see
Shakespeare during these years, it is typically in reference to the topoi cluster
circumscribed by this concept. And so, in "If I Were Four-and-Twenty"
(1919), we find the poet reflecting on Ireland's direction in exactly these
terms:

> When Dr. Hyde delivered in 1894 his lecture on the necessity of "the de-
> anglicization of Ireland," to a society that was a youthful indiscretion of my
> own, I heard an enthusiastic hearer say: "This lecture begins a new epoch in
> Ireland." It did that, and if I were not four-and-fifty, with no settled habit but
> the writing of verse, rheumatic, indolent, discouraged, and about to move to
> the Far East, I would begin another epoch by recommending to the nation a
> new doctrine, that of unity of being. [25]

Of course Yeats never did move to the Far East, but this article, published in
the *Irish Statesman*, provides a useful measure of Yeatsian anxiety, and, in
concert with another article for the *Irish Statesman* in 1919, "A People's
Theatre," supplies significant evidence for the changing valence of Yeats's
Shakespeare.

As the title suggests, "If I Were Four-and-Twenty" is a retrospective
piece whose significance lies primarily in its reflection on revivalist ambi-

tions, as well as the clarity with which it articulates the threefold nature of Yeatsian thought: "I would set out once again to found a little school of Irish thought," writes Yeats, "but this time I would not confine myself to literature and to drama."[26] What follows at this point is an enlightening anecdote:

> One day when I was twenty-three or twenty-four this sentence seemed to form in my head, without my willing it, much as sentences form when we are half-asleep: "Hammer your thoughts into unity." For days I could think of nothing else, and for years I tested all I did by that sentence. I had three interests: interest in a form of literature, in a form of philosophy, and a belief in nationality. None of these seemed to have anything to do with the other, but gradually my love of literature and my belief in nationality came together. Then for years I said to myself that these two had nothing to do with my form of philosophy, but that I had only to be sincere and to keep from constraining one by the other and they would become one interest. Now all three are a discrete expression of a single conviction.[27]

Were he four-and-twenty, Yeats's ideal revivalist society would combine occult research, literary production, and reflection upon the issue of nationality. Of course, this is a somewhat disingenuous statement, since, as I have argued throughout, Yeats's work for the National Theatre did exactly this, but the key trope here is that of unity. Crucially, Yeats now moves from self-reflection to the collective: "It is just the same with a nation—it is only a cultivated nation when it has related its main interests one to another. We are a religious nation. . . . Yet is there any nation that has a more irreligious intellect, or that keeps its political thought so distinct from its religious thought?"[28] Clearly Yeats is pushing for a palatable synthesis of emotion and intellect here, of art, religion, and politics—this the basis of unity of being. By "religious," Yeats does not mean "Catholic" or "Christian," but "spiritual" in the sense of a shared belief in the reality of a transcendental realm. Yeats's "religious nation" is a pluralist one, united in mystical sensibility, not in dogma:

> Then, too, I would associate that doctrine of purgatory, which Christianity has shared with Neo-Platonism, with the countryman's belief in the nearness of his dead "working out their penance" in rath or at garden end: and I would find in the psychical research of our day detail to make the association convincing to intellect and emotion. I would try to create a type of man whose most moving religious experience, though it came to him in some distant country, and though his intellect were wholly personal, would bring with it an imagery to connect it with an Irish multitude now and in past time.[29]

The creation of a "type of man" therefore underpins the poet's imagined work, and this type would provide an "imagery" capable of collecting the Irish "multitude" across time, symbols which might permit contact between

the living and the dead. The slightest familiarity with Yeats's religious philosophy allows us to understand that this is no metaphor, and indeed, my
argument in previous chapters has been exactly this: Yeats had thought himself to be such a man, and Shakespeare too.

Much of the rest of Yeats's essay is concerned with outlining the various
antimonies which, when fused appropriately, might unite a nation in a shared
awareness of its spiritual, social, and aesthetic heritage: family and the individual, intuition and logic, good and evil. Of particular interest here is the
promotion of Balzac as a modern artist whose novels form a vast scheme of
family and individual conflict, much in the same way that Yeats understood
Shakespeare's history plays to comprise "five plays, that are but one play."[30]
In a concession to modernity, Balzac is promoted above Shakespeare: "When
I was a child I heard the names of men whose lives had been changed by
Balzac, perhaps because he cleared them of Utopian vapours, then very prev-
alent; and I can remember someone saying to an old lion-painter: 'If you had
to choose, would you give up Shakespeare or Balzac?' and his answering, 'I
would keep the yellow backs.'"[31] Balzac enters the Yeatsian literary pantheon here as a witness to the struggles inherent in the social order:

> [H]is social order is the creation of two struggles, that of family with family,
> that of individual with individual, and . . . our politics depend upon which of
> the two struggles has most affected our imagination. . . . For a long time after
> closing the last novel one finds it hard to admire deeply any individual strength
> that has not family strength behind it. He has shown us so many men of talent,
> to whom we have denied our sympathy because of their lack of breeding, and
> has refused to show us even Napoleon apart from his Corsican stock, its strong
> roots running backward to the Middle Ages.[32]

Six years after writing this, Yeats was to place Shakespeare, Balzac, and
Napoleon at the same phase of personality in *A Vision*, so it is fascinating to
see all three figures here in what clearly constitutes an assertion of the vital
role of aristocracy in the ideal nation. "Family" provides a key concept here,
and Yeats goes on to expand its meaning to include "all institutions, classes,
orders, nations that arise out of the family and are held together, not by a
logical process, but by historical association."[33] The nation as a "family"
bound by an intuitive "religious" sensibility and by historical forces is the
Yeatsian ideal: a "social species . . . bound together by its emotional quality."[34] Art is the formal manifestation of the magical bonds connecting family members.

In fairly typical Yeatsian fashion, the prose in this essay vacillates between clarity and obfuscation, but we can read here a refiguring and recycling of the familiar idea that the mystical, emotional connections among
members of the Irish nation (alive and dead) are fashioned by artists and
visionaries. Logical "proof" for these connections is to be furnished by

"psychical research." What is being emphasized here, moreover, is the precondition for the ideal nation in a hierarchical social organization. In this sense, "If I Were Four-and-Twenty" restates Yeats's revivalism in the context of a perceived political threat to the landowning gentry. When Shakespeare is referenced, it is in the context of a literary canon whose members were, in Yeats's view, preoccupied with the holy trinity of art, religious philosophy, and nationality:

> When we compare any modern writer, except Balzac, with the writers of an older world, with, let us say, Dante, Villon, Shakespeare, Cervantes, we are in the presence of something slight and shadowy. It is natural for a man who believes that man finds his happiness here on earth, or not at all, to make light of all obstacles to that happiness and to deny altogether the inseparable obstacles seen by religious philosophy. The strength and weight of Shakespeare, of Villon, of Dante, even of Cervantes come from their preoccupations with evil.[35]

Certainly, modernity itself is on the hook here, and contemporary artists (Balzac exempted) are guilty of ignoring the spiritual realm in their preference for an aesthetics of the material world. "Bernard Shaw," for instance, "has invented a drama where ideas and not men are the combatants, and so dislikes whatever is harsh or incomprehensible that he complains of Shakespeare's 'ghosts and murders.'"[36] However, as I have argued above, Yeats's antipathy to modernity infuses all of his work, throughout his career. The difference here is the local context of a struggle within Ireland for national identity. The enumeration of writers from "an older world" finds its correlative in Yeats's later, overtly political rhetoric during his Senate years, when, in an "Undelivered Speech" written during the divorce controversy of 1925, he identifies himself as part of the "great stock" of Anglo-Irish figures: "We are the people of Burke and of Swift, of Grattan, of Emmet, of Parnell."[37] Clearly Yeats is keen to excavate room within the incipient Irish nation-state for the survival of an aristocratic class whose vitality ensures a unifying national sensibility conceived in highly mystical terms. Ireland here is envisioned at a turning point, but at this time—1919–1925 or so—there is still hope: "If we could unite our economics and our nationalism with our religion, that, too, would become philosophic . . . and we, our three great interests made but one, would at last be face to face with the great riddle, and might, it may be, hit the answer."[38] It is this ambivalence, this uncertainty, that infuses Shakespeare during the 1920s, and it is palpable in another significant essay from 1919, "A People's Theatre," which was also published in the *Irish Statesman.*

"We set out to make a 'People's Theatre,'" writes Yeats at the outset of this open letter to Lady Gregory, "and in that we have succeeded."[39] And yet, he concedes a little later, "we did not set out to create this sort of theatre, and its success has been to me a discouragement and a defeat."[40] Here we find precisely the ambivalence that permeates Yeats's prose during this period: the Abbey was indeed proving to be a success, but its drama was aligning with popular taste, moving away from the antirealist, symbolic, and ritualistic plays Yeats had promoted during the early years of the Irish Literary Theatre. Throughout the letter, we find this same mixture of satisfaction with the Abbey's popular success and disappointment with its content:

> We have been the first to create a true "People's Theatre," and we have succeeded because it is not an exploitation of local colour, or of a limited form of drama possessing a temporary novelty, but the first doing of something for which the world is ripe, something that will be done all over the world and done more and more perfectly: the making articulate of all the dumb classes each with its own knowledge of the world, its own dignity, but all objective with the objectivity of the office and the workshop, or the newspaper and the street, of mechanism and of politics.[41]

The key term here is "objective," a concept opposed in the scheme of Yeats's metaphysics to the preferred "subjective," and synonymous with the spiritual bankruptcy of modern, urban life: "the office . . . the newspaper . . . politics." This passage at first appears to trumpet the new Irish drama until the conjunction "but" directs the encomium into a cluster of Yeatsian metonyms for the detested (English) "objectivity" of the age. Moreover, as Yeats reflects on the genesis of the "People's Theatre," we are again greeted with the Shakespeare of the 1900s. It is worth reading the following passage at length:

> Shakespeare set upon the stage kings and queens, great historical or legendary persons about whom there is nothing unreal except the circumstance of their lives which remain vague and summary, because he could only write his best—his mind and the mind of his audience being interested in emotion and intellect at their moment of union and at their greatest intensity—when he wrote of those who controlled the mechanism of life. Had they been controlled by it, intellect and emotion entangled by intricacy and detail could never have mounted to that union which, as Swedenborg said of the marriage of the angels, is a conflagration of the whole being. But since great crowds, changed by popular education with its eye always on some objective task, have begun to find reality in mechanism alone, our popular commercial art has substituted for Lear and Cordelia the real millionaire and the real peeress, and seeks to make them charming by insisting perpetually that they have all that wealth can buy, or rather all that average men and women would buy if they had wealth. Shakespeare's groundlings watched the stage in terrified sympathy, while the British working-man looks perhaps at the photographs of these lords and ladies, whom he admires beyond measure, with the pleasant feeling that they will all be robbed and murdered before he dies.[42]

This is a fascinating reiteration of the second stage of Yeats's Shakespeare. In common with his audience, Shakespeare possesses unity of being—"his mind and the mind of his audience being interested in emotion and intellect at their moment of union"—and the experience of watching his drama is a mystical one, associated with "that union" defined by Swedenborg. This passage could have been written fifteen years prior, were it not for the critical social commentary that forms its rhetorical context. Clearly, a "People's Theatre" is a multivalent term, signifying both a theatre "of the people," with its revivalist connotations, and a theatre "of the masses," the latter term replete with elitist distaste for popular, modern aesthetics. Ultimately, Yeats argues, the mystical unity of emotion and intellect that bound Shakespeare to his audience came from the dramatized subject matter: "those who controlled the mechanism of life." Such people, "kings and queens, great historical or legendary persons," constitute both an aristocratic class, and an enlightened order of truth seekers from the "secret tradition" whose pursuit of gnosis had liberated them from hylic blindness. Again, Shakespeare is implicated in the topoi cluster of art, nationality (understood as the forces that constitute nationhood), and the occult. Following this recycling of Shakespearean qualities, Yeats pivots to bemoan the forces of a destructive modernity: "great crowds," "popular education," and "reality in mechanism." Again, much of this distaste for popular, commercial art is to be found in earlier writings, but the tone here is different. Certainly, as I have argued, Yeats had believed in the possibility of achieving Irish nationhood (not a state, specifically) on his terms via the transformative potential of an occultist dramaturgy housed in a new Irish cultural institution. Shakespeare was his model. By 1919, it was apparent that revivalist ambitions were playing second fiddle in Ireland's public life to a popular nationalism that demanded representation on the stage, and whose dominant aesthetic was political realism. For Yeats, the social order circumscribing the ideal nation was organic but hierarchical, and in this essay we find Yeats once more turning to Shakespeare for a historical analogy: "We know that the songs of the Thames boatmen, to name but these, in the age of Queen Elizabeth had the same relation to the great masterpieces [as Gaelic folk songs to the new Irish drama]."[43] The purported organicism of Elizabethan culture—folk songs feeding into Shakespearean verse drama—supplies one model for his vision of a united Ireland, and clearly Yeats here is bemoaning the current reception of his cultural agenda. Following the *Playboy* riots, and complaints in the press that the Abbey was not concerned enough with propagandizing the struggle for independence, Yeats had become increasingly disillusioned. "Shakespeare had nothing to do with objective truth,"[44] writes Yeats in this essay, implying that neither should the new Irish drama.

What would an ideal Irish theatre look like now? Here we find perhaps the clearest articulation of that vision:

I want to create for myself an unpopular theatre and an audience like a secret society where admission is by favour and never to many. . . . In most towns one can find fifty people for whom one need not build all on observation and sympathy, because they read poetry for their pleasure and understand the traditional language of passion. I desire a mysterious art, always reminding and half-reminding those who understand it of dearly loved things, doing its work by suggestion, not by direct statement, a complexity of rhythm, colour, gesture, not space-pervading like the intellect, but a memory and a prophecy[.][45]

Again, this passage contains much of the same prescriptions for a national drama that we find in Yeats's earlier writings, but here the audience has become a small "secret society," and the theatre is "unpopular." Clearly Yeats has retained the model of an occultist dramaturgy, "doing its work by suggestion," but the participants in this ritual have been decimated. This can only be read as a surrender to the forces of modernity inhering in a dominant Irish political nationalism. Once more the tone shifts toward futility and retrospective disillusionment; "You and I and Synge," he writes to Lady Gregory, "not understanding the clock, set out to bring again the theatre of Shakespeare."[46] Characteristically, Yeats here folds his critique of popular taste into a familiar, esoteric commentary on the alternating "primary" and "antithetical" (or "objective" and "subjective") phases of history, and it is worth recalling that this essay was written during the period of experimentation with automatic writing that led to the 1925 edition of *A Vision*, in which Yeats fully defines his metaphysical system, and only two years after *Per Amica Silentia Lunae*, *A Vision*'s gnostic predecessor. Ever the mystic, Yeats has recourse to the movement of the gyres to account for the failure of Shakespearean drama in contemporary Ireland: "Shakespeare, more objective than Dante—for, alas, the world must move—was still predominantly subjective, and he wrote during the latest crisis of history that made possible a theatre of his kind."[47] Once more, then, Yeats's nationalism and aesthetics are seen to be inextricably connected to his spiritual beliefs, and modernity is positioned at the cusp of a new epoch in which the desired unity of being is largely impossible: "The two great energies of the world that in Shakespeare's day penetrated each other have fallen apart."[48] So long the Shakespearean nation of Irish aristocrat-adepts leading a hierarchical society in a vast mythopoetic ritual. Yeats closes the door on his revivalist ambitions, but doesn't lock it. Just as the occult society maintained a secret history against the forces of mainstream religion, a smaller, "unpopular" theatre could keep the flame alight, awaiting the inevitable movement of the gyres:

[W]e have to prepare a stage for the whole wealth of modern lyricism, for an art that is close to pure music, for those energies that would free the arts from imitation, that would ally acting to decoration and to the dance . . . but as I read the world, the sudden changes, or rather the sudden revelations of future changes, are not from visible history but from its antiself. Blake says somewhere in a "Prophetic Book" that things must complete themselves before they pass away[.][49]

Throughout this book I have been arguing for a tripartite development of Yeats's Shakespeare; however, we might profitably nuance this further and acknowledge between the 1920s and 1930s both continuity and a degree of change. This, then, is the definitive Shakespeare of the 1920s: both a victim of the modern episteme and a figure awaiting a second coming. Like the "Prophetic Book" of Blake, Yeats predicts that Shakespeare will have to wait for the gyres, and for Ireland, to change. Yeats's revivalist agenda transitions from a project to produce the Irish nation to a strategy for keeping alive a spark of the antithetical. Shakespeare during this period moves from the stage into the realm of abstract systematizing, with its apotheosis in *A Vision*.

Before turning to that text, however, I want to briefly provide another fascinating instance of Shakespeare's deployment in the localist context of a defense of revivalist cultural nationalism against its political rivals. Yeats's despised critics attacked the work of the Irish National Theatre on essentially three bases: its refusal to produce overtly political drama, its staging of foreign masterpieces, and its perceived misrepresentation of the Irish people. The policing of national cultural production by clergy and press was anathema to Yeats, as witnessed by his public statements and work for the Senate during the 1920s. Furthermore, post-Treaty, Yeats found himself defending the Anglo-Irish minority against the "Gaelicizers" who wished to make Gaeilge the national language and the primary language of instruction in Irish schools. In 1924, Yeats published "Compulsory Gaelic" in the *Irish Statesman*, but the issue of Ireland's linguistic hybridity is also tackled in "The Irish Dramatic Movement," published in the *Voice of Ireland* (1923) and addressed to the students of a school in California that Yeats had previously visited. Here the poet, now a Nobel Prize winner, again reminisces on early revivalism and its transformative agenda, and once more he bemoans the current state of the popular Irish audience, this time turning to the use of Anglo-Irish dialect in Abbey productions. Writing about his early work with Synge and Lady Gregory, he remembers how "We had gone, all three, from cottage to cottage, collecting stories and hearing songs, and we thought that in these we had discovered that portion of the living mind of Ireland that was most beautiful and distinguished, and we wished to bring what we had discovered to Dublin, where, it seemed to us, the popular mind had grown harsh and ugly."[50] He continues to reiterate revivalist aspirations in the context of the stage—"We thought that Irish drama would be historical or legendary, and in verse or romantic prose"[51] —before turning to the issue of rural dialect: "this strange English, born in the country cottages, is a true speech

with as old a history as the English of Shakespeare, and . . . it takes its
vocabulary from Tudor England and its construction from the Gaelic."[52] We
find a further elaboration of this idea in "A Defense of the Abbey Theatre"
(1926): "That dialect—the dialect spoken in the west and south of Ireland—
is an ancient form of the English language. It has a history of some hundreds
of years, and is derived from two main sources. Its syntax is partly that of
Irish, and its vocabulary is partly that of Tudor English."[53] It is fairly clear
why a popular Irish nationalism in its reactionary phase would call for a
purification and de-Anglicization of the national language, and it should also
require little explanation why Yeats opposed this; he was later to write of his
own cultural hybridity, "Gaelic is my national language, but it is not my
mother tongue."[54] What is significant to my argument here is that Shakespeare always provided the poet with a means of negotiating his own identity, as well as prescriptions for Irish nationhood as a whole, and that Shakespeare's deployment in the 1920s and 1930s responds to internally generated
threats to revivalism. As with "A Popular Theatre," Yeats voices distaste for
contemporary Irish audiences—and so the cultural life of the new nation—
along with a sense that things might improve in the future:

> Should our Abbey Theatre come to an end, should our plays cease to be acted,
> we shall be remembered, I think, because we were the first to give to the
> English-speaking Ireland a mastery of style by turning a dialect that had been
> used hitherto with a comic purpose to a purpose of beauty. . . . The audience,
> though it has coarsened under the influence of public events and constant
> political discussion, is yet proud of its intelligence and of its old hospitality,
> and may be won over in time. Yet it may be a bitter struggle.[55]

This is certainly a less hostile view of Irish cultural life than we find articulated at the end of the poet's life, and in 1926 at least, Yeats was able to
declare the work of the Irish Literary Theatre a success: "an Irish school of
drama has been created and does not need the same anxious fostering."[56] But
the issue of an ideal audience for a difficult, symbolist drama aloof from the
vicissitudes of "public events and constant political discussion" was to remain a vexed one. With an annuity from the Cosgrave government, the
Abbey could sever its somewhat embarrassed fiscal ties to London; however,
the Irish audience Yeats desired was certainly not free from the political and
commercial influences of the day. "You cannot have a national theatre without creating a national audience," he writes in "A Defence of the Abbey
Theatre," "and that cannot be done by the theatre alone, for it needs the help
of schools and newspapers, and of all teachers of the people."[57] Much of
Yeats's work for the Senate was concerned with the proper prescriptions for
Irish education, and I think it is fair to say that a number of his ideas (transla-
tions from Greek to Gaelic, and back again; reading Shakespeare's history
plays for their historical content) were intended to inculcate revivalist aes-

thetics and their tacit conservative social ideologies. In short, Yeats's drama had "failed" because his audience was not sufficiently prepared to receive it. In the 1920s, Yeats retreats increasingly into elitist polemic, and, while calling for revivalist educational policies that might bring about such an audience in the future, he also finds solace in the metaphysics of the gyres, promising future change and renewal. "Of one thing we may be quite certain," he asserts: "at no time, neither in the beginning nor in its final maturity, does an intellectual movement express a whole people, or anybody but those who are built into it, as a victim was built into the foundation of a bridge."[58] Yeats rhetorically backs away from the universality of his nationalistic prescriptions; revivalist art is the art of the revivalists. Yet "[s]ometimes," he continues, "if those people are great enough, if there is among them a Sophocles or a Shakespeare, or even some lesser genius who has the sincerity of the Great Masters, they give their character to the people."[59] Given the right conditions, a transformative individual genius might shape national character. Such is the valence of Yeats's Shakespeare in the 1920s: he remains a symbolic, folkloric producer of high art, binding social strata via his mythopoetic stage rituals, and possessed of an audience whose premodern sensibility responded sympathetically to the play of rhythm and symbol. Increasingly, however, he is elevated above "the people." What we find at the end of Yeats's life is a Shakespeare who scorns the crowd, for whom there is no audience, but instead a modern, bourgeois, and philistine mob.

CAUGHT IN THE GYRES: SHAKESPEARE AND *A VISION* (1925 AND 1937)

Shakespeare features prominently in Yeats's occult manifesto, *A Vision*, a text which, until fairly recently, has typically been read merely as a guide to Yeatsian symbolism. Its extraordinary genesis in the automatic writings of Yeats's wife, George, is by now well known and fully documented, as are its major preoccupations: the journey of the soul beyond death, the correspondence of historical periods to the movement of gyres, and the categorization of human personality types from fully "primary" or "objective" to "antithetical" or "subjective." Much of *A Vision*'s metaphysics can be found in an occultist piece from 1917, *Per Amica Silentia Lunae*, in a much more readable form, but the scope of the later text's ambitions are unparalleled: the entirety of human civilization and character explained in terms of a vast, deterministic cosmic system. For a thorough dissection of Shakespeare's position on the "Great Wheel" of personality types, I would refer the interested reader to Rupin Desai's *Yeats's Shakespeare*, but since I am here concerned with the function of Shakespeare within Yeats's occultist nationalism, I want to argue for the text's significance in terms of Yeats's cultural agenda and his palpable distaste for Irish political and aesthetic life post-Treaty. Certainly I am not alone in doing so, and perhaps the most important critical precedent is Declan Kiberd's assessment in *Inventing Ireland* that *A Vision*, "for all its arcane law, was intended by him to provide a spiritual foundation for the new nation-state."[60] Kiberd's argument is persuasive and nuanced: the twin forces at work in the movement of the gyres—primary and antithetical—can be seen as corresponding to the antimonious qualities of "Anglo" and "Celt" operating through Anglo-Irish cultural hybridity and within Yeats's own ethnic identity. The interpenetration of these forces therefore maps onto a vision of contemporary Ireland: approaching unity of being requires equilibrium between these forces, and so an Irish nation must strive to balance its "Celticism" with its "Anglicism," although, as Kiberd indicates, "the system is so manipulated as to favour the antithetical Celtic over the primary English elements."[61] In this way, argues Kiberd, *A Vision* bears witness to Yeats's desire to excavate room within the Irish polity for the Anglo-Irish, and within the new nation's cultural life for its modes of thought and self-representation. It is in this sense that the text relates to Yeatsian anxiety about a potential sociocultural hegemony intolerant of revivalist aesthetic prescriptions. As we have seen, Yeats's early Shakespeare, born from Yeats's response to Arnold's treatment of "the Celt," evolves with the development of these categories, with which Yeats attempted to negotiate his position within the English literary tradition. In the context of post-Treaty Ireland, however, *A Vision* provides Yeats with a means to argue for cultural pluralism, and, crucially, a psychological resource: the cyclical movement of the gyres guaranteed a return to a more propitious episteme.

Shakespeare is located at phase 20 in Yeats's system, in the company of Balzac and Napoleon. Placing him at this position, Yeats argues for a Shakespearean creative process that draws from the external world, as well as the imagination: "At Phase 19 we create through the externalized *Mask* an imaginary world, in whose real existence we believe, while remaining separate from it; at Phase 20 we enter that world and become a portion of it; we study it, we amass historical evidence, and, that we may dominate it the more, drive out myth and symbol, and compel it to seem the real world where our lives are lived."[62] Thus, following Kiberd, "Celtic" and "Anglo" elements are fused in Shakespearean art. Phase 20 is a "phase of ambition; in Napoleon the dramatist's own ambition; in Shakespeare that of the persons of his art; and this ambition is . . . a creative energy."[63] Since people are driven to pursue their "mask," either by trying to become it, as is the case with Napoleon, or by creating it in their art, Shakespeare's plays are peopled with ambitious characters drawn from observation of real life, but who exist within worlds shaped by the writer's imagination. By contrast, the Romantic poets occupied more "subjective" positions, while phase 21 was exemplified by the realism of Bernard Shaw, perpetually an object of Yeats's scorn. Evidence for Shakespeare's location at phase 20 is therefore derived from the disparity between the lives of the playwright and those of his characters:

> Shakespeare, the other supreme figure of the phase, was—if we may judge by the few biographical facts, and by such adjectives as "sweet" and "gentle" applied to him by his contemporaries—a man whose actual personality seemed faint and passionless. Unlike Ben Jonson he fought no duels; he kept out of quarrels in a quarrelsome age; not even complaining when somebody pirated his sonnets; he dominated no Mermaid Tavern, but—through *Mask* and Image, reflected in a multiplying mirror—he created the most passionate art that exists. . . . Both Shakespeare and Balzac used the False *Mask* imaginatively, explored it to impose the True, and what Thomas Lake Harris, the half-charlatan American visionary said about Shakespeare might be said of both: "Often the hair of his head stood up and all life became the echoing chambers of the tomb."[64]

This passage recalls Yeats's earlier suggestion that Shakespeare's symbolism drew from the *anima mundi*, and that his inclusion of folk materials denoted an acceptance of rural mysticism—"his hair stood up"—and yet the implication of classifying Shakespeare as a "supreme figure of the phase" is that his drama is dependent on observations of the phenomenal world. Shakespeare in *A Vision* appears to be more realist than symbolist, an aberration in Yeats's thinking. Rupin Desai explores this point in *Yeats's Shakespeare*, noting how Yeats, in "The Tragic Generation" (1922), had suggested that Shakespeare was a man of phase 16, occupied in *A Vision* by Yeats's visionary hero William Blake: "The mid-Renaissance could but approximate to the full moon [phase 15] . . . but we way attribute to the next three nights of the moon the men of Shakespeare, or Titian, of Strozzi, and of Van Dyck."[65] We should also recall how, in "The Symbolism of Poetry" (1900), Yeats had firmly identified Shakespeare as a symbolist. So why might Shakespeare move from a putative phase 16 to phase 20? Desai's answer is that "here, perhaps unfortunately, he has allowed the logic of his system to prevail over personal conviction."[66] One of the principles of Yeatsian occultist aesthetics is that great art is born of conflict, and perhaps no conflict is greater than that between an individual and his historical "phase." "Were he not himself of a later phase," writes Yeats, "were he of the 16th phase like his age and so drunk with his own wine, he had not written plays at all, but as it is he finds his opportunity among a crowd of men and women who are still shaken by thought that passes from man to man in psychological contagion."[67] Desai's verdict seems right: since the Elizabethan age is antithetical—"the 16th phase"—Shakespeare must be somewhat primary. The logic of the system demands a reevaluation of the playwright's sensibility, and the later section of *A Vision*, entitled "Dove or Swan?" employs Shakespeare to validate the cyclicality of gyre-driven history:

I see in Shakespeare a man in whom human personality, hitherto restrained by his dependence upon Christendom or by its own need for self-control, burst like a shell. Perhaps secular intellect, setting itself free after five hundred years of struggle, has made him the greatest of dramatists, and yet because an *antithetical* age alone could confer upon an art like his the unity of a painting or of a temple pediment, we might, had the total works of Sophocles survived—they too born of a like struggle though with a different enemy—not think him the greatest.[68]

Since the exposition of epochal cyclicality precedes that of personality types in Yeats's thought—the individuals are assigned to a predetermined historical system—Shakespeare is moved to phase 20 to lend weight to the theory that great artists are in conflict with their times. Desai is right that he is the victim of the system's logic, but I think there is more to say on this issue, given the role of Shakespeare within Yeats's occult nationalism. Yeats certainly regarded himself as an artist "out of phase," and this sense of dislocation from his own time clearly increased over time. I have been arguing in this chapter for a correspondence between the changes in Shakespeare during the 1920s and Yeats's disillusionment with contemporary Irish cultural and political life. What we see in *A Vision* is a slightly different Shakespeare. His historical alienation is emphasized, he is more objective, and his art is therefore less symbolic. The use of symbols, whether in occult rituals or in poetry, was, for Yeats, a means of facilitating communication with spirits, accessing the *anima mundi*, and preparing the mind for visionary experience. As such, Shakespeare's ritualistic drama, replete with its folkloric and mythical content, was typically viewed as a mystical art and, as I have argued, provided Yeats with a model for his own revivalist ambitions. A less symbolic Shakespeare is therefore one who is less capable of affecting an audience via the occult technologies of imaginative transformation. We have to be careful not to overstate the case; situated at Phase 20, Shakespeare is no mechanical realist, and much of his power stems from his incorporation of reality into the imaginative realm: "Do we not feel an unrest like that of travel itself when we watch those personages, more living than ourselves, amid so much that is irrelevant and heterogeneous, amid so much *primary* curiosity, when we are carried from Rome to Venice, from Egypt to Saxon England, or in the one play from Roman to Christian mythology?"[69] However, when we consider these points together—an increased objectivity signifying "Anglo," epistemic alienation and a less symbolic art—the Shakespeare of *A Vision* speaks to his creator's own anxieties during a period when he was fighting against the exclusion of the Anglo-Irish from national cultural and political life, and relinquishing his ambitions for the new Irish drama in light of an Irish audience demanding a realistic, didactic, and accessible aesthetics.

THAT OLD SHAKESPEAREAN CONTEMPT

Yeats's vituperative pamphlet of 1938, published the following year as "On the Boiler," has long been mined for its harsh reactionary sentiment, and its writer certainly knew that its publication would ruffle feathers. It was to be the first of a series of sociocultural screeds—this one concerned primarily with "the multiplication of the uneducatable masses"[70] —but Yeats of course died before a second issue (on religion) could be composed. Much has been made of Yeats's flirtation with fascism during his final years, but while "On the Boiler" certainly refines Yeatsian cultural elitism to a degree unpalatable to postmodern sensibilities, I defer to Elizabeth Cullingford for a more nuanced reading, and I think it is worth reading her at length here. According to Cullingford, Yeats's interest in Mussolini's Italian politics turns out, on close inspection, to be a search for a coherent political doctrine that promised internal order alongside a conservative preservation of individual rights and hierarchical class interests:

> The nature of his convictions makes it wrong to place him in any political category save that of a nationalist of the school of John O'Leary. His devotion to Ireland, which survived circumstances that drove most other Irish writers into despairing exile, also dictated his attitude to other political philosophies. He was not a socialist, though he was sympathetic to some socialist ideals, because socialism seemed to him contrary to the Irish spirit of individualism and inappropriate to a peasant-based economy. He was not in theory a democrat, though in practice he conformed meticulously to democratic principles, because democracy in Ireland, in his eyes the tyranny of the lower-middle class, was destructive, mean-minded, and conformist. He was not a Tory, though he approved the predominance of the landed gentry, because the union of Church and State in Ireland threatened liberty of conscience. He was not even a conservative, though he loved tradition, because his commitment to the Irish cause made him a revolutionary against the *status quo*. Of all political stances he was probably closest to that of Burke's Old Whigs: an aristocratic liberalism that combined love of individual freedom with respect for the ties of the organic social group. But modern liberals, identified as they were with *laissez-faire* capitalism, had little appeal.[71]

It is better, then, to understand Yeats's politics as antique liberal than simply authoritarian or fascist. As Cullingford points out, by the time Italian fascism had been subsumed into National Socialism, Yeats had lost all interest; he "began the process of disengagement as early as 1934, and repudiated anti-Semitism, State-worship, censorship, interference with individual liberty, and the cruelty of all totalitarian regimes."[72] This seems to me an accurate reading both of Yeats's work for the Senate, and his public discourse. It might also be added that this tension between tradition and individual liberty is similarly visible in his work for the various literary and occult societies to which he attached himself. Still, "On the Boiler" is a blistering attack on the long-despised forces of modernity now seemingly triumphing in the anemic, clerically policed cultural life of contemporary Ireland. Of further interest, given the topic of this study, is the deployment of Shakespeare. In this final Shakespearean text we find the bard removed entirely from the salvific cultural nationalism of earlier, more optimistic years. Shakespeare in 1938 recycles a number of familiar topoi, but, as I have argued above, the rhetorical context significantly alters his signification within Yeatsian discourse: once the representative of an organic and hierarchical society, Shakespeare is now a metonym for a harsh, elitist social ideology; once the flowering of a national, folk sensibility awaiting restoration in contemporary Ireland, now he is a mirror for Ireland's perceived cultural and racial degeneration; once the writer of dramatic ritual, collecting the multitude via a body of myth and history, now he is the proponent of a Nietzschean "tragic joy," a solitary, existential position of laughter in the face of defeat.

From its opening lyric to its peroration, "On the Boiler" takes aim squarely at the forces shaping contemporary Irish cultural life—the newspapers, politicians, and educators—as well as "the masses," understood here not as the idealized rural folk of Ireland's West and South, but as the inheritors of precisely that tawdry, utilitarian sensibility against which Yeats had constructed his own, romantic prescriptions for Irish nationhood. Much of the content of "On the Boiler" is familiar from Yeats's earlier writings, but again, the tone is markedly more harsh and antidemocratic; in the wake of revivalism's failure, enmity is transferred from the powerful to the popular:

> The whole State should be so constructed that the people should think it their duty to grow popular with the King and Lord Mayor instead of King and Lord Mayor growing popular with them; yet, as it is even, I have known some two or three men and women who never, apart from the day's natural kindness, gave the people a thought, or who despised them with that old Shakespearean contempt and were worshipped after their death or even while they lived. [73]

Almost immediately, Shakespeare is introduced into a vituperative, elitist rhetoric. Here the descriptor "Shakespearean" carries several significations: the plays, their characters, the playwright, and the Elizabethan age as a whole. While Yeats is specifically attacking what he sees at the lord mayor of Dublin's pandering to voters, his rhetoric quickly expands to Ireland's sociopolitical arrangements, mediated through Shakespeare. It is important to remember that Yeats's Shakespeare of earlier years had provided a kind of ideological cement within a hierarchical social arrangement via his incorporation of folk materials—betokening the mystical life of the nation—into a challenging but universal nationalist drama. Not so now: that "old Shakespearean contempt" signifies not merely an aristocratic and artistic aloofness from the quotidian, but an attitude of disgust. What follows is a series of profoundly antidemocratic assertions:

> it seems probable that many men in Irish public life should not have been taught to read and write, and would not have been in any country before the middle of the nineteenth century. . . . Forcing reading and writing on those who wanted neither was a worst part of the violence which for two centuries has been creating that hell wherein we suffer. . . . Our representative system has given Ireland to the incompetent. [74]

Clearly popular education is on the hook for what Yeats regards as an insufferable contemporary politics, and Yeats follows with one of the essay's numerous prophetic caveats: "I say to those that shall rule here: 'If ever Ireland again seems molten wax, reverse the process of revolution. Do not try to pour Ireland into any political system. Think first how many able men with public minds the country has, how many it can hope to have in the near future, and mould your system upon those men.'" [75] Again we find a reiteration of the Yeatsian belief that a national transformation should be guided by the sociocultural elite, but the moment now is past. Of course, as we have seen, the ideal theatrical audience functioned within Yeats's nationalist thought as a (highly mysticized) metaphor and model for the ideal nation, hence Shakespeare's utility. It should come as no surprise, then, when Yeats pivots to the same topoi: "the theatre has not . . . gone my way or in any way I wanted it to go. . . . We who are opposites of our times should for the most part work at our art and for good manners' sake be silent. . . . I gave certain years to writing plays in Shakespearean verse about Irish kings for whom nobody cared a farthing." [76] Of significance here is the shifting valence of the Shakespearean signifier: having once stood in Yeatsian rhetoric for a challenging symbolist drama capable of affecting a spectrum of social classes, Shakespeare is now the cultural property of the elite. The phrase "we who are the opposite of our times" needs to be understood as a final judgment on the possibility of an organic Irish nation, prompting a notorious articulation of eugenicist principles:

> Since about 1900 the better stocks have not been replacing their numbers, while the stupider and less healthy have been replacing theirs. Unless there is a change in the public mind every rank above the lowest must degenerate, and, as inferior men push up into its gaps, degenerate more and more quickly. The results are already visible in the degeneration of literature, newspapers, amusements (there was once a stock company playing Shakespeare in every considerable town)[.] [77]

What had been, in the 1920s, ruminations on the function of aristocracy and "great families" in the social life of successful nations has become, by 1938, full-blown eugenics, and Shakespeare now functions as a yardstick of cultural degeneration: Shakespeare no longer played in "every considerable town."

For the student of Yeatsian thought, it is fascinating to see him folding contemporary racial "science" into a narrative of decline for which Yeats had previously supplied highly esoteric evidence. The cyclicality of the gyres, by now fully developed and disseminated in *A Vision*, promised the eventual return to a more favorable episteme, and I think the turn to eugenics here should not be read as a major shift away from metaphysical speculation, but rather as another example of Yeatsian bricolage. The signal phrase "We who are opposites of our times" reveals a familiar metaphysics, and having tipped his hat to contemporary pseudoscience, Yeats recycles the tenets of an idiosyncratic nationalism with its roots in decades of philosophical speculation and, more recently, "psychical" (spiritualist) research. "[W]e Irish are nearer than the English to the Mythic Age,"[78] he writes, following with a critique of the "English" sensibility apparently now threatening the newly sovereign Irish nation-state: "The English are an objective people; they no longer have a sense of tragedy in their theatre; pity, which is fed by observation instead of experience, has taken their place; their poets are psychological, looking at their own minds from without."[79] This is an important reminder that Yeats's antipathy to the "masses" was never a straightforward "modernist" response to social destratification and popular education, as it is frequently read.[80] Yeats's nationalism posited Ireland's defining sensibility as rural, antiutilitarian, and antipositivist, its people possessed of a folk art which permeated "high" and "low" culture, and whose symbolic content furnished evidence for the preservation of modes of existence permitting communication between the living and the dead. To the extent that Yeats's rhetoric partakes of a "modernist" critique of a commercial, popular art and an increasingly urbanized, destratified social arrangement, it needs to be understood less as an articulation of the high modernist zeitgeist, but rather in the context of his occult nationalism and romanticism.

In terms of "On the Boiler," Yeats's vituperative assault on mass culture constitutes a shift from the introspective, disappointed nostalgia of the 1920s into a harsh, polemical mode, but the topos remains essentially unchanged from decades earlier: "Instead of hierarchical society, where all men are different, came democracy; instead of a science which had re-discovered *Anima Mundi*, its experiments and observations confirming the speculations of Henry More, came materialism: all that Whiggish world Swift stared on till he became a raging man."[81] Once more Yeats traces out a familiar metahistory of epistemological change, within which the political struggle between England and Ireland figures as a final conflict between the "primary" and the "antithetical." The disintegration of an organic Irish audience for Shakespearean, revivalist drama spells the triumph of the new gyre, and, in an apocalyptic note, Yeats advises his readers to "[d]esire some just war, that big house and hovel, college and public house, civil servant—his Gaelic certificate in his pocket—and international bridge-playing woman, may know that they belong to one nation."[82] This is a conspicuous change; in the 1900s Yeats had believed that an Irish dramatic movement could unite the nation's social classes, and in the 1920s he had written that a "Sophocles or Shakespeare" might "give their character to the people."[83] By 1938, only a war could do so.

"On the Boiler" closes with a series of telling references to *Hamlet*. Having claimed earlier that "[t]he English are an objective people [who] no longer have a sense of tragedy in their theatre,"[84] Yeats proceeds to critique contemporary English productions of *Hamlet*:

> English producers slur over the scene where Hamlet changes the letters and sends Rosencrantz and Guildenstern to their deaths, because they define him through his thought and think that scene but old folk material incompatible with Shakespeare's *Hamlet*. Yet no imaginative man has ever complained, and Shakespeare when he made Hamlet kill the father of Fortinbras in single combat showed that he meant it. Hamlet's hesitations are hesitations of thought, and are concerned with certain persons on whom his attention is fixed; outside that he is a mediaeval man of action.[85]

This passage requires a little explication. This is taken from the essay's peroration, in which Yeats is applying his scorn of all things modern to literary hermeneutics. In much the same way that a theatrical audience represented a nation in Yeats's thought, "English producers" stand in for a host of pernicious agents of modernity. At one level, then, Yeats is supplying a genuine literary-critical assessment: contemporary productions of *Hamlet* portray him entirely as a thinker, and therefore tend to elide moments in the play text that make him a "mediaeval man of action." He then moves to situate the cause of this interpretive error in "[t]his new art, the art of the circulating libraries," which "has no interest in anything that cannot be understood through opinion."[86] He continues, "[U]nlike ancient art, it is urban, it belongs not to the small ancient town serrated by its green gardens but to the great modern town where meditation is impossible, where action is a mechanical routine, where the chest narrows and the stature sinks, where 'individuality' or intellectual coherence is the sole distinction left."[87] So, through a process of conflation and suggestion, Yeats identifies a hermeneutic error associated with "English" producers, connects it to commercial, bourgeois, "popular" art ("the art of the circulating libraries"), and therefore with the "objective" or "primary" gyre, and in doing so within the context of the essay's assault on contemporary Irish society, he implies that Ireland, far from de-Anglicizing, has adopted English modes of thought. This is a fascinating reiteration of his earlier claims that the rural Irish were the true inheri-

tors of Shakespeare, and again the "new art" is "urban" and "mechanical." Of
course, as I hope to have shown throughout this book, Yeats had been making such claims for a long time, enfolding Shakespeare into an occult nationalism. But the context makes the difference. "English" signifies "modern,"
and "Irish" signifies "ancient" or "premodern" such that a critique of modernity is also a nationalist credo, and vice-versa. Here we also find a restate-
ment of the Yeatsian understanding of artistic creation. Since the artist
creates from his "mask," Hamlet has become a man of action: Shakespeare,
we should remember, "fought no duels [and] kept out of quarrels in a quarrelsome age."[88] Unpacking the multivalent significations of Yeats's rhetoric
helps to account for the apparent non sequiturs and swift intuitive leaps in his
prose. Of course, since the advent of English cultural imperialism, talking
about Shakespeare had meant also talking about the relationship between art,
language, society, and power.

"On the Boiler" ends on a decidedly Shakespearean note and furnishes us
with the final incarnation of Yeats's Shakespeare, the tragedian beating a
hasty retreat from the political realm. Yeats's late-life musings on "tragic
joy" are familiar critical ground; a Nietzschean commonplace, "tragic joy"
describes a seemingly paradoxical sense of gaiety in the face of immanent
catastrophe, a heroic fatalism, and is most readily discussed in reference to
Yeats's final lyrics, such as "Lapis Lazuli." Typically, Yeats had recourse to
Shakespearean tragedy for examples of this attitude, and "On the Boiler" is
no exception:

> No tragedy is legitimate unless it leads some great character to his final joy.
> Polonius may go out wretchedly, but I can hear the dance music in "Absent
> thee from felicity awhile," or in Hamlet's speech over the dead Ophelia, and
> what of Cleopatra's last farewells, Lear's rage under the lightning, Oedipus
> sinking down at the story's end into an earth "riven" by love?[89]

Such literary-critical pronouncements must be read in the context of Yeats's
senescence and his withdrawal from the world of contemporary politics and
action. In terms of my argument here, Shakespearean tragic joy completes
the process of abstraction and dislocation I have outlined: what Yeats
chooses to emphasize in the Shakespearean canon—tragedy, aristocracy,
worldly failure, and withdrawal—responds to the obsolescence of his aesthetic prescriptions and the attendant reactionary elitism of his cultural politics. He closes "On the Boiler" with a reiteration of the coterie culture that
had circumscribed both his literary-nationalist endeavors and his membership in occult secret societies. Referencing the recent publication by the
Cuala Press of *Broadsides*, containing both traditional and modern Irish and
English poets, intended to be sung "as the country people sing Gaelic words,
mainly for the sake of their words,"[90] Yeats explains how "[w]hen our mod-

ern movement began it attempted not only dramatic literature but new popular songs."[91] He then turns to the issue of the songs' ideal audience:

> We [F. R. Higgins, Dorothy Wellesley, and Yeats] live in the country or in Dublin where one can see the mountains through a gap between two houses, and the largest audience we think of is a dinner of the Irish Academy of Letters, some group of friends in a public house, or else some house-party like that which saw the first production of Milton's *Comus*. Those who listen must be few that the words may keep their natural intonation, and those few must share a knowledge of good literature, and sometimes, when the poem is Irish of Irish national tradition, no churl must be present. We, like all good poets, turn our backs on the heterogeneous, seek out our own kindred.[92]

There is much that is familiar here in this description of a coterie of the enlightened, listening to the chanting of ancient and neo-folk songs. Yeats is clearly thinking of revivalist literary culture with its emphasis on renewing a connection to rural Irish cultural materials and their attendant magical properties. It also resembles a secret society, replete with the camaraderie of a shared sacred pursuit. We have seen this "audience" in Yeats's account of his visit to Stratford in 1901 and in the ambivalence toward a "People's Theatre" in 1928. However, by 1938, there is no longer a sense that such an organization might effect change or unite the social classes; "No churl must be present," he writes, employing an Anglo-Saxon word loaded with class prejudice, not to mention Spenserian overtones.[93] As I have argued throughout, the nation as an audience is a consistent refrain of Yeatsian thought, combining nationalist and occultist tenets and placing the ritualistic poet at the spiritual center of the Irish national community. Shakespeare provided Yeats with his most consistent model for expressing this vision, as well as a measure of cultural capital to support its credibility during the early years of the Irish National Theatre. Writing about Shakespeare in the past had always meant entering into a preexisting discourse—whether academic, theatrical, or mystical—and so one practical function of Shakespeare had been to enlarge the capillaries through which Yeats might disseminate his various nationalist and spiritualist prescriptions, as well as construct his own literary reputation. This is most obviously the case in his early disputes with Edward Dowden, and in his involvement with theatrical heavyweights like Harley Granville-Barker. At the close of "On the Boiler," however, following the evocation of Shakespearean "tragic joy," we find the revivalist organization severed from the national community. The solitary artist joyfully pouring scorn on the cultural catastrophe of contemporary Ireland—indeed modernity as a whole—and secure in the company of only the like-minded: such is the final incarnation of Yeats's Shakespeare. Elizabeth Cullingford writes of Yeats that he "approached his country with mystical ideas of nationality, but his country swiftly taught him that such ideas had little relation to reality."[94]

This is a perceptive point, and one that can be usefully extended: increasingly dissatisfied with his country, Yeats had recourse to an alternate reality, taking refuge in an apolitical realm of literature and in the vast metaphysical abstractions conveyed to him from beyond the veil. As we have seen, Yeats's Shakespeare was not left behind: like his creator, he climbed up into the winding tower.

NOTES

1. Ironically, Yeats's initially provincial poetics—which had ignited the fin-de-siècle "Dowden controversy"—would have likely fit the times. By the 1920s, Yeats's cultural nationalism had evolved to assert a more cosmopolitan outlook, albeit one tempered by the same distaste for overtly political, propagandizing literature. The irony inherent in Yeats's early dispute with the cosmopolitans is also indicated by Andrew Murphy in his essay, "An Irish Catalysis: W. B. Yeats and the Uses of Shakespeare," *Shakespeare Survey* 64 (2011): 209–19.

2. Brian Arkins provides a useful summary here: "If Yeats had a vision of the ideal society, it was that of a hierarchical system that exhibited his cherished ideal of Unity of Being, and was presided over by an enlightened aristocracy, with the consent of the peasantry, and the help of a religious class: 'The workman, noble and saint.' Since no contemporary society matched up to these requirements, Yeats made a series of forays into history in an attempt to locate his ideal. Two of these forays—those in the Italian Renaissance and into eighteenth-century Ireland—are problematic, while a third, into early Byzantium, is much more authentic." See Brian Arkins, *The Thought of W. B. Yeats* (Bern: Peter Lang, 2005), 69. Arkins neglects to mention Renaissance England, certainly a "problematic" foray given the contemporary political context.

3. See Brenda Maddox, *George's Ghosts: A New Life of W. B. Yeats* (New York: Picador, 2000). Also see Margaret Mills Harper, *Wisdom of Two: The Spiritual and Literary Collaboration of George and W. B. Yeats* (New York: Oxford University Press, 2006).

4. Pascale Casanova, *The World Republic of Letters*, trans. M. B. DeBevoise (Cambridge, MA: Harvard University Press, 2007), 35.

5. See Bryan Reynolds, *Performing Transversally: Reimagining Shakespeare and the Critical Future* (New York: Palgrave Macmillan, 2003), 9. "Shakespace," writes Reynolds, "is a term coined by Donald Hedrick and myself for the particular articulatory space through which discourses, adaptations, and uses of Shakespeare have suffused the cosmopolitan landscape transhistorically."

6. The source for this data is Allen Wade, ed., *A Bibliography of the Writings of W. B. Yeats* (London: Rupert-Hart Davis, 1958).

7. In his essay "Yeats and the English Renaissance," T. McAlindon accounts for Yeats's interest in Renaissance writers—particularly Spenser and Jonson—in terms of his "aristocratic myth": "The aristocratic morality which he recommended is based on the triumphant 'self-glorification' or 'self-enjoyment' of the noble soul and on its insolent opposition to the ascetic, anti-life ethic of the mob—that is, of Christian democratic society." T. McAlindon, "Yeats and the English Renaissance," *PMLA* 82, no. 2 (1967): 158. By 1904, after writing *The King's Threshold* and publishing *Ideas of Good and Evil*, this "myth" was fully assembled in his thought and subsequently used satirically against opponents in the press, and encomiastically on behalf of his coterie and the "aristocratic" culture that they represented. Similarly, Conor Cruise O'Brien sees 1902—following the controversial reception of *Cathleen ni Houlihan*—as the crucial year. Stephen Regan summarizes it this way: "[O'Brien's] contention is not that Yeats ceased to be an Irish nationalist but that his nationalism became conservative and aristocratic rather than popular and active. . . . After 1902, Yeats was no longer able to disguise his contempt for the rising Catholic middle class." Stephan Regan, "W. B. Yeats: Irish Nationalism and Post-Colonial Theory," *Nordic Irish Studies* 5 (2006): 96. As I argue here, this change is also visible in his Shakespeare, increasingly deployed as a metonym for "high" art and "noble" values.

8. See appendix 1 in Rupin Desai, *Yeats's Shakespeare* (Evanston, IL: Northwestern University Press, 1971), 225–27.

9. From 1906 Yeats was also carefully reading Ben Jonson, and McAlindon sees Yeats's interest in Ben Jonson as indicative of a hardening of attitudes toward the Catholic "masses" during the opening decades of the twentieth century: "Between 1905 and 1915 Yeats's dissatisfaction with 'this age' and the middle class acquired an intensity and a personal bitterness akin to Jonson's, and for familiar reasons: the public's reaction to Synge, the loss of the Lane pictures, and Moore's mockery of Yeats's aristocratic pretensions." McAlindon, "Yeats and the English Renaissance,"166.

10. Letter from Ezra Pound to John Quinn, May 1, 1916. See *The Selected Letters of Ezra Pound to John Quinn, 1915–1924*, ed. Timothy Materer (Durham, NC: Duke University Press, 1991), 55.

11. Declan Kiberd, *Inventing Ireland: The Literature of the Modern Nation* (London: Vintage, 1995), 316.

12. Michael Boss, "Root Music," in *Fins de Siecle/New Beginnings*, ed. Ib Johansen (Aarhus, Denmark: Aarhus University Press, 2001), 80–81.

13. R. F. Foster, *The Irish Story: Telling Tales and Making It Up in Ireland* (New York: Oxford University Press, 2004), 64–65.

14. Ibid., 65.

15. Ibid., 72.

16. Richard English, *Irish Freedom: The History of Nationalism in Ireland* (London: Macmillan, 2006), 448.

17. John Hutchinson, *The Dynamics of Cultural Nationalism* (London: Allen and Unwin, 1987), 41.

18. Ibid., 12.

19. Ibid., 13.

20. Ibid.

21. Ibid., 4.

22. Ibid.

23. Ibid., 10.

24. Ibid., 16.

25. W. B. Yeats, *The Collected Works of W. B. Yeats*, vol. 5, *Later Essays*, ed. William H. O'Donnell (New York: Scribner, 1994), 46.

26. Ibid., 34.

27. Ibid.

28. Ibid., 35.

29. Ibid., 37.

30. W. B. Yeats, *The Collected Works of W. B. Yeats*, vol. 4, *Early Essays*, ed. Richard J. Finneran (New York: Scribner, 2007), 82.

31. W. B. Yeats, *Later Essays*, 38.

32. Ibid., 39.

33. Ibid., 41.

34. Ibid.

35. Ibid., 42.

36. Ibid., 43.

37. W. B. Yeats, *The Collected Works of W. B. Yeats*, vol. 10, *Later Articles and Reviews*, ed. Colton Johnson (New York: Scribner, 2000), 191.

38. W. B. Yeats, *Later Essays*, 44.

39. W. B. Yeats, *The Collected Works of W. B. Yeats*, vol. 8, *The Irish Dramatic Movement*, ed. Richard J. Finneran and Mary FitzGerald (New York: Scribner, 2003), 244.

40. Ibid., 250.

41. Ibid., 249.

42. Ibid., 125.

43. Ibid., 130.

44. Ibid., 246.

45. Ibid., 255.

46. Ibid., 252.
47. Ibid., 251.
48. Ibid., 258.
49. Ibid.
50. W. B. Yeats, *Later Essays*, 156.
51. Ibid., 157.
52. Ibid., 160.
53. Ibid., 204.
54. Ibid., 212.
55. Ibid., 157, 163.
56. Ibid., 206.
57. Ibid.
58. Ibid., 207.
59. Ibid.
60. Declan Kiberd, *Inventing Ireland*, 316.
61. Ibid., 325.
62. W. B. Yeats, *A Vision*, 2nd ed. (New York: Macmillan, 1966), 154.
63. Ibid.
64. Ibid., 153–54.
65. W. B. Yeats, *The Collected Works of W. B. Yeats*, vol. 3, *Autobiographies*, ed. Douglas Archibald and William O'Donnell (New York: Scribner, 1999), 175. Cited in Desai, *Yeats's Shakespeare*, 84.
66. Desai, *Yeats's Shakespeare*, 99.
67. W. B. Yeats, *A Vision*, 294.
68. Ibid.
69. Ibid.
70. W. B. Yeats, *Later Essays*, 231.
71. Elizabeth Cullingford, *Yeats, Ireland, and Fascism* (New York: New York University Press, 1981), 234.
72. Ibid., 235.
73. W. B. Yeats, *Later Essays*, 222.
74. Ibid., 223.
75. Ibid., 225.
76. Ibid., 226–27.
77. Ibid., 230.
78. Ibid., 233.
79. Ibid.
80. See John Carey, *The Intellectuals and the Masses: Pride and Prejudice among the Literary Intellectuals, 1880–1939* (New York: St. Martin's, 1993).
81. W. B. Yeats, *A Vision*, 237.
82. W. B. Yeats, *Later Essays*, 241.
83. Ibid., 207.
84. Ibid., 233.
85. Ibid., 244.
86. Ibid., 246.
87. Ibid.
88. W. B. Yeats, *A Vision*, 153.
89. W. B Yeats, *Later Essays*, 247.
90. Ibid.
91. Ibid.
92. Ibid., 248.
93. The *OED* offers seven meanings for "churl." The meaning intended by Yeats corresponds to its use as "a term of disparagement or contempt; base fellow, villein. In modern times usually: rude low-bred fellow." *Oxford English Dictionary Online*, 2nd ed., s.v., "churl," http://www.oed.com/view/Entry/32843 (accessed May 21, 2012).
94. Cullingford, *Yeats, Ireland, and Fascism*, 157.

Chapter Four

Yeats's Modern(ish) Shakespeare

Irish Revivalism and Literary Modernism

> When an Englishman explores the mysteries of the Cabala, one knows one's
> opinion of him, but Mr. Yeats on any subject is a cause of bewilderment and
> distress.
> —T. S. Eliot, reviewing *The Cutting of an Agate*

In *Reinventing Shakespeare: A Cultural History from the Restoration to the
Present* (1991), Gary Taylor makes the following claim concerning the impact of Irish writers on Shakespeare's reception and interpretation at the start
of the twentieth century: "Malone and Dowden in their different ways each
shaped the international perception of Shakespeare for a generation or more,
while Harris and Shaw and Yeats and Joyce collectively helped shape his
modernist image."[1] "They still teach Shakespeare in Eire," he continues, "but
in 1921 he became a foreigner again."[2] This is a somewhat provocative
assertion, but one certainly worth considering. Taylor argues that Edmond
Malone and Edward Dowden, by virtue of their nationality and immense
influence on Shakespeare scholarship, had made Shakespeare "Irish," in a
sense. However, by 1921—when Joyce finished *Ulysses*—"Harris and Shaw
and Yeats and Joyce" had recast Shakespeare's image, each Irishman approaching Shakespeare's work in ways that broke decisively with the dominant practices of Victorian scholarship and theatrical production. For Joyce,
this rupture was signaled in the parodic mode, and Taylor accordingly reminds his reader that Joyce devotes around seventy pages or so to the quasi-
academic Shakespearean banter of Dedalus et al. in the National Library at
Dublin, playfully lampooning the dusty antiquarianism and biographical ex-
cesses of Victorian Shakespeare studies. Evidence for Yeats's contribution to

the modern Shakespeare is inferred from his critical dispute with Trinity College's Dowden and supported by his attempts, along with T. S. Eliot, to revive verse drama. In particular, notes Taylor, Yeats's adoption of avant-garde, nonnaturalistic dramaturgy signals his allegiance to modernist aesthetics: "The Ballets Russes, [Gordon] Craig's designs, [Harley] Granville-Barker's productions of Shakespeare were all examples of the 'new decorative method' [which] appealed to Yeats because it satisfied his own prescriptions for poetic drama."[3] Taylor's larger narrative here is the "modernist" refashioning of Shakespeare's drama during the early decades of the twentieth century, including the eschewal of Victorian biography and character critique by T. S. Eliot and his followers, and so the implications of his assertion that Shakespeare lost his "Irish accent"[4] by 1922 are left unexplored. Tellingly, his 1921 marker refers to the completion of *Ulysses*, not the Irish War of Independence. In Taylor's rhetoric, Shakespeare's putative change of nationality thus functions as a metaphor for a hermeneutic shift in Shakespeare reception.

There's a kernel of truth here; the scholarly heavyweights, Malone and Dowden, had indeed dominated an increasingly professionalized field of Shakespeare studies, and both men were Irish. However, Taylor's nationality trope elides some crucial nuance. Dowden had embraced the English literary canon at the expense of indigenous Irish material. Yeats's first published article, it should be remembered, took him to task for exactly this. Perhaps this is what Taylor had in mind when he wrote of Shakespeare's "Irish accent," but it would be more accurate to say that Malone and Dowden, figuratively speaking, lost their own Irish accents in service to England's Bard.[5] From Yeats's perspective, Dowden's Shakespeare was categorically an Englishman, a utilitarian, and, it could be argued, an imperialist. Echoing Matthew Arnold's assertions of the "Celtic substratum"[6] in English letters, Dowden subsumed Irish literature into an Anglo-American tradition, thus opening himself to charges of West Britonism from those, like Yeats, who reductively figured Dowden's view of Ireland as a "backwater to the 'one noble river' of English culture."[7] As for Yeats, since his cultural identity was complicated, so was his Shakespeare. As I hope to have demonstrated in the first chapter of this book, the Shakespeare that emerges from his writing at the turn of the century is both Irish *and* English; by locating in Elizabethan England a certain folk sensibility akin to the inhabitants of Ireland's rural West and then arguing for their kinship with all other "ancient" races, Yeats effectively deracinated the Bard, this a highly subversive maneuver in the context of an Irish cultural nationalism. In the opening decades of the twentieth century, Yeats's Shakespeare responded to the ideological anxieties attendant upon Yeats's revivalist coterie in the face of domestic sectarian politics and an aesthetic agenda fundamentally at odds with the tastes and mores of Irish literary consumers. So, to the extent that Yeats's construction of

Shakespeare registers the sociocultural agenda of its creator, refracted through a hermetic, occultist lens, it would be far safer to label this Shakespeare "Anglo-Irish," or perhaps more accurately, an Anglo-Irish, aristocratic revivalist.

Taylor's language is reductive, but his larger point remains valid. The valence of the Shakespeare signifier *was* changing. Between William Poel, Harley Granville-Barker, and Gordon Craig, productions of Shakespeare's plays were modernized. Almost single-handedly, T. S. Eliot opened the canon to a host of Shakespeare's contemporaries—Dekker, Webster, and Middleton—and, by promoting G. Wilson Knight, altered the dominant hermeneutic in Shakespeare studies. Diana E. Henderson sees the paradigm shift in Shakespeare criticism as responding in part to the nineteenth-century "disintegrators," scholars who, in identifying the hands of Shakespeare's contemporaries in his texts, "recognized the collaborative dimension of Shakespeare's art."[8] As such, she views the professional criticism of Knight, the New Critics, and Northrop Frye in terms of a "counteremphasis on the formal integrity and thematic unity of Shakespeare's plays [that] took shape in response to this perceived threat."[9] Interpreting Shakespeare reception as a sociocultural phenomenon, the urge to find unity in Shakespeare's plays can therefore be read in terms of an anxious response to epistemic change characterizing modernist aesthetics; "[t]hus," writes Henderson, "these moderns continued to look to Shakespeare as a marker of integrity and order, seeking comfort in an insecure new world."[10] By the 1930s, Shakespeare's plays were to be studied as long, musical poems replete with overarching "themes" and employing powerful rhythms and myths that recalled the ritualistic origins of dance and drama. This approach permeates Knight's essays on Shakespeare, as well as Wyndham Lewis's influential work, *The Lion and the Fox: The Role of the Hero in the Plays of Shakespeare* (1926). Moreover, as Richard Halpern argues in *Shakespeare among the Moderns* (1997), if one effect of modernist thought "was to set the terms for our century's reading of Shakespeare, it did so partly by displacing him from his given niche in English culture":[11]

> Today, whether viewing Akira Kurosawa's adaptations or Ariane Mnoutchkine's productions of Shakespearean drama, or reading an essay by Clifford Geertz on the Balinese cockfight or by Stephen Greenblatt on colonial encounters with the New World, we are likely to confront a Shakespeare moved somewhat outside the boundaries of Europe. This fact is not a mere curiosity or sidelight; it is central to our century's reception of Shakespeare and of the English Renaissance more generally.[12]

Yeats's writings on Shakespeare, I argue, contribute significantly to this process. Examined carefully, they demonstrate the Anglo-Irishman's attempts to sidestep the discursive containment of nation-states and thus to construct his own identity as the poet of a confederation of "ancient" peoples. This ontology is what lies behind such statements as "Gaelic is my national language, but it is not my mother tongue."[13] My focus on Gary Taylor's rhetoric here is not intended to suggest a substantial disagreement. Taylor's reference to Shakespeare's "accent" is merely a convenient metaphor. I also agree that Yeats "helped shaped [Shakespeare's] modernist image."[14] However, the contours of Yeats's Shakespeare were in place before Knight was a professor and Eliot a modernist poet, and prior to Pound's influence on Yeats. If Yeats's Shakespeare is to be considered a "modernist" Shakespeare, then, he must be considered such avant la lettre.

There is another way of thinking about these relationships between Yeats and Shakespeare, English and Irish letters, and Victorian and modernist reception. Certainly Yeats was no professional academic. Arguably he was also no modernist. However, taken together as a body of thought, Yeats's writing on Shakespeare demonstrates a remarkable proximity to these "modernist" trends, and in this more limited sense, Taylor is right about Yeats's position within the shifting field of Shakespeare reception. In what remains of this book, then, I want to consider Yeats as (co)producer of a "modern" body of knowledge about Shakespeare and to demonstrate how Shakespeare maps onto these critical dynamics. Between his first foray into "Shakespace" in 1897[15] and his appointment as a senator of the Irish Free State in 1922, Yeats made a series of claims about Shakespeare and his plays that would later be echoed, elaborated upon, and consecrated by T. S. Eliot, Wyndham Lewis, and G. Wilson Knight: Shakespeare was a symbolist, visionary poet situated on the cusp of a pernicious modernity, his work mythological and ritualistic, his characters archetypal, his drama powered by a complex, self-referential pattern of imagery and musical qualities of pitch, tone, and rhythm. Housed in a national theatre, his drama could elevate and enrich a nation's cultural life; deployed against the "masses," his cultural signification was elitist and aristocratic. In the previous chapters I have argued that each of these strands of thought constitutes an important aspect of Yeats's occultist cultural nationalism. As such, it is worth asking whether it might be more accurate to associate Yeats's Shakespeare with Irish nationalism. This, then, is my final claim in this book: a critical analysis of Yeats's Shakespeare not only sheds light on the Irishman's syncretic, idiosyncratic nationalism; it also underscores what Terence Brown has called a "historical accident":[16] the Irish Revival's remarkable yet accidental similarity to the international literary movement that followed.

THE MYTHICAL METHOD AND SHAKESPEARE'S PRIMITIVE MUSIC

Brown arrives at this conclusion in his assessment of the lamentable state of avant-garde cultural production in Ireland during the 1920s and 1930s, the heyday for international high modernism. His explanation for this is significant: since modernist aesthetics paralleled those of literary revivalism in so many respects, Irish disillusionment with the quasi-independence afforded by the Treaty translated into a rejection of Irish revivalism: "post-revolutionary literary Ireland seems to have thrown out the modernist baby with the romantic bathwater of the Literary Revival, leaving the 1930s to produce only a few writers . . . who wrote in varying degrees of awareness of the Revival's formal originality or of modernism's revolution of the word."[17] Irish revivalism, as Brown notes, most often draws critical comparison with aspects of Victorian romanticism, notably in its "obsession with the past . . . veneration of the primitive and the rural [and] cults of the hero and of blood sacrifice."[18] However, in its treatment of time, Brown suggests, Irish literary revivalism closely paralleled the formal qualities of modernism:

> In nationalism the nineteenth century's sense of time is challenged. No longer a secular, sequential process in which progress unfolds, time becomes an element in which the sacred national sage of ancient glory and recurrent defeat can be played out in the iterative and, it is hoped, climactic fashion. The past intrudes on the present to offer typologies and prophetic instances. . . . Past and present instances are significantly juxtaposed like images in some symbolist text. Historical time and mythological timelessness are woven together in a seamless garment of national imagining. . . . Literary production conducted in the context of nationalist feeling accordingly revives and translates texts from the dim past not for antiquarian reasons but to allow them to exist again in the timeless spirituality of the nation's continuous being.[19]

Revivalist texts like Yeats's dramatic Cuchulain cycle, or Douglas Hyde's *Love Songs of Connacht*, which present ancient texts in modern guises can thus be seen to mirror works like Eliot's *Waste Land* or Pound's *Cantos* in their mythic treatment of time. These are not histories but literary works that break formally with the narrative logic of sequential, Hegelian time; they announce a break from the master narratives of progress inscribed in Enlightenment texts. Further, argues Brown,

> [t]hat the revival depended for its sources as a revived national literature on the Celtic sagas, on folktale and on the self-conscious interlacing narratives of the story-teller's oral art, as well as on the revelatory capacities of myth, assuredly meant that the defining characteristics of its key texts would have little in common with the prevailing literary norms of Victorian literature where the

realist novel, the discursive essay and the subjective lyric met the expectations
of a bourgeois audience.[20]

Brown resists the move to fold this revivalist treatment of mythic time into
literary modernism. Instead, the most he can say without further analysis is
that this similarity betokens "an historic accident."[21] This is a significant
theoretical maneuver: in terms of its rejection of Victorian norms and its
employment of a "mythic method," Irish revivalism is "modern," but not
"modernist." It should come as no surprise that critical confusion exists on
this issue; reviewing *Ulysses* in 1923, Eliot famously defined the "mythic
method" as a "continuous parallel between contemporaneity and antiquity . . . a way of controlling, of ordering, of giving a shape and a significance
to the immense panorama of utility and anarchy which is contemporary history."[22] Less frequently cited is his assertion in the same article that this is a
"method already adumbrated by Mr. Yeats, and of the need for which I
believe Mr. Yeats to have been the first contemporary to be conscious."[23] In
his review, Eliot provides no examples of Yeats's "mythical method," but
Denis Donoghue suggests that the Yeatsian technique Eliot must have been
considering "entailed redeeming a mere fact from its penury by presenting it
in the light of a higher or larger perspective . . . in such poems as 'A Woman
Sung Homer' and 'No Second Troy.'"[24] Eliot certainly did not consider
Yeats's syncretic religious philosophy to constitute such a technique for
"ordering . . . contemporary history," despite the omnipresence of its symbolic content in Yeats's later poetry (which Eliot admired). Instead, Eliot looked
askance at Yeatsian occultism, writing in *The Use of Poetry and The Use of
Criticism* of how Yeats "was very much fascinated by self-induced trance
states, calculated symbolism, mediums, theosophy, crystal-gazing, folklore
and hobgoblins";[25] "[o]ften the verse has a hypnotic charm," he continues,
"but you cannot take heaven by magic, especially if you are, like Mr. Yeats, a
very sane person."[26] Similarly, delivering the Page-Barbour Lectures at the
University of Virginia in 1933, Eliot continued in this vein, remarking that
Yeats's mythology "was not a world of spiritual significance, not a world of
real Good and Evil, of holiness or sin, but a highly sophisticated lower
mythology summoned, like a physician, to supply the fading pulse of poetry
with some transient stimulant so that the dying patient may utter his last
words."[27] Taken together, these statements appear paradoxical. It seems that
Eliot approved of Yeatsian mythologizing when it was derived from antiquity—specifically Greek antiquity—but not from the eclectic Neoplatonic system articulated in *A Vision* (1925). In this sense Eliot's critique drew upon
his prejudicial division of mythology into an official, orthodox tradition and
an eclectic, idiosyncratic bunk. Trying to make sense of Yeats, Eliot points to
his nationality; Eliot "thought that to be an Irishman was to be deprived of
certain attributes of sensibility, notably of wit,"[28] writes Donoghue, and in

his essay on Andrew Marvell, Eliot locates Yeats "outside of the tradition altogether."[29] Eliot's admiration for Yeats's work is tempered by distaste for his occultism and a prejudicial stance concerning the perceived peculiarity of Irish letters.[30]

Of course, Eliot was right to see a "mythic method" in Yeats. But what for Eliot constituted an aesthetic technique was for Yeats an expression of metaphysical speculation. For instance, in the final two sections of his 1901 essay, "At Stratford-on-Avon," Yeats characteristically waxes philosophical. He begins with an exposition of "Shakespeare's Myth":

> The Greeks, a certain scholar has told me, considered that myths are the activities of the Daimons, and that the Daimons shape our characters and our lives. I have often had the fancy that there is some one Myth for every man, which, if we but knew it, would make us understand all that he did and thought. Shakespeare's Myth, it may be, describes a wise man who was blind from very wisdom, and an empty man who thrust him from his place, and saw all that could be seen from very emptiness.[31]

Yeats continues to think through this hypothesis in terms of the Shakespeare corpus; thus, "[i]t is in the story of Hamlet . . . and of Fortinbras. . . . And it is in the story of Richard II, that unripened Hamlet, and of Henry V, that ripened Fortinbras."[32] This is a form of speculative archetypal criticism, but one that proceeds from an unorthodox metaphysics, the "activities of the Daimons." Although here Yeats rhetorically hedges his assertion—"I have often had the fancy . . . it may be"—his contemporaneous essay, "Magic," removes any doubt that such statements are key doctrines in his evolving Neoplatonism.[33] Moreover, Yeats legitimizes the "Shakespeare Myth" by grounding it in classical antiquity. It is, after all, the Greeks who "considered that myths are the activities of the Dæmons." Whether or not such considerations have any kind of empirical basis is beside the point, and in fact the entire essay constitutes an attack on the utilitarian strand of Victorian Shakespeare criticism, and Edward Dowden's work in particular. Here the "Shakespeare Myth" aligns classical Greece and Elizabethan England within an atemporal order governed by a set of supernatural operators, and in the essay's final section, Yeats reduces the history cycle he has watched at Stratford to a singular myth: "The five plays, that are but one play, have, when played one after another, something extravagant and superhuman, something almost mythological. These nobles with their indifference to death and their immense energy seem at times no nearer to the common stature of men than do the Gods and the heroes of Greek plays."[34] In the second chapter of this book I have argued that Yeats's Stratford visit was crucial to the development of his own ritualistic and mythological drama, and therefore that Yeats's Shakespeare occupies a paradoxical space within the cultural politics of the Revival. So, the line from the Greeks to Shakespeare to, say, *On the*

King's Threshold (1903) or *On Baile's Strand* (1904) can reasonably be drawn in Yeats's thought at the turn of the century. My point here is that Yeats's "mythic method," as it applies to Shakespeare at least, has to be understood in the twin contexts of his religious philosophies and his cultural nationalism. A national dramatic cycle resting on a mythologized national history: this is what Yeats saw when he looked to the Greeks, to Shakespeare's histories, and what he sought to create on the Irish stage. He writes toward the end of "At Stratford" of how "English history" might have become as important to the English imagination as Greek mythology had been to the Greeks, were it not for the "Renaissance and [the] Italian influence."[35] Putting this in the context of his earlier statements regarding the activities of Dæmons, we can infer Yeats's neoromantic thinking about artistic creation: under the guidance of a supernatural entity, the dramatist enlarges (or perhaps reduces) individuals to the status of archetypes and elevates their actions to metaphysical proportions. In a famous passage from "A General Introduction for My Work," we see him articulating a similar set of ideas: "Dante and Milton had mythologies, Shakespeare the characters from English history or of traditional romance; even when the poet seems most himself . . . he is never the bundle of accident and incoherence that sits down to breakfast. . . . He is part of his own phantasmagoria."[36] For an artist presiding over the cultural and spiritual awakening of his nation, then, this "mythic method" must be understood—per Terence Brown—as a revivalist technique. In addition, Yeats anticipates several strands of modernist Shakespearean hermeneutics: archetypal or myth criticism, and the mysticized interpretation of G. Wilson Knight.

"At Stratford-on-Avon," also provides a clear set of prescriptions for Yeatsian dramaturgy. Yeats favors the "half-closed fan"[37] of Wagner's theatre for its ability to create a singular perspective; directors' "pictures" could thus be "composed for eyes at a small number of points of view . . . and what is no better than a trade might become an art."[38] He pays particular attention to the need for nonnaturalistic staging, and his admiration for Gordon Craig's scenery and the new pictorial method, it should be remembered, is cited by Gary Taylor as evidence for Yeats's contribution to the modernizing of Shakespeare's plays. I have, in the second chapter of this book, argued that these innovations appealed to Yeats because of their potentially transformative effect upon an audience's imagination, and that this visionary technology drew largely upon the ritualistic magic of the Golden Dawn, as well as his work on rites for the Celtic Mysteries. In this sense, Yeats's interest in the new staging techniques that were transforming the performance of Shakespeare stemmed largely from his occult activities in a nationalist context. Clearly Yeats was drawing from the same well as his contemporary moderns, but assuredly for different purposes, and this, it seems to me, is precisely the point Terence Brown makes in his assessment of Irish avant-garde literary production. Moreover, the fact that Yeats conceptualized the Shakespeare history cycle—when staged correctly—as a vast ritual of stylized movement and rhythmic utterance furthers this line of argument. In his own verse drama, of course, Yeats developed a series of rhythmic speech types over and above Shakespearean blank verse, and in "A General Introduction for My Work," he reflects at length on the rationale for his choices:

> When I wrote in blank verse I was dissatisfied; my vaguely mediaeval *Countess Cathleen* fitted the measure, but our Heroic Age went better . . . in the ballad metre of *The Green Helmet*. There was something in what I felt about Deidre, about Cuchulain, that rejected the Renaissance and its characteristic metres, and this was a principal reason why I created in dance plays the form that varies blank verse with lyric metres. When I speak blank verse and analyze my feelings, I stand at a moment of history when instinct, its traditional songs and dances, its general agreement, is of the past. I have been cast up out of the whale's belly though I still remember the sound and sway that came from beyond its ribs, and . . . I smell the fish of the sea. The contrapuntal structure of the verse . . . combines the past and present. If I repeat the first lines of *Paradise Lost* so as to emphasise its first five feet I am among the folk singers. . . . But speak it as I should I cross it with another emphasis, that of passionate prose. . . . The folk song is still there, but a ghostly voice, an unvariable possibility, an unconscious norm. What moves me and my hearer is a vivid speech that has no laws except that it must not exorcise the ghostly voice. I am awake and asleep, at my moment of revelation, self-possessed in self-surrender; there is no rhyme, no echo of the beaten drum, the dancing foot, that would overset my balance.[39]

Of course Yeats's taste for highly stylized, abstract, and ritualistic drama led him away from European models and toward Japanese Noh; his 1917 play, *At the Hawk's Well*, represents the culmination of this process. What I want to highlight in the above passage, however, are the overarching principles governing his experiments with metrical speech: first, it should be appropriate for presenting legendary Irish material—"our Heroic Age went better"—and second, it should, by virtue of a certain primitive or elemental power, transport both speaker and listener to a transcendent plane of experience. Once lulled into this state—"I am awake and asleep"—the speaker/listener experiences an atemporal order; the past is present in the form of a "ghostly voice." Blank verse, by itself, alienates by virtue of its associative connection to a specific period: the Renaissance. By mixing blank verse with passionate prose (that is, metrical prose), the "ghostly voice" or "folk song" is felt, but divorced from the *pastness* of the past,[40] Again, this relates to Yeats's revivalist mythic method—"Historical time and mythological timelessness are woven together in a seamless garment of national imagining"[41] —and the interchangeability of "ghostly voice" and "folk song" conveys the palimpsest of Yeatsian spiritualism and cultural nationalism. Further, though pure blank

verse was ultimately rejected by Yeats for these reasons, it should be recalled
that his de-Anglicizing of Shakespeare had rested largely on claims that rural
Irish culture had maintained an Elizabethan sensibility now lost to the English, and "that Ireland had preserved longer than England (the rhythmical
utterance of the Shakespearean stage)."[42]

Fourteen years prior, T. S. Eliot had also reflected upon the primitive
power of verse drama in an article for *The Nation and Athenaeum*, entitled
"The Beating of a Drum."[43] The piece begins with a critique of a recently
published scholarly work, *Studies in the Development of the Fool in Elizabethan Drama*, by Olive Mary Busby. "Miss Busby's facts are good facts and
worth having," writes Eliot, "[but] she has assembled them and chosen them
as a chronicler rather than as an anthropologist of folly."[44] In a single sentence, Eliot captures the "modernist" evolution of Shakespearean historicism.
Busby is guilty of a limited scope, locating the sources for Shakespeare's
fools in the drama of classical antiquity. Eliot instead calls for a different
method: "If literary critics, instead of perpetually perusing the writing of
other critics, would study the content and criticize the methods of such books
as 'The Origin of Species' itself, and 'Ancient Law,' and 'Primitive Culture,'
they might learn the difference between a history and a chronicle, and the
difference between an interpretation and a fact."[45] Scholars of literary history, insists Eliot, must take advantage of the new anthropological science. So,
King Lear's fool is "a *possessed*; a very cunning and very intuitive person; he
has more than a suggestion of the shaman or medicine man."[46] For a better
understanding of the "original impulse" toward comedy and tragedy, we
must look to those cultures whose art retains its ancient, ritualistic forms:
"the antecedent of the comic, is perhaps present, together with the tragic, in
all savage or primitive art; but comedy and tragedy are perhaps impermanent
intellectual abstractions."[47] From here, Eliot swiftly moves to situate the
primitive power of Shakespeare's drama in its cultural DNA: "It is the
rhythm, so utterly different from modern drama . . . which interpreters of
Shakespeare do their best to suppress, which makes Massine and Charlie
Chaplin the great actors that they are. . . . The drama was originally ritual;
and ritual, consisting of a set of repeated movements, is essentially a
dance."[48] Yeats, too, saw great drama as ritualistic and closely related to
dance, as he makes clear throughout his writings in *Samhain*. I am arguing,
however, that Yeats's prescriptions for ritualistic plays and rhythmic utterance need to be understood in the context of Irish revivalism and his ambitions for a spiritual reawakening in Ireland. Again, Yeats and Eliot seem to
be speaking with one voice, but the Irishman is concerned primarily with a
new *national* drama. Besides which, there is an important epistemological
distinction to be made here. The source of Eliot's approach is scientific and
anthropological, as evidenced by his allusions to "such books as 'The Origin
of Species' itself, and 'Ancient Law,' and 'Primitive Culture.'"[49] So, having

asserted the ritualistic origins of drama, Eliot pushes further into human history, way beyond the Dionysian rites of ancient Greece:

> [P]rimitive man acted in a certain way and then found a reason for it. An unoccupied person, finding a drum, may be seized with a desire to beat it, but unless he is an imbecile, he will be unable to continue beating it . . . without finding a reason for doing it. The reason may be the long continued drought. The next generation or the next civilization will find a more plausible reason for beating a drum. Shakespeare and Racine . . . each found his own reason. The reasons may be divided into tragedy and comedy. We still have similar reasons, but we have lost the drum. [50]

This is a fascinating idea, and one that succinctly folds a kind of anthropological hermeneutic into an implicit critique of modern culture. Modern artists, implies Eliot, maintain empty rituals shorn of their original, primordial impulse. In a statement of supreme iconoclasm, Eliot ventures that "the juggling of Rastelli [is] more cathartic than a performance of 'A Doll's House.'"[51] Yeats, I think, would have agreed, and social realism was certainly anathema in Yeatsian aesthetics.

There are, moreover, some strikingly similar statements in Yeats's prose, not least of which is his assertion of a cultural and spiritual rupture during, or immediately following, the Renaissance, which had ultimately produced an anemic modern culture in England.[52] In "Art and Ideas," an essay collected in *The Cutting of an Agate* (1913), Yeats writes of how "works of art are always begotten by previous works of art . . . and all our art has its image in the Mass that would lack authority were it not descended from savage ceremonies taught amid what perils and by what spirits to naked savages."[53] Yeats alludes approvingly to Heinrich Heine, whose *Shakespeare's Maidens and Women* (1839) posited a pagan antecedent for *Macbeth*'s witches: the Valkyries of Norse mythology.[54] "The old images, the old emotions," he writes, "awakened again to overwhelming life, like the gods Heine tells of, by the belief and passion of some new soul, are the only masterpieces."[55] In a move characteristic of Yeats's prose, these "old images [and] emotions" are then framed in religious terms: "The soul which may not obscure or change its form can yet receive those passions and symbols of antiquity."[56] What I want to emphasize here is the epistemological distance between Yeats and Eliot. Eliot maintains a dramatic tradition whose changing forms nevertheless respond to an original, primordial impulse. He posits a dramatic bloodline as old as mankind itself, but he doesn't offer a religious explanation for this impulse. Rather, by alluding to Darwin, Henry Maine, and Edward Burnett Tylor, he aligns his hypothesis with the newly fashionable sciences of evolutionary biology and cultural anthropology. Yeats, on the other hand, has no qualms about folding archetypal criticism into his eclectic, Neoplatonic philosophy of the soul, and while Eliot asks us to see the rhythmic power of

Shakespeare as evidence for a kind of cultural or psychological continuity, Yeats's take on rhythm is firmly implicated in visionary metaphysics. This can be easily demonstrated by referring to the passage on rhythm in "The Symbolism of Poetry":

> The purpose of rhythm, it has always seemed to me, is to prolong the moment of contemplation, the moment when we are both asleep and awake, which is the one moment of creation, by hushing us with an alluring monotony, while it holds us waking by variety, to keep us in that state of perhaps real trance, in which the mind is unfolded in symbols. If certain sensitive persons listen persistently to the ticking of a watch . . . they fall into the hypnotic trance; and rhythm is but the ticking of a watch made softer . . . while the patterns of the artist are but the monotonous flash woven to take the eyes in a subtler enchantment. . . . I have been swept, when in more profound meditation beyond all memory but of those things that came from beyond the threshold of waking life.[57]

Thus ever the occultist. Yeats, in fact, did not see much similarity between himself and Eliot. In his introduction to *The Oxford Book of Modern Verse* (1936), he wrote critically of Eliot's earlier poetry, calling him an "Alexander Pope, working without apparent imagination."[58] "Nor can I put the Eliot of these poems among those that descend from Shakespeare and the translators of the Bible," he adds; "I think of him as satirist rather than poet. . . . Not until 'The Hollow Men' and 'Ash Wednesday,' where he is helped by the short lines, and in the dramatic poems where his remarkable sense of actor, character, scene, sweeps him away, is there rhythmical animation."[59]

I am arguing here for a continuity of thinking about Shakespeare, about dramatic ritual, and about literary tradition, in the writings of Yeats and Eliot, but it is interesting to note how both men detached the other from a literary tradition extending back to Shakespeare and beyond. For Eliot, Yeats's weird otherworldliness constituted an unknowable Irishness, while Yeats disapproved of Eliot for producing "his effects by a rejection of all rhythms and metaphors used by the more popular romantics rather than by the discovery of his own."[60] In any case, both men pushed back against a classicist's narrow understanding of Shakespeare's sources. Shakespeare's fool, Eliot has it, is an English shaman, while Yeats, in "At Stratford-on-Avon," approves of the new pictorial method for staging Shakespeare since it "remember[s] the time when, as my nurse used to tell me, herons built their nests in old men's beards!"[61] As we have seen, Eliot's method is anthropological, while Yeats's is mystical and esoteric. When, in April 1901, Yeats wrote in a letter to Lady Gregory that he was "getting deeper into Shakespeare's mystery than ever before,"[62] the "mystery" was not the plays' authorship, the identity of the Dark Lady, or the "lost years," but the question of Shakespeare's relationship to the supernatural world governing artistic creation and reception. What we are witnessing here is the overlapping of two phenomena of the late nineteenth and early twentieth centuries—the Occult Revival and the impact of cultural anthropology—which can both be related to the decline of orthodox religious faith in Western Europe. Both galvanized literary modernism, and both played major parts in the Irish Revival.[63]

POINTS OF CONTACT: MODERNISM, MAGIC, AND MYTH CRITICISM

Yeats's Shakespeare, I have argued throughout this book, is fundamentally a product of fin-de-siècle Irish cultural nationalism. However, he is also distinctly "modern" in the sense that the discourses within which Yeats implicates him reject Victorian norms of theatrical production and biographical character critique. It is in this sense that Yeats's Shakespeare parallels the modernist Shakespeare and provides a way of understanding the Irish Literary Revival as a cultural phenomenon with an aesthetics akin to literary modernism. Perhaps the most significant source of cross-pollination, however, is the "cultural turn" away from racial determinism. For instance, Matthew Arnold's "On the Study of Celtic Literature" (an essay that precipitated Yeats's first public deployment of Shakespeare) constitutes a discursive reorientation of the philological inquiry into national literatures. Although Arnold employs terms that smack of the racial "sciences"—"Teutonic," "Cymric," "Celt," etc.—his argument that the study of English letters reveals a synthesis of Celtic and Teutonic elements is made without reference to somatic traits. Instead, he situates the historical process of assimilation in the cultural realm with reference to literature, sensibility, and social history in broad brushstrokes. As I have discussed in chapter 1, this turn to culture is what permitted Yeats, in 1897, to rework Arnold's hypothesis into a valorization of the "Celtic element," and to claim Shakespeare for the Irish and for all other "ancient" nations. In terms of the nineteenth century's obsession with Shakespeare's racial pedigree, Arnold's essay signifies a watershed moment. Moreover, as Richard Halpern makes clear in *Shakespeare among the Moderns*, the turn from racial to cultural hermeneutics set the stage for the "modernist Shakespeare," and indeed for twentieth-century approaches to Shakespeare, which are "fundamentally mediated by a primitivist discourse whose disciplinary language is anthropology—even when, as in the case of the New Criticism, this influence is not direct or immediately apparent."[64] While this "discourse of primitivism," explains Halpern, "distinguishes the modernist reception of Shakespeare from the late-Victorian one,"[65] "the practice of reading him through an anthropological lens actually began with the Victorians, who were less concerned with situating Shakespeare in a non-Western context than with establishing his racial pedigree within the European family."[66] It is, I think, through this "primitivist discourse" that we can account for the similarities between Yeats's and Eliot's Shakespeares while distinguishing between literary modernism and Yeatsian cultural nationalism. During the late Victorian period, writes Halpern, "the emphasis would shift from racial to cultural or ritualist explanations [of Shakespeare], and from a mainly European arena to a genuinely global one."[67] "Shakespeare criticism of the early twentieth century," he continues, "was often influenced by the same array of anthropological sources that fertilized high modernism in general: the Cambridge Hellenists . . . and comparative mythologists such as J. G. Frazer."[68] The influence of Frazer's groundbreaking work, *The Golden Bough: A Study in Magic and Religion*, is well documented, and readers of Eliot's seminal poem "The Waste Land," for instance, are familiar with its impact in the realm of avant-garde literature. First printed in two volumes in 1890, the third edition was published in twelve volumes between 1906 and 1915. Frazer offered a totalizing narrative of human religious behavior developing in stages from magic, through religious belief, to science. Famously, *A Golden Bough* also posits a universal myth of the dying and reviving god.

The emergence of Frazer's paradigm in Shakespeare criticism can be found in Wyndham Lewis's *The Lion and the Fox: The Role of the Hero in the Plays of Shakespeare* (1927). Lewis rests his claims about Shakespeare's kings and fools, and about the archaic origins of tragedy, firmly on the shoulders of the scholarly ritualists, citing, for example, F. M Cornford's *The Origin of Attic Comedy* (1914), H. M. Chadwick's *The Heroic Age* (1912), Walter Leaf's *Homer and History* (1915), Robert Lowie's *Primitive Society* (1920), A. B. Ellis's *The Ewe-Speaking Peoples of the Slave Coast* (1890), and most frequently, Frazer: "The function of the king is curiously bound up with the idea of sacrifice,"[69] he asserts at the heart of his exposition; "[o]verwhelming evidence to this effect is provided by Sir James Frazer in his wonderful series of books, *The Golden Bough*."[70] Lewis's analysis of the role of the king adheres firmly to Frazer's thought, and particularly to the concept of the king as the earthly representative of a god whose death expunges malevolent spiritual forces and whose resurrection ensures continued fertility and societal well-being. Lewis's exposition begins with a historical narrative about the establishment of European monarchy:

> The feudal European king was essentially not a patriarch, but a stranger and an *enemy*. The king and his nobles were usually of another race to the subject, their mastery beginning in physical conquest. . . . These russian or anglo-saxon serfs had their *individual* stranger (a small personal god) quartered on them, giving a personal form to all the anonymous outer power of the universe. . . . He was their *enemy*, a representative of the outer hostile world, between whom and themselves the terms of propitiation and sacrifice had been systematized. It was a pagan, human arrangement, and naturally with the Reformation it disappeared.[71]

The divinity of kings, he argues, was a phenomenon established bottom-up by conquered races. It developed from the racial difference between peasant-ry and nobility and rested upon "[t]he superstitious dread that the primitive man has always felt for a stranger, endowing him with supernatural attrib-utes."[72] From here, Lewis expands his thinking beyond European borders to consider parallels among, for instance, the "thonga kings," "the former kings of Dakomi," the Aztecs, the scourging of Christ (which Frazer considered a Roman Saturnalian ritual), and a number of tribes examined by the ethnogra-pher A. B. Ellis. In the society of the African thonga especially, Lewis finds correlatives for Shakespeare's clowns and court jesters in the form of the king's herald, whose "duty it is to appear before the king's door every morn-ing and to exalt the exploits of the ruler's ancestors, which is followed by vigorous disparagement of the present incumbent,"[73] and the "public vituper-ator," "who may hurl the most offensive insults at anyone in the country, from the king down."[74] Lewis builds his case for an anthropological reading of Shakespeare's kings incrementally and arrives at a Frazerian understand-ing of the king's role in Shakespeare's drama: "He was, from the moment he entered the arena, the bull to be attacked and sacrificed if possible."[75] If the king is a sacrificial other—both at court and on the stage—then Shake-speare's role as a playwright must be understood in functionalist terms as "a public executioner."[76] The cathartic element in tragedy therefore derives from a primitive, superstitious psychology, and so "[t]he innocent-looking, compassionate representation of an agony and death, like that of Othello, with its catharsis by means of tears and pity, is thus . . . revealed as some-thing else. It is a show of the same nature as a public execution."[77] As a synthesis of ritualist scholarship, Lewis's book deftly reveals the modernist turn toward "the primitive" and expands the discourse beyond a nativist, nationalist reading of Shakespeare. As such, one effect of this modernist Shakespeare is to weaken English cultural capital. In *Shakespeare among the Moderns*, Halpern argues precisely this, noting how "Lewis intentionally disrupts any sense on the part of the English that they 'own' Shakespeare as a distinctively national patrimony."[78] "Lewis's 'international' Shakespeare," he continues, "mirrors the early modernists' own sense of cosmopolitanism and disrupts the Victorians' desire to hold some kind of racial or national 'property' in Shakespeare."[79] Lewis's thesis has its weaknesses. It proceeds both inductively—in his analysis of kingship—and impressionistically: for instance, he later suggests that Falstaff "has a tincture of the *shaman* about him."[80] Certainly, its totalizing approach and scant attention to Shake-speare's immediate cultural context mean that it does not hold up to twenty first-century critical paradigms. However, its significance in terms of the history of Shakespeare reception cannot be overstated. Together, Lewis and Eliot constructed an international playwright working within an archaic tradi-tion of myth, ritual, and superstition, setting the stage for the twentieth century's Shakespearean structuralist schools of myth theory and archetypal criticism.

Nowhere in Yeats's work do we find such an elaborate reading of Shakespeare in this context.[81] However, he alludes to *The Golden Bough* in "Sailing to Byzantium" and references it at greater length in "The Ten Principal Upanishads" (1937):

> When I was young we talked much of tradition, and those emotional young men, Francis Thompson, Lionel Johnson, John Gray, found it in Christianity. But now that *The Golden Bough* has made Christianity look modern and fragmentary we study Confucius with Ezra Pound, or like T. S. Eliot find in Christianity a convenient symbolism for some older or newer thought, or say with Henry Airbubble, "I am a member of the Church of England but not a Christian." Shree Purohit Swami and I offer to some young man seeking, like Shakespeare, Dante, Milton, vast sentiments and generalisations, the oldest philosophical compositions of the world. . . . European scholarship with many doubts has fixed their date, or the date of the most important, at a little before 600 B.C. when Buddha was born, but Indian scholarship prefers a far earlier date.[82]

This passage is significant for a number of reasons, not least of which is its assertion that Shakespeare (like Dante and Milton) was a truth seeker, a religious writer in the sense of an artist exploring and trying to express a unified philosophical vision of the world. At the time of writing, Yeats was also putting the finishing touches to the second edition of *A Vision* (1937), his own poetic, esoteric treatise on metaphysics, the life of the soul, and the cyclicality of historical epochs. The importance of *The Golden Bough*, claims Yeats, was its impact on Christianity, or rather its impact on those who sought to find "tradition" in Christianity. *The Golden Bough*, of course, argued for an anthropological rather than a theological approach to Christianity (provoking a scandalized reception), but Yeats clearly regards it as clearing the way for the study of more ancient sacred texts: Confucius for Pound, the *Upanishads* for Yeats. Eliot's response, meanwhile, was merely to use Christianity for "a convenient symbolism." In "A General Introduction for my Work," Yeats distinguishes himself from the "modern man, *The Golden Bough* and *Human Personality* in his head,"[83] since a "modern man" can read, repeat, and even believe St. Patrick's Creed "without a thought of the historic Christ, or ancient Judea, or of anything subject to historical conjecture and shifting evidence."[84] "I repeat it," he continues, "and think of 'the Self' in the Upanishads."[85] The distinction I am attempting to make here concerns Frazer's reception among the literati most frequently associated with a modernist school of poetics. Despite its secularist teleology (man's primitive belief in magic leads ultimately to a scientific perspective), *The Golden Bough* helped make the case for Yeats's syncretic religious beliefs, which at this point in his life synthesized East and West in a highly idiosyn-cratic hodgepodge of Buddhism, Vedanta, Rosicrucianism, Caballah, and Hermeticism. Read against the grain, and treated as a sort of hermetic text, *The Golden Bough* claims to reveal the kind of universal myth to which Yeats was attracted on the basis of his Neoplatonic weltanschauung. It dis-misses Christianity as a mere reiteration of a far more ancient and universal archetype, one which Yeats was inclined to import into his religious bricol-age: the dying god and his resurrection maps onto Yeats's vision of the soul's incarnation, and of the gyre-driven cyclicality of civilizations' rise and fall.

Why does Yeats reference Shakespeare here at all? Dante and Milton are easier to account for as religious systematizers. Certainly, Yeats did not regard the three poets as similar types: while he places Shakespeare at phase 20 in *A Vision*, Dante occupies phase 17, for example. Milton was much admired by Yeats, but situated on the wrong side of the epistemic rupture which Yeats saw in England following the rise of Puritanism.[86] However, the prose is pretty clear; Shakespeare was a truth seeker. But in order for Shake-speare to fit here, among Milton and Dante, Yeats must be suggesting that the man's works reveal a unified metaphysical vision. The "Shakespeare Myth" he proposed in "At Stratford-on-Avon," it should be remembered, also had a certain Frazerian quality to it: "a wise man who was blind from very wisdom, and an empty man who thrust him from his place."[87] The tendency to find unifying mythological patterns in the fabric of archaic litera-tures—and especially in Shakespeare's works—is one of the hallmarks of twentieth-century criticism: a direct line can be drawn from Frazer and the Cambridge ritualists to the schools of myth and archetypal criticism. Psycho-analytic criticism also belongs to this family tree. Frequently, such studies profess the objectivity of scholarly inquiry but hint at something altogether more mysterious in terms of the mechanism by which archetypal elements are transmitted and the conclusions that can be drawn from the observation of such patterns. Robert Graves thus claimed that his *The White Goddess* (1948) boldly finished what Frazer had been too timid to complete, isolating a matriarchal divinity whose worship was central to Western mythology and positing this as the skeleton key that unlocked its mythological symbolism. In 1991, Ted Hughes published his voluminous *Shakespeare and the God-dess of Complete Being*, a book that cites Yeats twice in its series of epi-graphs. In fact, in the first of these epigraphs (deserving a page all to itself), Hughes transcribes the "Shakespeare Myth" passage from "At Stratford-on-Avon." Tellingly, in a 1990 letter to Donya Feuer, a director at the Royal Dramatic Theatre in Stockholm, Hughes voiced anxiety about the nature of his thesis and its reception: "I hope I don't seem to be arguing that the living complex of these plays is nothing but the allegorical staging of the private theology of an eccentric, syncretic Occult Neoplatonist."[88] Neither Graves nor Hughes, almost fifty years apart, were willing to present their works as

revelatory or visionary texts in a religious sense, but Hughes' tome opens
with the words of a "syncretic Occult Neoplatonist," W. B. Yeats. What I am
suggesting here is that the school of myth criticism that grew out of comparative mythology occupies an epistemological borderland between empiricism
and spiritualism which recalls, perhaps, the origins of literary interpretation
in the exegesis of sacred texts. Yeats's "Shakespeare Myth" proceeds from
the mind of an occultist turned to consider the Shakespeare corpus. Furthermore, read in the contexts of "At Stratford-on-Avon" as a whole, and Yeats's
contemporaneous involvement with the Celtic Mysteries and the new Irish
drama, it is clear that his "Shakespeare Myth" derives from a unique cluster
of interests and activities. Yeats's Shakespeare, I contend, is sui generis.

Yeats's approach to Shakespeare in the 1890s and 1900s resembles both
Eliot's and Lewis's in terms of the proximity of its revivalist tropes of folk
and faery to those of the "primitivist discourse" outlined above. Initially,
Shakespeare is a folklorist. Glossing the "Pooka" character in *Irish Fairy and
Folk Tales* (1888), Yeats explains how "[s]peculative persons consider him
the forefather of Shakespeare's Puck";[89] "Homer, Aeschylus, Sophocles,
Shakespeare . . . were little more than folk-lorists with musical tongues,"[90] he
writes in 1893. Then, coinciding with the period of Yeats's involvement with
the Celtic Mysteries and an incipient Irish National Theatre, Shakespeare is a
purveyor of rituals and, to the degree that Yeats associates him with symbolism, a magician. In "The Symbolism of Poetry," he cites *Timon of Athens* to
show how "[a]ll sounds, all forms . . . call down among us certain disembodied powers, whose footsteps over our hearts we call emotions."[91] Eliot and
Lewis see archaic psychological rituals at work in Shakespeare's archetypal
characters, his blank verse, and the tragic form itself. So does Yeats. But for
Yeats, Shakespeare's kings and nobles represent ideal forms that the playwright accessed through a spiritualist creative technology: an imagination
attuned to the life of the unseen world. Completing his demolition of the
Dowden thesis in "At Stratford-on-Avon," for example, he concludes that
"Shakespeare watched Henry V. not indeed as he watched the greater souls
in the visionary procession, but cheerfully, as he watches some grand spirited
horse."[92] But it is in the larger context of a profound anxiety about modernity
that the resemblances between these Shakespeares can be seen to fit clearly
into a larger discourse, and through which we can gain a better understanding
of the correlation between the Revival and the aesthetics of high modernism.

SHAKESPEARE AMONG THE MODERNS: WYNDHAM LEWIS
AND G. WILSON KNIGHT

One key point of contact between Lewis's thinking in *The Role of the Hero*
and Yeats's in "At Stratford-on-Avon" is the "failed" king of the history

cycle: Richard II. In the section of his book beginning with a chapter titled "Shakespeare a Feminine Genius," Lewis searches for the elusive "gentle Will," so joining the ranks of countless scholars, poets, and amateurs who claim to have distilled the man from the works. He begins with a refreshingly anti-bardolatrous statement of intent: "There is no intention here of representing Shakespeare as a philosopher, or as one of those great generalizing minds that fecundate the world from time to time with new and dazzling principles of truth."[93] No intentional fallacy is at work here, it seems. Instead of "Shakespeare as a philosopher," however, Lewis gives us Shakespeare as "a sort of feminine genius."[94] "I propose, then," he reiterates a little later, "to consider Shakespeare's attitude to the world somewhat as that of a woman."[95] Shakespeare is female, or rather, Shakespeare's attitude to the world is a "feminine" one, which means to Lewis that he disapproves of worldly action and prefers contemplation. The larger project here is to oppose Shakespeare's worldview to that of Machiavelli, and to align him instead with Montaigne, who shares "the same curiosity and discouragement, wonderful flexibility of expression, passionate friendship for another man, humour and skepticism."[96] "Both are critics of action," he explains, "but Shakespeare paradoxically criticizes it by showing you its adepts in *action*. . . . All Shakespeare's work can be regarded as a criticism of action and of the agent-principle."[97] Shakespeare's "feminine genius" is explicitly dramatized in *Hamlet*, but it is evident in his "execution" of the tragic protagonists: "When the misfortune arrives, they automatically become Shakespeare."[98] Within this schema, Richard II demands special consideration:

> As a good example of this Richard II.'s well-known speech when he finds that he has lost his kingdom can be cited. This second Plantagenet, who up till then has shown in his harangues in the play no sign of especial intelligence, has been only crossly harsh and pompous by turns, lets drop a series of remarks that certainly no Plantagenet would ever have made[.][99]

Lewis seizes on the peculiarity of Richard's monologue in act 3, scene 2—transcribing the entire speech—and then accounts for the uncharacteristic remarks as "the irruption of the mind of the author into the midst of the shallow events it was his task to depict."[100] "For God's sake, let us sit upon the ground, / And tell sad stories of the death of kings,"[101] cries Richard/Will; this, per Lewis, is precisely the task of Shakespeare, Executioner.

Almost thirty years prior, of course, Yeats had also singled out Richard in "At-Stratford-on-Avon" as the centerpiece of his critical engagement with Edward Dowden.[102] His assessment of Richard is remarkably similar: "I cannot believe that Shakespeare looked on his Richard II. with any but sympathetic eyes, understanding indeed how ill-fitted he was to be King, at a certain moment of history, but understanding that he was lovable and full of capricious fancy."[103] In promoting Richard over Dowden's hero, Henry V, Yeats was of course taking a stand not just against Dowden, but against Victorian academe and its prevailing Shakespearean hermeneutic. "To suppose that Shakespeare preferred the men who deposed his King is to suppose that Shakespeare judged men with the eyes of a Municipal Councillor weighing the merits of a Town Clerk," writes Yeats; "He saw . . . in Richard II. the defeat that awaits all, whether they be Artist or Saint, who find themselves where men ask of them a rough energy and have nothing to give but some contemplative virtue."[104] It is at this point in his Shakespeare essay that Yeats folds his exegesis into a larger narrative of social decline, positioning the Renaissance as a watershed when the "courtly and saintly ideals of the Middle Ages were fading, and the practical ideals of the modern age had begun to threaten the unuseful dome of the sky."[105] As we have seen, despite fluctuations in his thinking about the situation of the Renaissance on the cusp of an incipient modernity, Yeats's Shakespeare belongs to the older "Merry England," which "was fading, and yet . . . was not so faded that the poets could not watch the procession of the world with that untroubled sympathy for men as they are."[106] Similarly, in the opening pages of *The Lion and The Fox*, Lewis positions Shakespeare "with one foot in the old world of chivalrous romance and the other in the new one of commerce and science."[107] Yeats's Richard also deserved especial consideration since he appeared in possession of the visionary sensibility of "Artist and Saint."[108] Almost forty years later, in 1937, Yeats wrote to Dorothy Wellesley and wondered, "Did Shakespeare in *Richard II* discover poetic reverie?"[109] I have argued in these pages that Yeats's Richard II is a product of Irish cultural nationalism. Although Yeats shared with certain fellow moderns an antipathy toward the popular tastes and mores of contemporary society, his belief in the cyclicality of historical epochs meant that the Irish Revival signified more than the restoration of an indigenous literary tradition and an accumulation of national cultural capital. It was a watershed moment in of itself. In the early years of the twentieth century, Yeats plotted a European spiritual revival whose epicenter was Ireland. Further, as we have seen in the previous chapter, later Shakespeare responds to its creator's disappointment with Ireland's cultural provincialism and the political marginalizing of the Anglo-Irish.

So, both Yeats and Wyndham Lewis singled out Richard II in their interpretations, and both stressed that Richard's failure in the affairs of state should be measured alongside the elegiac beauty of his utterance. Moreover, both men used the example of Richard in their construction of Shakespeares embedded in larger ideological critiques of modernity. Lewis, for instance, characterizes Elizabethan drama as "unexpectedly wild, providing the renaissance with its primitive antiquity,"[110] thus invoking a primitivist discourse, before asserting that "no English audience to-day can get any meaning or pleasure out of it."[111] Contemporary audiences, claims Lewis, are "not so much civilized as fatigued, stereotyped and inert,"[112] prompting the following polemical turn:

> A stiffness, partly of the old puritan pasteboard, and partly of age is beneath most english shirt-fronts, whatever the physiological age of the wearer, at an average play; or else its wearer is relaxed to some snobbish decay. The mind of the same playgoer has been drilled out of, and watered down from, other franknesses as well. It is no longer a possible earth for such wild seeds as the tragedies of Webster or of Shakespeare. At the most the moneyed crust of our time affects a pedantically cynical wildness that is often whorish enough, but so overlaid with a sweetening of sentiment . . . that its representative is able to rival in repulsiveness the miltonic prude.[113]

Contemporary English audiences have lost the wild joy and primitive energy of their Elizabethan predecessors. Indeed, Lewis continues, it is "because they [the English] were so very near to a savage condition, very fresh to life . . . that this great art occurred."[114] This is a fascinating reiteration of Yeats's earlier writing, and (as we have seen) it is precisely on the basis of this premodern sensibility that Yeats was able to draw the line from Shakespeare's original audiences to the rural Irish and so to de-Anglicize England's most potent cultural icon. However, it would be misleading to map Lewis's Shakespeare entirely onto Yeats's. Lewis's larger argument is that Elizabethan drama staged the "machiavellian nightmare"[115] taking place in the Italian states during the Renaissance, which the English watched with a kind of wondrous stupefaction. "It was because that vivid and dramatic life was not going on to the same extent off the stage in England that it occurred on the stage so naturally,"[116] he explains. In "At Stratford," we should remember, Yeats claimed that English history might have fueled an indigenous mythology like that of the ancient Greeks had it not been for the "Italian influence."[117] These are points of contact and divergence: Yeats found the survivors of a cultural catastrophe in Galway, Sligo, Leinster, and Connacht; Lewis saw only decay. Like Yeats, Lewis emphasized Shakespeare's dispassionate nature, his reputation as a quiet man who, to use Yeats's terms, "kept out of quarrels in a quarrelsome age."[118] In their analysis of Shakespeare and the Elizabethan age, then, Yeats and Lewis shared discursive traits, tropes, and topoi. But writing almost thirty years before Lewis, Yeats's Shakespeare served an Irish nationalist agenda, and it is precisely this salvific nature of Shakespeare that distinguishes him from the modernist Shakespeare.

I want to return to Richard Halpern's study of *Shakespeare among the Moderns* to clarify this point. Modernists produced a "Shakespeare lodged firmly in the twentieth century,"[119] and their construction of Shakespeare is particularly notable for the "presence" of what he calls "historical allegory." Modern-dress productions of Shakespeare, for instance, playfully violate the distance between past and present, and so while "anachronism naively collapses two different historical periods by absorbing one into the other, historical allegory willfully violates distinctions without obliterating them. . . . Historical allegory is anachronism raised to the level of policy."[120] However, he continues, "[m]odernist historical allegory does not light on just any period with equal interest; the late sixteenth and early seventeenth centuries offer it a privileged image of cultural decline. . . . Modernism's historical allegory is not a salvific project but a juxtaposition of losses; only in the early modern period does it find a sufficiently dark reflection of its own catastrophes."[121] Similarly, theorizing the modernist paradigm shift in Shakespeare studies, Hugh Grady indicates how Eliot and his fellow poet-scholars "celebrated a defunct past somehow recreated through art and literature in the present" in response to a "capitalist civilization [they viewed] as empty, bureaucratic, and soulless."[122] Yeats's attention to the Renaissance clearly fits the bill in its focus on "cultural decline," but as I have argued in this book, Shakespeare's construction in the context of Irish revivalism implicates him not in a "juxtaposition of losses," but precisely as part of a "salvific project": the restoration in Ireland of a culture possessing "unity of being."

Beyond Shakespeare, there are greater points of contact between Wyndham Lewis and W. B. Yeats, many of which are enumerated by Peter L. Caracciolo and Paul Edwards in their article, "In Fundamental Agreement: Yeats and Wyndham Lewis."[123] As Caracciolo and Edwards make clear, Lewis and Yeats corresponded and admired each other's work; famously, *A Vision* references Lewis's art as an analogue for its "stylistic arrangement of experience comparable to the cubes in the drawing of Wyndham Lewis."[124] Despite differences in "style and ethos . . . [o]n closer inspection Yeats and Lewis prove to have a surprising amount in common."[125] They continue:

> Yeats's feudalistic Irish Nationalism, mysticism and eccentric historicism are the antithesis of the younger painter's cosmopolitan internationalism, anti-historicism and mechano-morphic vision of humanity [yet] [t]he cultural vision of both extended way beyond Europe and they shared the view that a willed struggle with a contradictory version of the self was the basis of achievement in the arts. Each valued his apparent opposite at crucial moments.[126]

"In Fundamental Agreement" makes the case for a philosophical correspondence between Lewis and Yeats in the 1920s and 1930s stemming from an antipathy toward theories positing the preeminence of phenomenal reality and extending to Lewis's intellectual flirtation with spiritualism. Lewis's position on the possible existence of a "spirit world" was ambivalent, but Caracciolo and Edwards point to instances where Lewis seems to endorse the kind of neoromanticism familiar from Yeats's writing. "In *Time and Western Man*" (1927), for instance, "Lewis would affirm that 'If you say that creative art is a spell, a talisman, an incantation—that it is *magic* in short . . . I believe you would be correctly describing it. That the artist uses and manipulates a supernatural power seems very likely.'"[127] Certainly, as we have seen, there are further correspondences in their interpretations of Shakespeare. I am arguing, however, that while analogous topoi in their writing on Shakespeare indicate both writers' profound anxieties about contemporary "modern" culture, ultimately the Irish nationalist context defines Yeats's Shakespeare, and here there are some significant points of departure. *The Lion and the Fox* closes with a series of short chapters scornfully dismantling Matthew Arnold's Celt/Saxon dichotomy: "How this myth has been built up is very curious," he begins; "[i]f you wish to study its evolution you cannot do better than go to Arnold's *Celtic Literature*. There you get this delusion presented in perhaps its craziest and most magnificent form."[128] Lewis blasts Arnold for constructing a false racial ontology in order to support his case against the "Philistine." The "Celt," he concludes, is "an absurdity."[129] In a passage in *Time and Western Man*, Lewis continues his attack on "Celticness" as an authentic ethnic identity: "The romantic persons who go picking about in the Aran Islands . . . for genuine human 'antiques,' are today on a wild-goose chase; because the sphinx of the Past, in the person of some elder dug out of such remote neighbourhoods, will at length, when he has found his tongue, probably commence addressing them in the vernacular of the *Daily Mail*."[130] Here Lewis ridicules the entire revivalist enterprise, at least in its first flush. As we have seen, Yeats's Shakespeare was constructed around the turn of the century in the pages of revivalist periodicals and in the context of a larger discourse affirming the survival of an archaic folk sensibility in locations like the Aran Islands. Although Caracciolo and Edwards point to a "fundamental agreement" between Yeats and Lewis, the correspondences they indicate derive primarily from Lewis's approval of Yeats's later work. Yeats's earlier writing produced at best a kind of critical ambivalence from Lewis, and following Yeats's death, Lewis wrote a "seemingly ungenerous obituary that shows his continuing ambivalence about the early work."[131] So, Lewis and Yeats constructed similar Shakespeares, but they did so at different times and for different purposes: the modernist and the revivalist Shakespeare, it seems, were not in fundamental agreement.

A likelier candidate for a Yeatsian Shakespearean is G. Wilson Knight, the prolific academic and producer whose first manuscript was carried personally to Oxford University Press by T. S. Eliot. There is no evidence for Yeats having read Knight's work, but the hermeneutic Knight advances in books like *The Wheel of Fire* (1930) reveals so many Yeatsian parallels that I would be remiss in omitting him from this analysis of the similarities between Yeats's revivalist Shakespeare and the one constructed by Eliot's modernist coterie. It is by way of a coda, then, that I want to briefly compare the two and to demonstrate Shakespeare's early contribution to a modern body of knowledge about Shakespeare. In this case the mutual source is not

Frazer and the new ritualism, but the influence of the French symbolists. Knight's thematic approach to Shakespeare's plays is utterly antihistoricist, but fundamentally rooted in the modern attention to poetic imagery that reached its apotheosis in the "New Criticism" of Cleanth Brooks and his *Well-Wrought Urn* (1947). [132] In the opening chapter of *The Wheel of Fire*, "On the Principles of Shakespeare Interpretation," Knight carefully defines what he calls "interpretation" and distinguishes it from "criticism": "Criticism is a judgment of vision; interpretation a reconstruction of vision." [133] It is the task of the interpreter to piece together Shakespeare's "vision" from the plays' "atmosphere," which is to say that each play possesses a unique "atmosphere" created by "a set of correspondences which relate to each other independently of the time-sequence of the story." [134] Setting out to rescue Shakespeare from centuries of plot-based critiques, Knight asks us to focus instead on the "spatial" rather than "temporal" qualities of the plays, and on symbols rather than characters, because "with Shakespeare a purely spiritual atmosphere interpenetrates the action . . . and where a direct personal symbol growing out of the dominating atmosphere is actualized, it may be a supernatural being, as the Ghost, symbol of the death-theme in *Hamlet*, or the Weird Sisters, symbols of the evil in *Macbeth*." [135] As with Yeats, Knight's prose mysticizes as much as it clarifies Shakespeare. "The Spatial," for instance, is defined as "the omnipresent and mysterious reality brooding motionless over and within the play's movement," [136] which lends the play its "metaphysical significance." [137] It is the play's "spiritual quality" [138] that determines its significance and requires that "interpretation must be metaphysical rather than ethical." [139] The interpreter "should regard each play as a visionary whole, close-knit in personification, atmospheric suggestion, and direct poetic-symbolism," [140] and it is precisely this "visionary whole" that accounts for the longevity of Shakespeare's appeal: "The soul-life of a Shakespeare play is an enduring power of divine worth," writes Knight; "[i]ts perennial fire is as mysterious, as near and yet as far, as that of the sun, and like the sun, it burns on while generations pass." [141] As with Wyndham Lewis's Frazerian Shakespeare, such tropes edge toward a Yeatsian mysticism, and it is left up to T. S. Eliot, in his introduction, to throw some cold water over the "perennial fire": "I do not think that Mr. Wilson Knight . . . has fallen into the error of presenting the work of Shakespeare as a series of mystical treatises in cryptogram, to be filed away once the cipher is read; poetry is poetry, and the surface is as marvelous as the core." [142] Ultimately, Knight's hermeneutic rejects a range of conventional critical approaches to Shakespeare's plot, characters, and ethical intentions; in the case of the latter, Shakespeare's intentions are rendered unknowable on the basis of a neoromantic, visionary conception of the creative process: "'Intentions' belong to the plane of intellect and memory: the swifter consciousness that awakes in poetic composition touches subtleties and heights and depths unknowable by intellect and intractable to memory."[143] Knight understands the process of poetic composition as one of marrying "spiritual" elements (i.e., symbols and images) to "material" events (characters, settings, and plot events) to form what he calls a "union between 'earth' and 'heaven'";[144] however, it is the vision that comes first. The poet then finds material vehicles with which to ground the vision: "It seems . . . that a great poet must, if he is to forgo nothing of concreteness and humanity, lose himself in contemplation of an actual tale or an actual event in order to find himself in supreme vision; otherwise he will tend to philosophy, to the divine element unmated to the earthly . . . the final poetic result is always a mystery."[145]

Although this is a somewhat cursory overview of Knight's approach, it is enough to serve my purpose here, and anyone familiar with Yeats's prose should immediately see the parallels I am foregrounding. Knight constructs Shakespeare as a visionary symbolist and the act of creation as a form of what Yeats called "poetic reverie." His approach to interpretation is antimaterialist and antihistoricist, stressing instead the sensitive interpreter's ability to sift through the play's figurative elements to reconstruct the singular poetic vision. In the 1930s, as Yeats explored the concept of "tragic joy," he wrote how the "heroes of Shakespeare convey to us through their looks, or through the metaphorical patterns of their speech, the sudden enlargement of their vision, their ecstasy at the approach of death."[146] An enlarged vision conveyed in metaphorical patterns seems to echo Knight's idea of a play. However, again context is key: "I have heard Lady Gregory say, rejecting some play in the modern manner sent to the Abbey Theatre, 'Tragedy must be a joy to the man who dies,'"[147] Yeats continues. An "enlarged vision" here once more signifies archetypal, ideal forms stored, as he would have it, in the world's memory, the *anima mundi*. Tragedy is not concerned with an individual's pain at a specific moment. It is "a timeless pattern";[148] "the rhythm is old and familiar,"[149] writes Yeats, and for the audience, the "imagination must dance, must be carried beyond feeling into the aboriginal ice."[150] Unlike Yeats, then, Knight's principles of interpretation do not engage directly with the existence of an atemporal, supersensory realm, though his signifiers dance around it. For instance, in *The Mutual Flame: On the Sonnets and the Phoenix and the Turtle*, Knight discusses the phoenix as a symbol of transcendence. "Whenever poetry has vigour, the Phoenix may come"[151] he writes, lending agency to the symbol itself: the phoenix comes, seemingly of its own volition, drawn from some unnamed realm of archetypal images by the power of the poetry itself. Tellingly, Knight then notes how the phoenix "lives today [in] W. B. Yeats' exquisite poem to *His Phoenix*."[152]

As we have seen throughout this book, Yeats's Shakespeare was constructed primarily during the 1890s and early 1900s, and many of the essays written during that time, collected as *Ideas of Good and Evil* (1903), implicate Shakespeare within nationalist, symbolist, and occultist contexts. So, in "Magic," Yeats claims a magical function for symbols, while simultaneously dismissing artistic intentionalism: "I cannot now think symbols less than the greatest of all powers whether they are used consciously by the masters of magic, or unconsciously by their successors, the poet, the musician and the artist."[153] And in "The Philosophy of Shelley's Poetry" we find a similar credo: "Any one who has any experience of any mystical state of the soul knows how there float up in the mind profound symbols, whose meaning . . . one does not perhaps understand for years."[154] In "At Stratford-on-Avon" Yeats demands that we judge Shakespeare neither by mimetic standards of realism, nor by the "ethical" approach. Shakespeare's plots are inspired by the activities of the "Daimons" and constitute reiterations of mythic patterns. Shakespeare's characters' actions are "no more than the expression of their personalities,"[155] and to critique them in practical, worldly terms is an error since "a man's business may at times be revelation, and not reformation."[156] In their mutual rejection of Victorian Shakespeare criticism—particularly biography and ethical character critique—and in their directions for staging Shakespeare, both Yeats and Knight are "modern." Clearly, too, Knight owes much to the symbolist school and to the elevation of the image in modernist poetry.

Knight's critical prose frequently verges on mysticism, as, for instance, in his essay on "Mystic Symbolism" (1931). For Knight, Shakespeare's final plays—the romances—comprise a singular metaphysical vision, and *The Tempest* deserves particular attention as "the most perfect work of mystic vision in English literature."[157] He cites a book by Colin Still, *Shakespeare's Mystery Play: A Study of The Tempest* (1921), explaining how "Still analyses *The Tempest* as a work of mystic vision, and shows that it abounds in parallels with the ancient mystery cults and works of symbolic significance throughout the ages."[158] However, he falls short of validating Still's occult hermeneutic altogether, instead suggesting that he and Still have reached similar conclusions via different approaches, "His reading of *The Tempest* depends on references outside Shakespeare," he writes, "whereas my interpretation depends entirely on references to the succession of plays which *The Tempest* concludes."[159] Knight's Shakespeare is a poet, and Still's is a mystic; but "if the art of poetry has its share of divine sanction and transcendent truth, then what limit can we place to the authentic inspiration of so transcendent and measureless a poet as Shakespeare?"[160] Given such statements, I think it is fair to say that Knight ascribes to great poets powers of mystic vision that permit them access to metaphysical, "transcendent" truths. Knight's Shakespeare *is* a mystic, even if not self-aware, and the fact that Knight arrives at this conclusion by attending to the plays' symbolism—what Eliot called their "subterrene or submarine music"[161] —surely makes him a candidate for the most Yeatsian of modernist Shakespeareans. Curiously,

Yeats paid little attention to *The Tempest*. In 1892 he twice references the "stuff that dreams are made on," first in reference to Irish mythology ("There alone is the stuff that dreams are made on") and then to Blake, for whom "the only real world was the mental world, and the rest was the stuff that dreams are made of."[162] In 1893 he alludes to the play again in reference to folklore, this time Slavonian: "The Slavonian peasants tell their children now, as they did a thousand years before Shakespeare was born, of the spirit prisoned in the cloven pine."[163] The final direct reference is to Beerbohm Tree's production of the play; Yeats disapproved of Tree's elaborate pictorialism, complaining in a letter to Lady Gregory that Tree had "turned *The Tempest* into a very common and vulgar pantomime."[164] These allusions are commensurate with Yeats's revivalist Shakespeare—first a folklorist, then a ritualistic dramaturge—but Desai also notes two allusions to the play in later poems, "The Old Stone Cross" and "Under Ben Bulben,"[165] and from these it can be assumed that what Yeats took from the play was primarily its vision of a transcendent spiritual reality operating beyond the realm of human sense perception. Again, what I am interested in here is the proximity of modernist Shakespeares to Yeats's revivalist Shakespeare: in this case we witness in Yeats and Knight a cross-fertilization of spiritualism and symbolism. It is far more explicit in Yeats's writing, but the suggestion that Shakespeare was a seer connects the two. Moreover, it is the treatment of Shakespeare's works as long poems replete with mystical symbols, and requiring modern staging techniques, that provides a major point of contact. Knight's poetic interpretation of Shakespeare's texts looks for unifying patterns of imagery, but he stops short of folding these discoveries into systems like Yeats's *A Vision* which claimed to represent a vast cosmic machinery governing human action. The vision is Shakespeare's alone, unearthed by the sensitive interpreter from the plays themselves, and this—for Knight—constitutes his peculiar genius.

INTERNATIONAL SHAKESPEARES AND AUTONOMOUS SHAKESPACE

In the previous chapters I have outlined a number of stages in the development of Yeats's Shakespeare: a symbolist, folkloric poet of "Merry England"; an artist situated within an idealized premodern culture on the brink of collapse; a creator of quasi-occult nationalist rituals; a high-culture revivalist. In each case Yeats's construction of Shakespeare demonstrates the contours of his evolving vision for Ireland's new cultural and spiritual life, and ultimately registers the failure of that vision to become manifest. His Shakespeare is genetically related to the Shakespeares constructed early in the twentieth century by writers whose various literary endeavors were underpinned by a polemical turn away from nineteenth-century aesthetics and fertilized by the elevation of "primitive" cultures, whether extinct or merely exotic. Although Yeats's Shakespeare served an Irish nationalist agenda, Yeats shared with Eliot and Lewis an understanding that the value of Elizabethan drama lay in its difference from popular literary modes, rather than its capacity for moral instruction or its usefulness as a repository of national virtue. This is a point Halpern makes in *Shakespeare among the Moderns*: early modern plays interested modernists since their "stylized, and sometimes grotesque qualities made them useful weapons in the battle against late nineteenth-century traditions of dramatic and psychological realism";[166] "yet," he continues, "these were the very same qualities that modernist playwrights sought in non-Western forms of drama."[167] After 1913, for instance, the Japanese Noh rapidly replaced early modern English drama in Yeats's prescriptions for a highly stylized, ritualistic theatre. Of course, Eastern mysticism permeated Yeats's thought from his dealings with Blavatsky's Theosophists through his friendship with Rabindranath Tagore, and so Yeats's interest in Noh might be seen to stem equally from a voguish Orientalism. But whatever the impulse, the result is a Shakespeare internationalized by association with writers outside of the English canon. This is witnessed for instance in his essay on "Certain Noble Plays of Japan," where Yeats explicates the social context of Noh's performance with reference to *Antony and Cleopatra*:

> Realism is created for the common people and was always their peculiar delight, and it is the delight to-day of all those whose minds, educated alone by schoolmasters and newspapers, are without the memory of beauty and emotional subtlety. The occasional humorous realism that so much heightened the emotional effect of Elizabethan tragedy—Cleopatra's old man with an asp, let us say . . . was made at the outset to please the common citizen standing on the rushes of the floor; but the great speeches were written by poets who remembered their patrons in the covered galleries.[168]

This piece comes from 1913, and Yeats's topoi are familiar ones from his work for the Abbey: a classist distaste for realism permeates his defense of a difficult, aristocratic theatre. "Let us press the popular arts on to a more complex realism," he exhorts; "[i]n the studio and in the drawing-room we can found a true theatre of beauty."[169] Yeats found his ideal theatre in Noh, and in his essay on the Japanese form he characteristically positions Shakespeare at the cusp of an aesthetic decline on the basis of its occasional realism, "the art of Shakespeare passing into that of Dryden, and so into the prose drama, by what has seemed when studied unbroken progress."[170] This abstract, stylized ideal is an "Asiatic" component whose presence in Europe derives from "half-Asiatic Greece and Egypt."[171] However, this element has largely expired, save in "our lyric poetry," which has "renewed itself, putting off perpetually what has been called its progress in a series of violent revolutions."[172] So, Yeats here isolates an "Asiatic" artistic genome in the evolution of European art and identifies it in the more "noble" parts of Shakespeare. "Poets from the time of Keats and Blake have derived their descent only through what is least declamatory, least popular in the art of Shakespeare," he writes, before drawing a historical analogy: "When for the first time *Hamlet* was being played in London, Noh was made a necessary part of official ceremonies at Kioto."[173] "Therefore," he concludes, "it is natural that I go to Asia for a stage-convention."[174]

As ever, the larger context of "Certain Noble Plays of Japan" is a nationalist one, and the essay proceeds from a "visit to the studio of Mr. Dulac, the distinguished illustrator of the *Arabian Nights*," where Yeats claims to have seen "the mask and head-dress to be worn in a play of mine who will speak that part of Cuchulain."[175] Yeats's passion for Noh spurs an optimism that "I shall . . . complete a dramatic celebration of the life of Cuchulain planned long ago."[176] Ultimately, as I see it, Yeats was attempting to find a place for Irish literature within an idiosyncratic tradition encompassing a wide array of national literatures, but excising virtually everything associated with a descent into realism, and thus virtually everything written in England between the Restoration and the present. "Modern England" had been born "when Bunyon wrote in prison."[177] Nor is it any accident that the locations associated with the ideal art are also closely connected to Yeats's religious bricolage: Greco-Egyptian hermeticism and Far Eastern spiritualism. Madame Blavatsky's Theosophy, it should be remembered, synthesized Eastern and Western esoteric traditions. Shakespeare thus earns his place within the Yeatsian canon while simultaneously bearing witness to the decline of the "Asiatic" qualities Yeats prized. We might then say that while Yeats inherited a Victorian Shakespeare caught up in the antagonistic nationalism of England and Germany, the net result of his treatment within the spiderweb of Yeatsian discourse was a somewhat Gaelicized, occasionally Orientalized, but thoroughly de-Anglicized Shakespeare.

More frequently—and perhaps naturally—Shakespeare appears in Yeats's prose alongside Homer or Sophocles, and I have demonstrated how Yeats saw in Shakespeare's history plays the nascent construction of a national mythology akin to that of ancient Greece. In "The Well of the Saints" (1903), for instance, Yeats positions Synge's work among "the great theatre of the world, with that of Greece and that of India, with the creator of Falstaff, with Racine."[178] The connecting tissue within this tradition is its folk sensibility, preserved within a highly stratified social arrangement and cultivated historically through folklore, folktale, and song: "The only literature of the Irish countrypeople is their songs, full often of extravagant love, and their stories of kings and of kings' children."[179] "Nobody ever trembled on a dark road because he was afraid of meeting the nymphs and satyrs of

Latin literature," he writes in "Oedipus the King," "but men have trembled
on dark roads in Ireland and in Greece. Latin literature was founded upon
documents, but Greek literature came like old Irish literature out of the
beliefs of the common people."[180] Again, we see Yeats constructing an idiosyncratic literary tradition, this time conflating Greek and Irish literatures,
while excising the "Latin" element. In a 1937 radio broadcast, Yeats explained that "modern Irish poetry moves in a different direction [from modern English poetry] and belongs to a different story [since] Irish poetry began
in the midst of that rediscovery of folk thought."[181] That Yeats was able to
envision this tradition—dismissing not only most modern English works, but
also Latin literature as a whole—was due largely to what Pascale Casanova,
in *The World Republic of Letters*, has labeled the "Herder effect."[182] At the
end of the eighteenth century, Johann Gottfried von Herder challenged
French hegemony in belles lettres with recourse to the "folk" element. As I
have discussed in the introduction to this book, Herder "changed the rules of
the international literary game"[183] by associating national cultural capital
with the vitality of a nation's folk traditions. Casanova sees literary history in
terms of nationalist struggles for self-identification and cultural autonomy.
Literatures are therefore not "a pure emanation of national identity; they are
constructed through literary rivalries, which are always denied, and struggles, which are always international."[184] Once a small nation has emerged
from cultural or political subjugation, however, its literary capital positions it
spatially in a new virtual territory of international letters, and its writers are
freed from writing on behalf of their nation of origin. Contemporary literary
space is essentially denationalized. I think it is useful to imagine this model
applied to the realm of Shakespeare's cultural influence, "Shakespace."
When Yeats wrote of his visit to Stratford and his disagreement with Dowden, Shakespeare was still firmly enmeshed in nationalist and imperialist
ideologies. By the 1930s, Shakespeare typically figured in Yeats's prose in
the company of others. Take, for example, this excerpt from his 1934 essay
"Louis Lambert":

> When I lectured in America the other day, I always invited questions and was
> constantly asked about books. . . . Once I said, "Lionel Johnson held that a
> man should have read through all good books before he was forty and after
> that be satisfied with six. Then somebody asked what would be my six books
> and I said I wanted six authors not six books and I named four authors,
> choosing not from those that should, but from those that did most move me,
> and I said I had forgotten the names of the other two. "First comes Shake-
> speare," I said. "Then the *Arabian Nights* in its latest English version, then
> William Morris, who gives me all the great stories Homer and the Sagas
> included, then Balzac who saved me from Jacobin and Jacobite."[185]

"First comes Shakespeare," but next comes the *Arabian Nights*: despite Yeats's initial deployment of Shakespeare in an Irish nationalist context, the net effect of Yeats's writing over time is to reposition England's culture hero within an idiosyncratic, pan-national tradition. Shakespeare may have signified numerous racial affiliations at various times—Anglo-French, Celtic, Anglo-Irish—but his resting place was an international canon. Today Shakespeare is no longer a British (or German) possession; rather he has become a polyvalent signifier, implicated within multiple frames of reference from Western popular culture to postcolonial appropriations on the stage. As London hosted the 2012 Olympics, for example, the Globe Theatre ran "Globe to Globe," a polyglot rendering of Shakespeare's corpus: thirty-seven plays performed in thirty-seven languages. "Shakespeare is the language which brings us together better than any other," writes artistic director Dominic Dromgoole, "and which reminds us of our almost infinite difference, and of our strange and humbling commonality."[186] From the 1916 *Book of Homage* to the 2012 Globe Theatre's publicity, a hundred years of Shakespeare reception has refashioned Shakespeare's verse drama from the vehicle of an Ur-Englishness into an autonomous poetic language.

I began this chapter with Gary Taylor's point about Shakespeare losing his "Irish accent"—that is to say, becoming a foreigner again—at the hands of Irish writers in the early decades of the twentieth century: Frank Harris in biography, George Bernard Shaw in theatrical criticism, Yeats in verse drama, and Joyce in prose fiction. However, I have been arguing that Yeats's Shakespeare occupies a more complicated ideological terrain. A product of Yeats's occultist cultural nationalism, Yeats's Shakespeare reflects the cultural hybridity of its creator and resembles so-called modernist Shakespeares by virtue of the larger discursive contexts shared by Yeats's revivalism and Eliot's modernism. Yeats waged a rhetorical war against many of the same ideological and aesthetic foes, but in the context of his work, such traditions were typically English imperial impositions. Reviving native Irish literature and spirituality meant expunging such pernicious "English" imports as commercialism, utilitarianism, and material positivism. Yeats's initial foray into "Shakespace" has to be understood in the context of the political antagonism between England and Ireland. But as we have seen in the case of his dispute with Dowden and in his later writings, Yeats's Shakespeare also registers the contours of intranational cultural politics: for instance, Yeats's later push for cosmopolitanism in Irish cultural life. From Yeats's perspective, Shakespeare had almost constructed a national mythology from English history, but his chronological position meant that this quasi-revivalist project was doomed to obsolescence and later to a narrow, nativist misappropriation. Yeats's work can thus be seen as a culturally nationalist eddy in the broader currents of Shakespeare reception, which ultimately reconfigured Shakespeare the Saxon culture hero and gave us the deracinated, international

Shakespeare produced over the course of the twentieth century. In this sense Taylor is certainly correct, and this is perhaps Yeats's most significant contribution to the modern Shakespeare. So, we have seen Yeats's Shakespeare move inexorably into the realm of "classic" or "universal" literature—terms signifying an atemporal, transcendent literary order—and while it might seem an exaggeration to claim that Shakespeare today no longer possesses his English identity, I think we can say that his nationality no longer matters beyond the commercial interests of an English heritage industry.[187] This situation, Hugh Grady reminds us, is largely due to the multiplicity of audiences, writers, and academics who have played a part in the history of Shakespeare's reception, "the collective impact of numerous private and public interpretations,"[188] and to the process he calls "iconization," whereby "an autonomous style becomes a historical icon, charged with countless meanings interpreted into the work(s)."[189] "This process of iconization," he argues, "becomes complete when an artwork—Shakespeare's canon is perhaps the supreme example—absorbs so much that it becomes transcendent of any particular historical epoch, one of the celebrated timeless masterpieces of traditional literary history."[190] Of course, paradigm shifts in the reception of Shakespeare are attributable both to a mass of individual interpretations—some more pioneering than others—and to the sociopolitical currents forming the larger context of hermeneutic change. Today's transnational Shakespeare owes perhaps as much to the decline of British political power globally, and to the ascendancy of America, as to the work of Dowden, or Bradley, or Eliot, or Knight. As we have seen, Yeats's Shakespeare is therefore also a Victorian Shakespeare, a revivalist Shakespeare, an Anglo-Irish Shakespeare, and a modern, universal Shakespeare, adhering both to the political struggle for Irish independence, and to the personal struggle of Ireland's national poet among the multiple voices of Irish cultural nationalism.

NOTES

1. Gary Taylor, *Reinventing Shakespeare: A Cultural History from the Restoration to the Present* (Oxford: Oxford University Press, 1991), 242.
2. Ibid.
3. Ibid., 275.
4. Ibid., 242.
5. In his chapter on Edward Dowden in *Ireland's Literature*, Terence Brown points out the irony in Dowden's admiration for American literature, considering his studied opposition to what he regarded as the provincialism of the Revival; on one occasion, Dowden himself brings up the Irish accent trope: "To set his noble words on the origins of American literature beside his later ungracious words about the beginnings of the Irish Renaissance ('I confess that I am not ambitious of intensifying my intellectual or spiritual brogue') is to understand the kinds of deformations of sensibility that colonial experience effected on one of Victorian Ireland's most attentive minds." See Terence Brown, *Ireland's Literature: Selected Essays* (Mullingar: Lilliput Press, 1988), 45.

6. Arnold, Matthew, "On the Study of Celtic Literature," in *The Complete Prose Works of Matthew Arnold*, vol. 3, *Lectures and Essays in Criticism*, ed. R. H. Super (Ann Arbor: University of Michigan Press, 1962).

7. See David Gardiner, "To Go There as a Poet Merely: Spenser, Dowden, and Yeats," *New Hibernia Review* 1, no. 2 (1997): 112–33. Gardiner goes on to note how, "[i]n an 1889 *Fortnightly Review* article, 'Hope and Fears for Literature,' Dowden asked, 'shall we in these islands of ours, who "spake the tongues that Shakespeare spake," nurse the dream of four separate streams of literature, or shall we have our pride and our joy in one noble river broadened and deepened by various affluent waters?'" (117).

8. Diana E. Henderson, *Collaborations with the Past: Reshaping Shakespeare across Time and Media* (Ithaca, NY, and London: Cornell University Press, 2006), 20.

9. Ibid.

10. Ibid.

11. Richard Halpern, *Shakespeare among the Moderns* (Ithaca, NY: Cornell University Press, 1997), 17.

12. Ibid.

13. See "A General Introduction for my Work," in W. B. Yeats, *Essays and Introductions* (New York: Macmillan, 1961), 520.

14. Taylor, *Reinventing Shakespeare*, 242.

15. For a definition of "Shakespace," see Bryan Reynolds, *Performing Transversally: Reimagining Shakespeare and the Critical Future* (New York: Palgrave Macmillan, 2003), 9. Reynolds defines the term as "the particular articulatory space through which discourses, adaptations, and uses of Shakespeare have suffused the cosmopolitan landscape transhistorically."

16. Terence Brown, "Ireland, Modernism, and the 1930s," in *Modernism and Ireland: The Poetry of the 1930s*, ed. Patricia Coughlin and Alex Davis (Cork: Cork University Press, 1995), 34.

17. Ibid., 38.

18. Ibid., 32.

19. Ibid.

20. Ibid., 34.

21. Ibid.

22. T. S. Eliot, "'Ulysses,' Order and Myth," *The Dial* (1923), in *Selected Prose of T. S. Eliot*, ed. Frank Kermode (London: Faber and Faber, 1975), 177.

23. Ibid.

24. Denis Donoghue, "Three Presences: Yeats, Eliot, Pound," *Hudson Review* 62, no. 4 (2010): 566–67.

25. T. S. Eliot, *The Use of Poetry and the Use of Criticism: Studies in the Relation of Criticism to Poetry in England* (Cambridge, MA: Harvard University Press, 1986), 133. Cited in Donoghue, "Three Presences," 567.

26. Ibid.

27. T. S. Eliot, *After Strange Gods: A Primer of Modern Heresy* (London: Faber and Faber, 1934), 50. Cited in Donoghue, "Three Presences," 567.

28. Donoghue, "Three Presences," 567.

29. T. S. Eliot, "A Foreign Mind," *Athenaeum*, July 4, 1919, 552. Cited in Donoghue, "Three Presences," 565.

30. Despite his apparent distaste for Yeats's religious bricolage, Eliot certainly maintained the mysterious power of the symbol, and Hugh Grady reminds us that "the occult was a conspicuous object of interest for such giant Modernist figures as Pound, Eliot, and, of course, W. B. Yeats—undoubtedly because of its status as an anti-positivistic mode of thought and because of its connections to such Modernist preoccupations as myth, symbol, and mystery." Hugh Grady, *The Modernist Shakespeare, Critical Texts in a Material World* (Oxford: Clarendon Press, 1991), 89.

31. W. B. Yeats, *The Collected Works of W. B. Yeats*, vol. 4, *Early Essays*, ed. Richard J. Finneran (New York: Scribner, 2007), 81.

32. Ibid., 81.

33. See "Magic": "I believe in the practice and philosophy of what we have agreed to call magic, in what I must call the evocation of spirits, though I do not know what they are, in the power of creating magical illusions, in the visions of truth in the depths of the mind when the eyes are closed." W. B. Yeats, *Early Essays*, 25.

34. W. B. Yeats, *Early Essays*, 82.

35. Ibid.

36. W. B. Yeats, *Essays and Introductions*, 509.

37. W. B. Yeats, *Early Essays*, 75.

38. Ibid.

39. W. B. Yeats, *Essays and Introductions*, 524.

40. In *The Lion and the Fox*, Wyndham Lewis asserts the power of blank verse, which "transforms everyone who uses it into a member of a race of heroes. A serving-man speaking blank verse is of a different race to us, who speak prose. If employed constantly by a man of genius it leads inevitably in the end to a world peopled by Othellos, Antonys, Timons and Lears entirely, except for a few prose intruders." Wyndham Lewis, *The Lion and the Fox: The Role of the King in the Plays of Shakespeare* (London: G. Richards, 1927), 162.

41. Terence Brown, "Ireland, Modernism, and the 1930s," 32.

42. W. B. Yeats, *Essays and Introductions*, 528. Yeats attributes this information to Frank Fay in "An Introduction for my Plays" (1937).

43. T. S. Eliot, "The Beating of a Drum," *The Nation and Athenaeum*, no. 34 (October 6, 1923): 11–12.

44. Ibid., 11.

45. Ibid.

46. Ibid.

47. Ibid.

48. Ibid., 12.

49. Ibid., 11.

50. Ibid, 12.

51. Ibid.

52. "The mischief began at the end of the seventeenth century when man became passive before a mechanized nature," he wrote in the introduction to *The Oxford Book of Modern Verse*. W. B. Yeats, introduction to *The Oxford Book of Modern Verse: 1892–1935* (New York: Oxford University Press, 1936), 194.

53. W. B. Yeats, *Essays and Introductions*, 352.

54. Rupin Desai, *Yeats's Shakespeare* (Evanston, IL: Northwestern University Press), 44–45. Heine's book on Shakespeare is one that we can be sure Yeats read, along with Dowden's *Shakspere: His Mind and His Art* (1875), G. G. Gervinus's *Shakespeare Commentaries* (1849–50), and Victor Hugo's *William Shakespeare* (1864).

55. W. B. Yeats, *Essays and Introductions*, 352–53.

56. Ibid., 353.

57. Ibid., 117.

58. W. B. Yeats, *Oxford Book of Modern Verse*, xxi.

59. Ibid., xxii.

60. Ibid.

61. W. B. Yeats, *Early Essays*, 76.

62. W. B. Yeats, *The Letters of W. B. Yeats*, ed. Allan Wade (London: Rupert Hart-Davis, 1954), 349.

63. Leon Surette explores the cross-pollination of fin-de-siècle occultism and literary modernism in *The Birth of Modernism: Ezra Pound, T. S. Eliot, W. B. Yeats, and the Occult* (Montreal and Kingston: McGill-Queen's University Press, 1993). In terms of the Irish Revival, I am thinking primarily of Yeats, the Golden Dawn, and the new Irish drama. Funds for the Abbey, for example, came from Annie Horniman, a fellow member of the secret society.

64. Halpern, *Shakespeare among the Moderns*, 16.

65. Ibid.

66. Ibid., 17.

67. Ibid., 22.

68. Ibid.

69. Lewis, *The Lion and the Fox*, 135.

70. Ibid.

71. Ibid., 125.

72. Ibid., 128.

73. Ibid., 131.

74. Ibid., 132.

75. Ibid., 129.

76. Ibid., 145.

77. Ibid.

78. Halpern, *Shakespeare among the Moderns*, 24.

79. Ibid.

80. Lewis, *The Lion and the Fox*, 223. In a later chapter, Lewis considers the comic power of Falstaff in terms of shamanism: "A shaman is a persona following the calling of a magician or priest: and the word shamanization that I have employed would refer to a shaman . . . who had in addition transformed himself. This phenomenon—that of sex-transformation—in our life to-day is . . . evident and . . . widespread. . . . Shamanism . . . consists generally in the reversal of sex: a man, feeling himself unsuited for his sex, dresses himself as a woman, behaves as a woman . . . or by means of this sexual abnegation prepares himself for the duties of a magician" (222). Lewis's exposition of the "shaman" factor in early modern drama reveals profound anxieties about transvestism and homosexuality. "Generally speaking," he writes, "the process of shamanizing himself confers on a man the feminine advantages. It signifies either a desire to experience the sensual delights peculiar to the female organization; or else an ambition to identify with occult powers" (222). Thus the cross-dressing element in Shakespearean comedy is identified with sensual pleasure and natural magic. Lewis uses this presumption to suggest that Falstaff "has a tincture of the shaman in him" (223). It is this "tincture," he claims, that manifests itself in Falstaff's humor, producing a "magical result": "namely, it makes him immune from . . . accidents" (223).

81. In 1905 Yeats turned down Bullen's invitation to contribute an article for his edition of Shakespeare. *The Letters of W. B. Yeats*, ed. Allen Wade (London: Methuen, 1962), 456–57.

82. W. B. Yeats, *The Collected Works of W. B. Yeats*, vol. 5, *Later Essays*, ed. William H. O'Donnell (New York: Scribner, 1994), 173.

83. W. B. Yeats, *Essays and Introductions*, 514.

84. Ibid.

85. Ibid.

86. References to Dante, Milton, and Shakespeare occur relatively frequently in Yeats's prose. For instance, in 1893 Yeats writes of "Dante, who revealed God, and Shakespeare, who revealed man." *Uncollected Prose by W. B. Yeats, First Reviews and Articles, 1888–1896*, vol. 1, ed. John Frayne (London: Macmillan, 1970), 266. The following year he puts "Homer, and Dante, and Shakespeare, and Spenser" among those great writers who have "begun to draw on" folktales (328). Dante is praised throughout Yeats's work as a poet of supreme imagination who drew upon a vast metaphysical system for inspiration. Milton is similarly praised, but his historical situation following the Renaissance marks him as tainted by England's supposed cultural and spiritual decline. Rupin Desai notes how, "[i]n a lecture, Yeats spoke of 'the old writers as busy with their own sins and of the new writers as busy with other people's' and ranked Shakespeare on one side and Milton on the other." Desai, *Yeats's Shakespeare*, 229.

87. W. B. Yeats, *Early Essays*, 81.

88. This letter, dated May 31, 1990, is cited in Theodore Leinwald's review, "Ted Hughes Reads the Complete Shakespeare," *New England Review* 30, no. 2 (2009): 10.

89. W. B. Yeats, *Uncollected Prose*, 100.

90. Ibid., 284.

91. W. B. Yeats, *Essays and Introductions*, 116.

92. W. B. Yeats, *Early Essays*, 81.

93. Lewis, *The Lion and the Fox*, 149.

94. Ibid.

95. Ibid., 158.

96. Ibid., 160.
97. Ibid.
98. Ibid., 164.
99. Ibid.
100. Ibid., 165.
101. William Shakespeare, *Richard II* (3.2.151–52), in *The Norton Shakespeare, Based on the Oxford Edition*, ed. Stephen Greenblatt, Walter Cohen, Jean E. Howard, and Katherine Eisaman Maus (New York: Norton, 1997), 984.
102. See the first chapter of this book for a detailed analysis of the Yeats/Dowden dispute and its significance within the framework of Yeats's cultural nationalism.
103. W. B. Yeats, *Early Essays*, 79.
104. Ibid.
105. Ibid., 79–80.
106. Ibid., 80.
107. Lewis, *The Lion and the Fox*, 11.
108. W. B. Yeats, *Early Essays*, 79.
109. Dorothy Wellesley, *Letters on Poetry from W. B. Yeats to Dorothy Wellesley* (London: Oxford University Press, 1940), 253.
110. Lewis, *The Lion and the Fox*, 59.
111. Ibid.
112. Ibid.
113. Ibid., 59–60.
114. Ibid., 61.
115. Ibid.
116. Ibid.
117. W. B. Yeats, *Early Essays*, 82.
118. W. B. Yeats, *A Vision*, 2nd ed. (New York: Macmillan, 1966), 153.
119. Halpern, *Shakespeare among the Moderns*, 3.
120. Ibid., 4.
121. Ibid., 9.
122. Grady, *The Modernist Shakespeare*, 180.
123. Peter L. Caracciolo and Paul Edwards, "In Fundamental Agreement: Yeats and Wyndham Lewis," *Yeats Annual* 13 (1998): 110–57.
124. W. B. Yeats, *A Vision*, 25.
125. Caracciolo and Edwards, "In Fundamental Agreement," 110.
126. Ibid.
127. Cited in Caracciolo and Edwards, "In Fundamental Agreement," 112.
128. Caracciolo and Edwards, "In Fundamental Agreement," 302.
129. Ibid.
130. Cited in Caracciolo and Edwards, "In Fundamental Agreement," 132.
131. Caracciolo and Edwards, "In Fundamental Agreement," 131.
132. See Taylor, *Reinventing Shakespeare*, 285–94. Taylor demonstrates how Cleanth Brooks's construction of a symbolist Shakespeare "associated him with a particular strand of modernist poetry pioneered by the French symbolists . . . championed in England by Arthur Symons' influential book on *The Symbolist Movement in Literature*, and epitomized in English by Eliot and Pound and Stevens." Taylor, *Reinventing Shakespeare*, 286. Yeats's Shakespeare, too, was a symbolist Shakespeare, and in his essay "Shakespeare as a Symbolist Poet," Brooks "substantiates his argument with numerous citations from appropriate authorities [including] Yeats." Ibid., 287. Yeats's own debts to the symbolists are well known, and in "A General Introduction to My Work," Yeats critiqued "modern" poets on the basis of their misappropriation of symbolist methods: "Young men teaching school in some picturesque cathedral town, or settled for a life in Capri or in Sicily, defend their type of metaphor by saying it comes naturally to a man who travels to work by Tube . . . but they seem to have rejected also those dream associations which were the whole art of Mallarmé." W. B. Yeats, *Essays and Introductions*, 525.

133. George Wilson Knight, *The Wheel of Fire: Interpretations of Shakespearian Tragedy, with Three New Essays* (London: Methuen, 1949), 1.

134. Ibid., 3.

135. Ibid., 4.

136. Ibid.

137. Ibid., 5.

138. Ibid., 6.

139. Ibid., 11.

140. Ibid.

141. Ibid., 14.

142. T. S. Eliot, introduction to G. W. Knight, *The Wheel of Fire*, xx.

143. Knight, *The Wheel of Fire*, 7.

144. Ibid., 8.

145. Ibid.

146. W. B. Yeats, *Essays and Introductions*, 522–23.

147. Ibid., 523

148. Ibid.

149. Ibid.

150. Ibid.

151. George Wilson Knight, *The Mutual Flame: On Shakespeare's Sonnets and the Phoenix and the Turtle* (London: Methuen, 1955), 223.

152. Ibid. Knight comments twice on Yeats's symbolism in *The Mutual Flame*. In a discussion of the symbols used by Shakespeare to denote eternity and infinity, he picks out "the dome and other packed symbols in Yeats's two *Byzantium* poems" (94).

153. W. B. Yeats, *Early Essays*, 39.

154. Ibid., 79.

155. Ibid., 77.

156. Ibid., 77–78.

157. George Wilson Knight, *Shakespeare and Religion: Essays of Forty Years* (London and New York: Routledge, 2002), 67.

158. Ibid., 67–68.

159. Ibid., 68.

160. Ibid.

161. T. S. Eliot, introduction to G. W. Knight, *The Wheel of Fire*, xix.

162. The first allusion comes from *Letters to the New Island*, 159, and the second from *Uncollected Prose*, 253. See Desai, *Yeats's Shakespeare*, 257.

163. W. B. Yeats, *Uncollected Prose*, 284.

164. W. B. Yeats, *The Letters of W. B. Yeats*, ed. Allen Wade (London: Methuen, 1962), 443.

165. Desai, *Yeats's Shakespeare*, 270.

166. Halpern, *Shakespeare among the Moderns*, 25.

167. Ibid.

168. W. B. Yeats, *Early Essays*, 167.

169. Ibid.

170. Ibid., 166.

171. Ibid.

172. Ibid.

173. Ibid., 168.

174. Ibid., 166.

175. Ibid., 163.

176. Ibid.

177. W. B. Yeats, *Essays and Introductions*, 365. This is from "Edmund Spenser" (1902), collected in *The Cutting of an Agate* (1902) and published in *Essays and Introductions*.

178. Ibid., 303.

179. Ibid.

180. W. B. Yeats, *The Collected Works of W. B. Yeats*, vol. 10, *Later Articles and Reviews*, ed. Colton Johnson (New York: Scribner, 2000), 222.

181. W. B. Yeats, *Essays and Introductions*, 506.

182. Pascale Casanova, *The World Republic of Letters*, trans. M. B. DeBevoise (Cambridge, MA: Harvard University Press, 2007). See my discussion of Casanova in the introduction to this book. As Casanova points out, nationalist writers also face competition from within. Yeats's aesthetic principles were readily challenged, and often rejected, by the "Gaelicizers"—those who regarded Gaelic as the only appropriate vehicle for Irish literature—and "a younger generation of English-language Catholic writers who upheld the claims of realism against those of poetic drama." Casanova, *World Republic*, 311.

183. Ibid., 77.

184. Ibid., 36.

185. "Louis Lambert" (1934), in *Essays and Introductions*, 447.

186. Dominic Dromgoole and Tom Bird, "Globe to Globe," http://globetoglobe. shakespearesglobe.com (accessed August 8, 2012).

187. See Barbara Hodgdon, "Stratford's Empire of Shakespeare; or, Fantasies of Origin, Authorship, and Authenticity: The Museum and the Souvenir," in *The Shakespeare Trade: Performances and Appropriations* (Philadelphia: University of Pennsylvania Press, 1998), 191–240.

188. Grady, *The Modernist Shakespeare*, 80.

189. Ibid.

190. Ibid., 80–81.

Bibliography

Arkins, Brian. *The Thought of W. B. Yeats*. Bern: Peter Lang, 2010.

Arnold, Matthew. "On the Study of Celtic Literature," in *The Complete Prose Works of Matthew Arnold*. Vol. 3, *Lectures and Essays in Criticism*, edited by R. H. Super, 291–395. Ann Arbor: University of Michigan Press, 1962.

Bate, Jonathan. *The Genius of Shakespeare*. Basingstoke and Oxford: Picador, 1997.

Bevan, Bryan. *Marlborough the Man*. London: Robert Hale, 1975.

Bloom, Harold. *The Anxiety of Influence: A Theory of Poetry*. New York: Oxford University Press, 1973.

Bourdieu, Pierre. *Distinction: A Social Critique of the Judgment of Taste*. Translated by Richard Nice. Cambridge: Harvard University Press, 1984.

Brown, Terence. "Ireland, Modernism, and the 1930s." In *Modernism and Ireland: The Poetry of the 1930s*, edited by Patricia Coughlin and Alex Davis, 24–42. Cork: Cork University Press, 1995.

———. *Ireland's Literature: Selected Essays*. Mullingar: Lilliput Press, 1988.

Burnett, Mark Thornton, and Ramona Wray, eds. *Shakespeare and Ireland: History, Politics, Culture*. New York: St. Martin's, 1997.

Caracciolo, Peter L., and Paul Edwards. "In Fundamental Agreement: Yeats and Wyndham Lewis." *Yeats Annual* 13 (1998): 110–57.

Carey, John. *The Intellectuals and the Masses: Pride and Prejudice among the Literary Intellectuals, 1880–1939*. New York: St. Martin's, 1993.

Carlyle, Thomas. *On Heroes, Hero-Worship and the Heroic in History* (1841). Notes and introduction by Michael K. Goldberg. Berkeley: University of California Press, 1993.

Cartelli, Thomas. *Repositioning Shakespeare: National Formations, Postcolonial Appropriations*. London and New York: Routledge, 1999.

Casanova, Pascale. *The World Republic of Letters*. Translated by M. B. DeBevoise. Cambridge, MA: Harvard University Press, 2007.

Chapman, Wayne K. *Yeats and English Renaissance Literature*. London: Palgrave Macmillan, 1991.

Cullingford, Elizabeth. *Yeats, Ireland, and Fascism*. New York: New York University Press, 1981.

Deane, Seamus, ed. *Celtic Revivals: Essays in Modern Irish Literature*. London: Faber & Faber, 1985.

Desai, Rupin. *Yeats's Shakespeare*. Evanston, IL: Northwestern University Press, 1971.

Desmet, Christy, and Robert Sawyer, eds. *Shakespeare and Appropriation*. London and New York: Routledge, 1999.

Donoghue, Denis. "Three Presences: Yeats, Eliot, Pound." *The Hudson Review* 62, no. 4 (2010): 563–82.

———. "Yeats's Shakespeare: 'There Is a Good Deal of My Father in It.'" *Yeats Annual* 18 (2013): 69–95.

Dowden, Edward. *Shakspere: A Study of His Mind and Art*. New York: Harper, 1918.

Eliot, T. S. "A Foreign Mind." *Atheneum*, July 4, 1919, 552–53.

———. *After Strange Gods: A Primer of Modern Heresy*. London: Faber and Faber, 1934.

———. "The Beating of a Drum." *The Nation and Athenaeum* 34 (October 6, 1923): 11–12.

———. *Selected Prose of T. S. Eliot*. Edited by Frank Kermode. London: Faber and Faber, 1975.

———. *The Use of Poetry and the Use of Criticism: Studies in the Relation of Criticism to Poetry in England*. Harvard, MA: Harvard University Press, 1986.

Ellmann, Richard. *The Identity of Yeats*. 2nd ed. New York: Oxford University Press, 1964.

———. *Yeats: The Man and the Masks*. London: Norton, 2000.

English, Richard. *Irish Freedom: The History of Nationalism in Ireland*. London: Macmillan, 2006.

Flannery, James W. *W. B. Yeats and the Idea of a Theatre: The Early Abbey Theatre in Theory and in Practice*. New Haven. CT: Yale University Press, 1976.

Foster, R. F. *The Irish Story: Telling Tales and Making It Up in Ireland*. New York: Oxford University Press, 2004.

———. "Protestant Magic: W. B. Yeats and the Spell of Irish History." *Proceedings of the British Academy* 75 (1989): 243–66.

———. *W. B. Yeats: A Life*. Vol. 1, *The Apprentice Mage: 1865–1914*. New York and Oxford: Oxford University Press, 1998.

———. *W. B. Yeats: A Life*. Vol. 2, *The Arch-Poet, 1915–1939*. New York and Oxford: Oxford University Press, 2003.

Foulkes, Richard. *Performing Shakespeare in the Age of Empire*. Cambridge: Cambridge University Press, 2002.

Gardiner, David. "'To Go There as a Poet Merely': Spenser, Dowden, and Yeats." *New Hibernia Review* 1, no. 2 (1997): 112–33.

Gollancz, Israel, ed. *A Book of Homage to Shakespeare*. Oxford: Oxford University Press, 1916.

Grady, Hugh. *The Modernist Shakespeare: Critical Texts in a Material World*. Oxford: Clarendon Press, 1991.

Granville-Barker, Harley. *Prefaces to Shakespeare*. London: Sidgwick and Jackson, 1927.

Habicht, Werner. "Shakespeare Celebrations in Times of War." *Shakespeare Quarterly* 52, no. 4 (2001): 441–55.

Halpern, Richard. *Shakespeare among the Moderns*. Ithaca, NY: Cornell University Press, 1997.

Harper, George Mills, ed. *Yeats and the Occult*. Toronto: Macmillan, 1975.

Harper, Margaret Mills. *Wisdom of Two: The Spiritual and Literary Collaboration of George and W. B. Yeats*. New York: Oxford University Press, 2006.

Henderson, Diana E. *Collaborations with the Past: Reshaping Shakespeare across Time and Media*. Ithaca, NY, and London: Cornell University Press, 2006.

Hennessey, Oliver. "Talking with the Dead: Leo Africanus, Esoteric Yeats, and Early Modern Imperialism." *English Literary History* 71, no. 4 (2004): 1019–38.

———. "Among the Academics: Yeats, Dowden, and 'West British' Shakespeare in the Irish Literary Revival." *South Carolina Review* 45, no. 2 (2013): 1–13.

Hodgdon, Barbara. *The Shakespeare Trade: Performances and Appropriations*. Philadelphia: University of Pennsylvania Press, 1998.

Howes, Marjorie. *Yeats's Nations: Gender, Class, and Irishness*. New York: Cambridge University Press, 1996.

Hutchinson, John. *The Dynamics of Cultural Nationalism*. London: Allen and Unwin, 1987.

Jackson, J. W. "Ethnology and Phrenology as an Aid to the Biographer." *Anthropological Review and Journal 2* (1864): 126–40.

Johansen, Ib, ed. *Fins de Siecle/New Beginnings*. Aarhus, Denmark: Aarhus University Press, 2001.

Kahn, Coppélia. "Remembering Shakespeare Imperially: The 1916 Tercentenary." *Shakespeare Quarterly* 52, no. 4 (2001): 456–78.

Kennedy, Dennis. *Looking at Shakespeare: A Visual History of Twentieth-Century Performance*. Cambridge and New York: Cambridge University Press, 2001.

Kiberd, Declan. *Inventing Ireland: The Literature of the Modern Nation*. London: Vintage, 1995.

Knight, George Wilson. *The Mutual Flame: On Shakespeare's Sonnets and the Phoenix and the Turtle*. London: Methuen, 1955.

———. *Shakespeare and Religion: Essays of Forty Years*. London and New York: Routledge, 2002.

———. *The Wheel of Fire: Interpretations of Shakespearian Tragedy, with Three New Essays*. London: Methuen, 1949.

Leinwald, Theodore. "Ted Hughes Reads the Complete Shakespeare." *New England Review* 30, no. 2 (2009): 9–25.

Lewis, Wyndham. *The Lion and the Fox: The Role of the King in the Plays of Shakespeare*. London: G. Richards, 1927.

Ludwigson, Kathryn R. *Edward Dowden*. New York: Twayne, 1973.

Maddox, Brenda. *George's Ghosts: A New Life of W. B. Yeats*. New York: Picador, 2000.

Magee, William Kirkpatrick. *Irish Literary Portraits*. London: Macmillan, 1935.

Marcus, Philip L. *Yeats and the Beginning of the Irish Renaissance*. Ithaca, NY, and London: Cornell University Press, 1970.

Marshall, Gail, and Adrian Poole, eds. *Victorian Shakespeare: Literature and Culture*. 2 vols. Basingstoke and New York: Palgrave Macmillan, 2003.

Materer, Timothy, ed. *The Selected Letters of Ezra Pound to John Quinn, 1915–1924*. Durham, NC: Duke University Press, 1991.

McAlindon, T. "Yeats and the English Renaissance." *PMLA* 82, no. 2 (1967): 157–69.

McLeod, Bruce. *The Geography of Empire in English Literature, 1580–1745*. Cambridge and New York: Cambridge University Press, 1999.

Murphy, Andrew. "An Irish Catalysis: W. B. Yeats and the Uses of Shakespeare." *Shakespeare Survey* 64 (2011): 209–19.

———. *But the Irish Sea betwixt Us: Ireland, Colonialism, and Renaissance Literature*. Lexington: University Press of Kentucky, 1999.

Nelson, Bruce. *Irish Nationalists and the Making of the Irish Race*. Princeton and Oxford: Princeton University Press, 2012.

Poole, Adrian. *Shakespeare and the Victorians*. London: Arden, 2004.

Pound, Ezra. *Pavannes and Divagations*. New York: New Directions Publishing, 1975.

———. *The Selected Letters of Ezra Pound to John Quinn, 1915–1924*. Edited by Timothy Materer. Durham, NC: Duke University Press, 1991.

Prince, Kathryn. *Shakespeare in the Victorian Periodicals*. London and New York: Routledge, 2008.

Putz, Adam. *The Celtic Revival in Shakespeare's Wake: Appropriation and Cultural Politics in Ireland, 1867–1922*. New York: Palgrave Macmillan, 2013.

Regan, Stephen. "W. B. Yeats: Irish Nationalism and Post-Colonial Theory." *Nordic Irish Studies* 5 (2006): 87–99.

Reynolds, Bryan. *Performing Transversally: Reimagining Shakespeare and the Critical Future*. New York: Palgrave Macmillan, 2003.

Rozmovits, Linda. *Shakespeare and the Politics of Culture in Late Victorian England*. Baltimore, MD, and London: Johns Hopkins University Press, 1998.

Schoenbaum, Samuel. *Shakespeare's Lives*. Oxford: Oxford University Press, 1993.

Schuchard, Ronald. *The Last Minstrels: Yeats and the Revival of the Bardic Arts*. Oxford and New York: Oxford University Press, 2008.

———. "Yeats's Letters, Eliot's Lectures: Toward a New Focus on Annotation." *Text* 6 (1994): 287–306.

Shakespeare, William. *The Norton Shakespeare, Based on the Oxford Edition.* Edited by Stephen Greenblatt, Walter Cohen, Jean E. Howard, and Katherine Eisaman Maus. New York: Norton, 1997.

Steinberger, Rebecca. *Shakespeare and Twentieth-Century Irish Drama: Conceptualizing Identity and Staging Boundaries.* Aldershot and Burlington: Ashgate, 2008.

Surette, Leon. *The Birth of Modernism: Ezra Pound, T. S. Eliot, W. B. Yeats, and the Occult.* Montreal and Kingston: McGill-Queen's University Press, 1993.

Sword, Helen. *Ghostwriting Modernism* . Ithaca, NY: Cornell University Press, 2002.

Taylor, Gary. *Reinventing Shakespeare: A Cultural History from the Restoration to the Present.* Oxford: Oxford University Press, 1991.

Taylor, Michael. *Shakespeare Criticism in the Twentieth Century.* Oxford: Oxford University Press, 2001.

Wade, Allen, ed. *A Bibliography of the Writings of W. B. Yeats.* London: Rupert-Hart Davis, 1958.

Walkley, A. B. "The Irish National Theatre." *Times Literary Supplement* 69 (May 8, 1903): 146.

Welch, Robert. *The Abbey Theatre, 1899–1999: Form and Pressure.* New York and Oxford: Oxford University Press, 1999.

———, ed. *W. B. Yeats: Writings on Irish Folklore, Legend, and Myth.* London: Penguin, 1993.

Wellesley, Dorothy. *Letters on Poetry from W. B. Yeats to Dorothy Wellesley.* London: Oxford University Press, 1940.

Yeats, John Butler. *Essays Irish and American.* Charleston, SC: Nabu Press, 2010.

Yeats, William Butler. *The Collected Works of W. B. Yeats.* Vol. 2, *The Plays.* Edited by David R. Clark and Rosalind E. Clark. New York: Scribner, 2011.

———. *The Collected Works of W. B. Yeats.* Vol. 3, *Autobiographies.* Edited by Douglas Archibald and William O'Donnell. New York: Scribner, 1999.

———. *The Collected Works of W. B. Yeats.* Vol. 4, *Early Essays.* Edited by Richard J. Finneran and George Bornstein. New York: Scribner, 2007.

———. *The Collected Works of W. B. Yeats.* Vol. 5, *Later Essays.* Edited by William H. O'Donnell. New York: Scribner, 1994.

———. *The Collected Works of W. B. Yeats.* Vol. 8, *The Irish Dramatic Movement.* Edited by Richard J. Finneran and Mary FitzGerald. New York: Scribner, 2003.

———. *The Collected Works of W. B. Yeats.* Vol. 9, *Early Articles and Reviews: Uncollected Articles and Reviews Written between 1886 and 1900.* Edited by John Frayne and Madeleine Marcheterre. New York: Scribner, 2004.

———. *The Collected Works of W. B. Yeats.* Vol. 10, *Later Articles and Reviews.* Edited by Colton Johnson. New York: Scribner, 2000.

———. *The Collected Works of W. B. Yeats.* Vol. 17, *Letters to the New Island.* Edited by George Bornstein and Hugh Weitmeyer. New York and London: Scribner, 1989.

———. "Commentary on the Three Songs." *Poetry* 45, no. 3 (1934): 130–34.

———. *Essays and Introductions.* New York: Macmillan, 1961.

———. *Explorations.* Selected by Mrs. W. B. Yeats. New York: Macmillan, 1962.

———. Introduction to *The Oxford Book of Modern Verse, 1892–1935.* Edited by W. B. Yeats. New York: Oxford University Press, 1936.

———, ed. *Irish Fairy and Folk Tales.* New York: Boni and Liveright, 1918.

———. *The Letters of W. B. Yeats.* Edited by Allen Wade. London: Methuen, 1962.

———. *Mythologies.* New York: Macmillan, 1959.

———. *The Poems.* Edited by Daniel Albright. London: David Campbell, 1992.

———. *Uncollected Prose by W. B. Yeats, First Reviews and Articles, 1888–1896.* Vol. 1. Edited by John Frayne. London: Macmillan, 1970.

———. *A Vision.* 2nd ed. New York: Macmillan, 1966.

Index

Abbey Theatre (Irish National Theatre Company), 57, 68, 70, 83, 96, 107, 109, 111, 112, 119, 121, 123–124, 163

adepts, 18, 71, 72, 73–76, 82, 87–91, 100, 108, 122, 156

Anglo-Irish community, 6, 47, 49, 110, 115, 116, 119, 123, 125, 128, 157

Anglo-Saxon race, 33–40, 59, 100, 151

anthropological turn in criticism, 16, 151–156

The Arabian Nights, 167, 168–169

Arnold, Matthew, 15, 26–27, 33–40, 44, 57, 59, 67, 97, 125, 140, 151, 160

Balzac, Honoré de, 118–119, 126–127, 168

Beltaine (theatrical magazine), 72, 77, 101

Benson, F. R., 6, 13, 44, 54, 67, 73, 81, 95, 101

blank verse, 43, 146–147, 156, 172n40

Blavatsky, Madame Helena, 30, 42, 165, 167

Brooks, Cleanth, 161, 174n132

Brown, Terence, 6, 49, 60n20, 142–145

Burke, Edmund, 115, 119, 129

Carlyle, Thomas, 19n11, 34, 40, 62n75

Casanova, Pascale, 7–9, 16, 21n39, 32, 57, 58, 68, 93, 109, 167, 176n182

The Celtic Mysteries (occult society), 13–15, 32, 57, 70–72, 71–72, 74–76, 80, 89, 146, 155–156

Celtic Studies, 34, 37

Celtic race, 27, 32, 33–40, 59, 67, 97, 125, 151, 160

Christianity, 40, 71, 117, 154

colonialism, 4, 8

cosmopolitanism, 45, 48, 49, 160, 169

Craig, Edward Gordon, 79–80, 81, 83, 139, 141, 146

Cuchulain, 41, 91, 143, 147, 167

cultural capital, 2, 21n39, 34, 57, 58, 74, 81, 100, 135, 153, 157, 167

daimon, 55, 60n6, 80, 99, 100, 145. *See also* Shakespeare, William, as daimon

Dante, 98–99, 119, 122, 145, 154–155, 173n86

Desai, Rupin W., 17, 18, 55, 62n71, 100, 125, 127–128, 164

Donoghue, Denis, 28, 44, 97, 99, 144

Dowden, Edward, 8, 10, 15, 25, 26–27, 32, 44–57, 67, 72, 74, 108, 135, 139, 145, 167, 169

Easter Rising, 1–2, 110, 112, 115

Eliot, T.S., 16, 30, 46, 107–108, 139, 141, 142, 143, 144–145, 148, 149–150, 152, 154, 156, 159, 161, 164, 165, 169

Elizabethan Age, 13, 26, 76, 77, 94, 100, 121, 127, 130, 140, 145

Elizabethan Stage Society, 69, 81, 84

Ellmann, Richard, 70, 71, 82, 101

About the Author

Oliver Hennessey lives in New Orleans and teaches courses in Shakespeare and early modern literature at Xavier University of Louisiana. He has an M.Phil. from Trinity College, Dublin, and a Ph.D. from the Hudson Strode Program in Renaissance Studies at the University of Alabama. His research interests include Shakespeare reception and appropriation in the nineteenth and twentieth centuries, as well as carnivalesque literatures. He has published essays in *English Literary History*, *English Literary Renaissance*, *Borrowers and Lenders: The Journal of Shakespeare and Appropriation*, and *Yeats-Eliot Review*.

CPSIA information can be obtained at www.ICGtesting.com
Printed in the USA
BVOW03*0009110814

362142BV00002B/3/P